THE CHALLENGE OF EPISTEMOLOGY

THE CHALLENGE OF EPISTEMOLOGY
Anthropological Perspectives

Edited by

Christina Toren and João de Pina-Cabral

Berghahn Books
NEW YORK • OXFORD
www.berghahnbooks.com

First published in 2011 by

Berghahn Books

www.berghahnbooks.com

© 2011 Berghahn Books

Originally published as a special issue of *Social Analysis*, volume 53, issue 2.

Library of Congress Cataloging-in-Publication Data

The challenge of epistemology : anthropological perspectives / edited by
    Christina Toren and João de Pina-Cabral.
        p. cm.
    Includes bibliographical references and index.
    ISBN 978-0-85745-435-5 (pbk. : alk. paper); ISBN 978-0-85745-516-1 (ebook)
        1. Anthropology—Philosophy. 2. Anthropology—Methodology. 3. Social
    epistemology. 4. Knowledge, theory of. I. Toren, Christina, 1947–
    II. Pina-Cabral, João de.

    GN33.C5 2011
    301.01—dc23

                                                                    2011036055

British Library Cataloguing in Publication Data

A catalogue record for this book is available from the British Library.

Printed on acid-free paper

CONTENTS

1   Introduction: The Challenge of Epistemology
        Christina Toren and João de Pina-Cabral

Chapter 1
19   Answering Daimã's Question: The Ontogeny of an Anthropological
        Epistemology in Eighteenth-Century Scotland
        Peter Gow

Chapter 2
40   Phenomenological Psychoanalysis: The Epistemology of Ethnographic
        Field Research
        Jadran Mimica

Chapter 3
60   Plural Modernity: Changing Modern Institutional Forms—Disciplines
        and Nation-States
        Filipe Carreira da Silva and Mónica Brito Vieira

Chapter 4
80   Ontography and Alterity: Defining Anthropological Truth
        Martin Holbraad

Chapter 5
94   Exchanging Skin: Making a Science of the Relation between Bolivip
        and Barth
        Tony Crook

Chapter 6
108   An Afro-Brazilian Theory of the Creative Process: An Essay in
        Anthropological Symmetrization
        Marcio Goldman

Chapter 7

130   Intersubjectivity as Epistemology
    Christina Toren

Chapter 8

147   Can Anthropology Make Valid Generalizations? Feelings of Belonging
    in the Brazilian Atlantic Forest
    Susana de Matos Viegas

Chapter 9

163   The All-or-Nothing Syndrome and the Human Condition
    João de Pina-Cabral

Chapter 10

177   Evidence in Socio-cultural Anthropology: Limits and Options for
    Epistemological Orientations
    Andre Gingrich

Chapter 11

191   Strange Tales from the Road: A Lesson Learned in an Epistemology
    for Anthropology
    Yoshinobu Ota

Chapter 12

207   Epistemology and Ethics: Perspectives from Africa
    Henrietta L. Moore

219   Index

INTRODUCTION

The Challenge of Epistemology

Christina Toren and João de Pina-Cabral

In proposing a discussion of 'an epistemology for anthropology', the editors intended a provocation, a challenge. Knowing all too well what comes of 'definitive solutions' to scientific problems, we did not seek to reach a consensus. Rather, given the contemporary focus in cultural studies and anthropology on ethnographic studies of scientific practice, attempts in cognitive science to build biologically and anthropologically valid models of mind, and new ethnographic endeavors to attain phenomenological validity, we wanted to explore the limits of current debate by bringing together views that clashed and subdisciplinary perspectives that diverged.

Challenged to consider what might be the primary condition for anthropological knowledge, certain of us were concerned with how we are to come to grips with what might be understood as changing conditions of theory building, for no one can deny that broader changes in the world at large have had an impact on the development of anthropological knowledge.[1] Most of us,

Notes for this section begin on page 17.

however, found our inspiration in ethnography, which is again unsurprising, for the ethnographic encounter has had a profound impact on the production of new ways of understanding what it is to be human. As will become evident in what follows, however, ethnography-as-inspiration takes different—even radically different—forms. For certain of our contributors, the writing of ethnography and theory building are mutually implicated aspects of one and the same activity, while others take ethnography to provide the basis for anthropological generalization. Certainly, the anthropological endeavor cannot be entirely comprehended by ethnography, but it is most decidedly marked by its principal analytical practice. So let us begin by asking, what do ethnographers want? The answers to this question inform what follows.

As ethnographers, we aim at phenomenological validity, such that our analyses can provide a way to understand any mode of human being-in-the-world, irrespective of whether the researcher is working with texts and archives that provide the material for a historical ontogeny of ideas or with rural Fijians in island villages, financial analysts in Paris and New York, social scientists in China, white working-class people in London, Tupinambá people in Brazil, or cosmopolitan intellectuals in Vietnam. The phenomenological validity of any ethnography rests on the human encounter between researcher and researched and cannot help but be based in the similarity that emerges out of our differences from one another, and the difference that resides in our similarities. We want to see a more general awareness that analyzing ethnographically the lived world of those closest to us (including ourselves) is just as tall (but no taller) an order as analyzing and understanding those distant others who seem most exotic to us. In no case is the relationship between researcher and researched to be taken for granted—not for reasons of an assumed mismatch of power that is bound to work in favor of the analyst, but because what is at stake here is the very possibility (or not) of an engagement with other human beings, whoever they may be, for the purpose of grasping the existential multiplicity of the human condition.[2]

We want an acknowledgment throughout the discipline of the necessity for an engagement with 'what it is to know' (epistemology) and 'what exists' (ontology), which themselves want finding out, with respect not only to others but also to ourselves, since the analyst's tendency is to take so very, very much for granted. This taking for granted has everything to do with the fact that, apart from studies of scientific practice, there is little ethnography concerning either our own processes of knowing (often held to be the province of psychology) or what exists for us (Western ontology is usually left to philosophers, and too rarely do anthropologists question the set of entities presupposed by the theories they use).[3]

Clearly, too, the human encounter that informs our ethnographies is not to be read in individualist terms (an ethnographer, an informant) because, in bringing these persons together, it entails acknowledgment of their lived histories and the social worlds in which they participate in face of an activity that aims at being mutually valid (phenomenologically valid). The mutuality of this human encounter is localized and particular but ultimately is to be understood in universal terms as a function of the similarities that reside in our differences from one another. This is where the focused analysis of life-as-lived by particular human beings with particular histories in particular places (ethnography) meets the comparative analytical project of understanding what it is to be human (anthropology).

Finally, we want a means for making other human scientists (neuroscientists, for example, or economists) understand that explaining the human condition requires that they (and we all) come to grips with the historicity that makes them and us—just like everyone else—accept the nature of our own lived world to be fundamentally self-evident. At the same time, we take note of Henrietta Moore's call (this volume) to heed the importance of self-questioning: "Languages of self-description are necessarily meta-languages, requiring a certain distance from experience ... They are not simply private and conceptual but are addressed to others, and as such they circulate publicly and are subject to contestation, recontextualization, and reinterpretation, providing a link between moral evaluations and actions in the world." In other words, they are "forms of objectification" bound up in processes of self-reflection that are inherent in all forms of action.

Given these considerations, what are the implications of undertaking ethnography for what we anthropologists know? In what ways does anthropology inform ethnography, and how does the latter shape future anthropological debates and ethnographic modes? Should we be concerned that some, considering anthropology too large a task, have fled the field to embrace cultural or area studies? That others have retreated into hermeneutic particularism, holding fast to a disembodied culture as the key to all knowledge? That yet others have espoused a cognitivism that makes neuroscientific models of brain function the measure of humankind everywhere?

We met in Lisbon in September 2007 at the Institute of Social Sciences, with the financial help of the Wenner-Gren Foundation and the Portuguese Foundation for Science and Technology. It will come as no surprise that during the three days of our meeting we often disagreed with one another, each participant being wedded to his or her own hard-won theoretical position and usually reluctant to give any ground. From the perspective of the editors of this book, this was not a bad thing. So often in the past, shyness at engaging openly in theoretical debate has left anthropologists at the mercy of backward and unsophisticated stereotypes concerning our main mode of data gathering (participant observation), our primary form of analysis (ethnography), and our principal process of concept building (anthropological theorizing).[4]

The challenge we posed initially to our contributors gave rise to twelve quite different responses, whose relation to one another is, as will become evident, in certain respects kaleidoscopic. Each chapter bears on the nature of the anthropological project (broadly conceived), so even where one analytical position implicitly or explicitly challenges another, each chapter has a relation to and reflects elements of the others. With each new turn of the authorial lens, adjacent patterns are broken up and reassembled, producing a new and sometimes surprising order. Thus, what we find here is a kind of unity-in-diversity that demonstrates the sheer importance both of radical ethnographic endeavor and of anthropology as a distinctive discipline.

Finding Out What It Is to Be Human

Common to all is the continuing commitment to understand genuinely what it is to be human in all its multiplicity and, in so doing, to find out and explain in its fullness human being in the world. We are all aware of the vastness (even the impossibility) of the task, but we believe that it is profoundly important to keep at it, to struggle with what it means to study our fellow human beings (and through them, ourselves), to acknowledge all the messily manifest, historically specific entailments (at once philosophical, political and personal, conscious and unconscious) that emerge as inherent in the endeavor, and still to keep on.

The twelve chapters collected here differ more or less greatly about what is meant by 'epistemology' and by 'ontology', and which of these is the central issue that should concern us. For Christina Toren, however, this problem is more apparent than real, a function of the analytical process itself in which, of necessity, certain issues are brought to the fore against a background whose character may remain implicit. She argues that epistemology and ontology always implicate one another and are best understood, therefore, in terms of a figure-ground relation. When epistemology is the figure, it can seem that too great an emphasis is being placed on processes that we seem largely, but by no means entirely, to have in common (how we know what we know) and that the ground (what the world is for us as particular human beings with particular histories) is being ignored. By the same token, when ontology is the figure, it can appear that the analyst is arguing for an idea of human being where un/consciousness can have no real purchase on the world and we are forever condemned to mutual incomprehension because the ground (here, how we know what we know) is left unexamined. The trick, then, is to hold onto the awareness that what exists for us and how we know what we know are, for any one of us, lived as inextricable from one another.[5]

Be that as it may, all of us are confident that we can find things out, and that what we find out can provide illuminating, if partial, answers to questions whose salience, whose very ontological foundation, emerges out of ethnographic analysis. Indeed, this is the heart and continuing strength of anthropology, for it is the only human science whose methods themselves engage the researcher directly in epistemological issues.[6] Often enough, too, ethnographic analysis leads the anthropologist to examine critically the presuppositions concerning what exists for us that underlie his or her own methodological practice. It follows that for all the contributors to this book, in one way or another, one of the central aspects of anthropology as explanation (or, we dare say, as science) is to find out what human being is for the people with whom we work, what the salient questions are for them, and what answers they themselves provide.

The concept of 'the people' (Scots, for example, or Cubans) is not to be taken for granted. Experienced ethnographers are plainly conscious that this is a methodological construct that they build out of their research material concerning human subjects who are never (and cannot be) a completely coherent collectivity. The very concept of the collective in its various forms is an anthropological device elaborated by modernist anthropology in order to allow for ethnography as a method of inquiry. In questioning the ontological status of such an idea, contemporary anthropological critique of sociocentrism takes a meta-linguistic position concerning the central presuppositions that grounded most of twentieth-century social scientific thought. Here, too, anthropology, because of its grounding in ethnography, can have a centrally creative role in the contemporary theoretical scene.

The very idea, however, that other peoples' ideas of human being and sociality have the same order of reality as our own, that their questions are as important and their answers as valid as those posed and answered by scientists (by economists and neuroscientists, for example, as well as anthropologists) is a difficult one to get across to those who hold that human reason finds its most perfect form in that specific kind of scientific rationality that insists on the necessity of setting up hypotheses and attempting to falsify them.[7] Indeed, it is difficult for anyone to grant credibility to ideas about what exists for us and how we know what we know that differ to any profound degree from their own. So many of us today—inside as well as outside the human sciences—still fail to understand that the specific nature of scientific knowledge is such that no life-world can be built on its basis. The days in which utopian thinkers believed that they could build a rational life-world (one that would be compatible with modes of everyday experience) appear not to have entirely passed away, however, even though scientific socialism is no longer the order of the day.

Sociality is a fundamental condition of human being, and the particular forms that sociality takes are a function of intersubjectivity, which is always and necessarily prior historically and, by the same token, developmentally. We humans have the peopled world in common, and intersubjectivity is always antecedent, but—and this is a big but—each of us lives the world as a function of his or her unique history, whose parameters each of us projects into the world with some confidence that we are right, only to come up against those of other people—our spouses, our children, our neighbors, our informants in the field who often enough become our friends—and discover differences that we may perhaps reject out of hand or strive to understand, depending on our stance toward the other. This is an aspect of the human condition: to assume sameness in others (whether considered collectively or as particular persons) and discover difference; to assume difference and discover sameness. It is the basic disposition that Donald Davidson (2001) calls the principle of interpretive charity, and it underlies all forms of human communication (see Pina-Cabral below). How we respond to it has everything to do with our own past histories and hence with our disposition to grant to others the same humanity (intelligence, perspicacity, passions, insight, depth of feeling, and so on) that we grant to ourselves, even while we have to realize that we may not be able to grasp fully the specific forms that their humanity takes.

It follows that doing anthropology in one's native country—'down the road' in Bahia (Brazil) or in the Scottish Highlands—poses problems of the same magnitude as doing anthropology far away from one's own place in Fiji, Papua New Guinea, Cuba, or Kenya. Even so, not all explicit knowledge is constituted in the same way, with the same purposes in mind, and within the same sets of binding parameters. It is an ethnographic task to inquire into the different nature of the different forms and modes of constituting knowledge (and that, of course, includes the practice of science).

In response to a searching ethnographic question from Daimã, a Yudja woman from the Xingú River in central Brazil, Peter Gow shows how, when the analyst turns the ethnographic endeavor on himself and his ancestors, an investigation of the ontogeny of ideas reveals that "common and scientific observation are the same thing." Gow's analysis finds its focus in an effort to understand the implications for his own ancestors (and for himself) of Scottish Enlightenment thinkers' specifically scientific concern: "Rather than being pursued for its own sake, reason was to be applied to the world and to the improvement of human life." One such thinker was James Hutton, whose *Theory of the Earth* "invented geology as a by-product of thinking about how landowners could improve the soil of their properties." Gow's analysis shows how standard agricultural practices were represented as irrational and how the Highland Clearances used this representation to justify the introduction of sheep farming. The Clearances at once treated as irrelevant the common people's knowledge of *duthchas*, which involved "hereditary right of access to specific parcels of land," and increased the rental value of land to which a titled landowner might hold the written title deeds. This ethnographic analysis of an ontogeny of related ideas is able to show that Adam Smith's profoundly influential idea of 'the four stages of society' was derived "directly from the transforming spatial forms of Scottish life." Gow's compelling analysis provides an answer to Daimã's question about what makes him the kind of human being he is, reveals new dimensions of the lived political economy of a brutal aspect of our intellectual history as anthropologists and human scientists, and manifests tellingly his view that anthropology has no need of any epistemology other than ethnography.

For all our contributors, the effort to find out and explain others entails an investigation of who they are themselves and how their own ideas and practices inform their fieldwork and their ethnographic analyses—indeed, this is one of the main methodological traditions that have emerged out of contemporary anthropological debate. Except where it is particularly germane to the material under discussion (as above), this self-investigation remains implicit, as do, often enough, aspects of the contributors' theoretical commitments. Jadran Mimica takes perhaps the most radical view of the ethnographic endeavor, making it the ethnographer's task to understand fully that his or her "character and personality structure are both the limiting and facilitating conditions of the ethnographic project itself," which entails a genuine self-critical exercise in reflection, as opposed to the "idealized self-representations … in so many would-be self-reflexive ethnographies." Real ethnographic knowledge and theoretical understanding demand "endless concrete work, a permanent self-modification that can be characterized as an intra-psychic surgery by one's own hand." This is because "[a]n ethnographer neither lives the life nor dies the death of the people s/he is working with … it is the interrelations between the two and the dynamics of human passions and radical imagination that constitute the ontological nexus of any given life-world." For Mimica, the life-world of the Yagwoia of Papua New Guinea, with whom he has worked for 30 years, is, just as it is for all of us, "the life-made-culture, made so by the plenitude of desires of the human embodied un/conscious psyche, whose primordial project is its own self-projection into and actualization as phantasy-which-is-the-world." Thus, his own work resides in the continuing endeavor to grasp this particular constellation of Papua New Guinean subjectivity and its life-world. Here he gives us an ethnographic insight into what it would be to live an "oneiric mode of experience, [which] makes it clear that, for the Yagwoia, their life-world is no less real in their dreaming than in their wakefulness." In so doing, Mimica invokes Castoriadis's "radical imaginary" as "literally, the ontological source of all human reality … the creative matrix by virtue of which there is any given human cultural life-world." Mimica's ethnographic-cum-psychoanalytic account is phenomenologically grounded in the Yagwoia life-world such that it at once "maintains and amplifies [its] ontological originality and existential integrity."

Questioning How We Know What We Know

Given that subjectivity is always and inevitably a function of intersubjectivity, any and every subject-object engagement with the world is historical through and through. Our present endeavor to interrogate the grounds of knowledge for our own discipline is a case in point. In short, none of us can escape his or her history, but we can strive to engage in good faith with others and, in so doing, grant constitutive power to their collective and personal histories and to our own. The struggle, then, is truly to understand others without merely assimilating them to our own ideas.

It follows that this desideratum is itself historically grounded. Throughout the twentieth century, the idea of cultural difference evolved, and even to this day it has not freed itself totally from conceptions of progress and cultural development (which are, in the long run, tantamount to assimilation). This principal guideline of contemporary ethnography is being taught all over the world to anyone who learns anthropology. Specifically, it emerged as a global human project in the twentieth century in the wake of the globalization of modernity. Of all the sciences, anthropology was a major player in this process, having made an extensive effort to free itself from Eurocentrism. In order to see how this might be the case, we have to question the stereotypical unitary view of modernity, which continues to associate modernness with the West, and to adopt instead a pluralist notion (cf. Pina-Cabral 2005: 121–125).[8] The contribution to this book by Filipe Carreira da Silva and Mónica Brito Vieira—looking at anthropology from the outside, as it were—is especially valid in this respect.

Of course, we want to bring home to other researchers in our own and other disciplines the continuing, even increasing, necessity to engage with ethnographic findings and anthropological abstractions in an age when it appears that for so many theorists the globalizing effects of capitalism tend to push all other considerations out of the way. How we are to do this, however, is a matter of some contention. For Carreira da Silva and Brito Vieira there is no sense in looking for "universal epistemological foundations, a search that is associated with the quasi-naturalistic agenda of liberal rationalism." Instead, the way forward is to engage in the "transdisciplinary flow between disciplines, methods, and theories that characterizes the cutting edge of science today." They see the best solution as an engagement in "dialogical pluralism," that is, "a meta-theoretical strategy that sees the history of theory and theory building as different sides of the same coin." As an example of dialogical pluralism in science, they discuss Honneth's critical response (using Hegel and G. H. Mead) to the task of understanding "the inner logic of the concrete forms that human conflict assumes in different social spheres, from the private/intimate domain to the realm of work relations." They emphasize "the need to complement a historically minded reconstruction of our predecessors with a theoretically sustained examination of the inescapable questions they sought to answer." Along the way, they provide us with a useful analysis of "[a] plural modernity, with several historically entangled varieties.' Their analysis meets the central concerns of most of the participants in this debate when, in the wake of Wittgenstein, they call for the central theoretical importance of making sure that "the 'thick' fabric of culture, sociality, and history does not 'go on holiday'." They claim that a contemporary preoccupation with theme-driven and problem-oriented research, which promotes a transdisciplinary mode of scientific production, is not incompatible and is, in fact, dependent on disciplinary forms of scientific reproduction. This historicist approach to scientific work, too, was largely consensual among our contributors.

Taking a quite different tack, Martin Holbraad sees a concern with how we know what we know as itself fundamentally wrong-headed, as inevitably bringing in its train "the epistemological assumption that truth must be a property of representations that make claims about the world" and thus logically entail the possibility of falsification. He argues that "the most distinctive characteristic of anthropological thought .... [is that] it is oriented toward difference" and that "[t]he questions that alterity poses to us anthropologists pertain to what exists rather than what can be known." He wants us at once to retain a hard distinction between ontology and epistemology and to recognize that "since anthropology is centrally concerned with alterity ... anthropology must reflect upon its modus operandi in ontological rather than epistemological terms." This entails the recognition that "some data resist collection ... because the concepts available to anthropologists for describing them are inadequate." By means of an examination of Cuban Ifá divination, in which the role of truth "is not to make a claim about the world but rather to change it—to interfere ... in its ontological constitution," Holbraad argues that anthropologists need a different concept of truth as "inventive definition." This idea of truth does not entail falsification as its opposite, precisely because "it emerged as an answer" to the kind of question that asks how far we, as anthropologists and analysts, "have to change our assumptions about what counts as truth before we could say that oracles give truth." Holbraad asks us to start with the assumption that "anthropology is not about 'how we think they think'. It is about how we could learn to think, given what they say and do."[9]

Beginning with Roy Wagner's observation that "every understanding of another culture is an experiment with our own," Tony Crook shows us how very enlightening ethnography can be when it takes seriously the relations between the researcher and those with whom he or she works—that is to say, when it does not pretend to screen out "the 'bodily-personal-relational' from the 'social science' by means of methods." Crook uses his work with the Min in Bolivip, Papua New Guinea, to show how Barth's ideas about Baktaman 'secrecy' were dependent on anthropology's own "field research metaphors of uncovering data, revealing connections, and entering initially opaque new cultural worlds in search of hidden meanings." For the Min, knowledge is 'skin'—substantial—and coming to know something is 'making skin'; here "knowledge always comes of and from someone, and never goes about on its own as if alienated as some kind of object or detached from the people who hold it." It follows that while people in general (and senior men in particular) attest to the necessity for secrecy and the danger of certain knowledge to the uninitiated (women, for example), secrecy cannot be all or nothing. Rather, as one man told Crook, "knowledge of important things can be given to those who have felt sorrow, who have looked after and respected them, provided that they hide it so that no one knows." Thus, men tell important knowledge to those particular women who respect and care for them and who, for this very reason, need to know what is required of initiated men. Moreover, it is evident to people—and discussed—that solving a problem or finding something out adumbrates a ground from which it springs, whose substance and extent is as yet unknown. As Crook explains: "For every time something is disclosed and becomes clear, people immediately perceive that it has revealed alongside it something else that remains hidden."

There are lessons here for us as anthropologists and as human beings. When we address one another as researchers and scholars engaged in the same task, immediately we encounter and make much of those differences in analytical vocabulary whose theoretical entailments we hold to compromise our effort toward understanding. This makes sense to us and is justified in part because it is indeed the case that our analytical categories set the parameters for our explanations, and in part because our own passions are engaged in what we do. What counts in the end, however, is what our ethnographies can bring to our anthropological understanding of what it is to be human. The anthropological endeavor is as profoundly important and urgent today as it has ever been.

Reclaiming Ethnography

By means of an ethnographic re-examination of so-called fetishism in the Afro-Brazilian religion *candomblé*, Marcio Goldman argues that there is no need to give pre-eminence either to epistemology or to ontology. In *candomblé*, the creative process that 'makes the saint' or 'makes the head' consists in finding in an object or person what cries out to be found and made—brought into being, as it were—because it is already there. This is a beautiful ethnographic demonstration of why particular manifestations of how we know what we know and what exists for us may be understood as aspects of one another. The fused possibilities thus provided for make it plain that being and becoming are likewise, that all the environing world of people and things (including ourselves and everything that we know) goes on and on, becoming what it already is—from which it follows that potential manifold possibilities are already there to be found out and actualized in a world in which "nothing is lacking." Goldman's analysis of *candomblé* exemplifies his implicit axiom that anthropologists should be using only the epistemologies and ontologies offered by the people with whom we work.

Christina Toren agrees with this view, even while she sees the primary difficulty for anthropologists as a particularly powerful case of the problem we have in our daily lives. If we are genuinely to credit other people's understandings of the world (what they take to exist or what might come to be as a function of how they know what they know), we have also to recognize, first, that the environing world provides for all the meanings that humans can make and, second, that our own understandings are no less amenable to historical analysis—that is, no less explicable by social analysis—than the next person's. It follows that because our own categories are of only limited use in understanding other people's, since they are at best initial approximations, the explanatory power of our ethnographies must reside in rendering our informants' categories analytical. Toren's chapter is an ethnographic argument for a model of human being and for ontogeny as a historical process that provides at once "for the analysis of social relations and for how they inform the constitution of meaning over time by particular persons in such a way as to produce meanings that are always unique ... even while they are always recognizable for what they have in common with meanings made by others." She argues that this model entails an ethnographic analysis that, when turned on ourselves, is bound to reveal aspects of our own understanding of what the world is for us, and how we know it, to which we would not otherwise have access.[10]

Susana de Matos Viegas argues in favor of a style of anthropological generalization that arises out of ethnographic experience. For her, generalizing can be based on an evaluation of diversity and need not require a postulation of uniformity. It is bound to be founded in processes that bring together ethnographic intersubjectivity with comparative abstraction. Her ethnographic demonstration of how, for the Tupinambá of Brazil, 'places' are at the very heart of sociality, kinship, and history first required long-term participant observer fieldwork. An understanding of intersubjectivity was at the heart of Viegas's initial close analysis of daily life in the small locality of Sapucaeira. Some five years later, this was followed, at the behest of the Brazilian government, by an extensive two-month survey of residential arrangements among Tupinambá throughout the region of Olivença. It was this study that enabled Viegas to generalize her findings and to argue convincingly against the idea that the Tupinambá people on the Atlantic

Coast had 'disappeared'. For even while acknowledging the diversity of existing arrangements and the fact of historical processes of expropriation of land, she was able to show how an "ethnography of the Tupinambá's lived experience in *lugares* provides us … with a different picture" of contemporary diversity and its history. The powerful conclusion of Viegas's chapter makes it plain that the "epistemological tools that allow us to reach valid generalizations correspond simply to the axis of anthropological training."

Toren has long argued that we have to be thoroughgoing in doing away with what Holbraad sees as "the dilemma between universalism and relativism … [which entails] that mainstream anthropological thinking relies on a remarkably uniform image of what counts as anthropological truth." For Toren, the solution lies, however, not in a redefinition of what constitutes truth, but in rethinking our models of human being such as to have as our focus a phenomenon that is through and through at once historical and material (see Toren 2002). It follows that the biological and the social, mind and body, the material and the ideal, subject and object, the relative and the universal, epistemology and ontology (and so on and so on) are in each case best understood not as separable and dialectically related analytical entities but as aspects of one another, like the two sides of the continuous surface that is a Moebius strip. In this view, the anthropologist's task is to show not only how all our ideas and practices (including his or her own) constitute the transforming world, but also how the fullness of the world is such that it is capable of confirming all our ideas of it, even while, often enough, we may question whether indeed we are right.

What constitutes confirmation for us is itself an artifact of our lived histories. The confirmation of a drug's efficacy that is required by a double-blind experiment differs from the confirmation that is discovered through the use of a herbal remedy when the placebo effect is not ruled out. And they both diverge markedly from the confirmation of a suspicion that ensues when new information comes to light about 'what was really going on' when a certain political deal was arrived at, or from our projections onto another person in which we find confirmation in their every action of our own ideas of their moral worth.

Science shares its history with all human thought, but, as Pina-Cabral reminds us, in the same way as there is no single theoretical foundation that will remain forever stable, there is no stable empirical base for it all. Ethnographic generalization alone would never have invented anthropology—that is ultimately an empiricist dream, and it can be contemplated only if we believe that one could have anthropology, historically, without having had earlier on an idea of science and an institutional investment in the production of science. Similarly, anthropological theory would be blind without ethnography.

At the same time, as we all recognize—and as Gow's chapter so cogently demonstrates—our scientific thought is enmeshed in certain forms of political economy along with all our other ideas. Indeed, the hierarchy of sciences can be argued to have more to do with the technologies of control that they make possible than with the breadth and quality of the knowledge that they produce. It is instructive to note, for example, how biology has become very much a 'hard science' (rivaling even physics) since the dream of controlling the human genome appeared on the horizon of possibility. Science as a mode of understanding the world is a particular human project, yet the kind of validity it produces cannot rule out other forms of validity that are not founded in scientific premises. Nor can science encompass what ultimately escapes control: the extraordinary fecundity of mind. From conception onwards, each of us is the autopoietic (self-creating) product of our transforming, intersubjective engagement in the environing world, whose lived contingencies may produce new, unlooked-for trajectories of existence. The fact that this process is in its very nature historical explains why the lived world of people and things is always co-extensive with the subject.

Considered as an epistemology and entailed ontology (or vice versa), this view at least has the virtue of realizing that we cannot help but project into the world those aspects of ontology that our own particular history makes salient to us and find them confirmed. That this is as true for the anthropologist as scientist as it is for his or her informants does not (and cannot) rule out the possibility of disconfirmation for either, for after all, as is plain in Pina-Cabral's reminder concerning the "all-or-nothing syndrome," the possibility of disconfirmation inheres in all knowledge processes (although of course this possibility may be denied or taken to be irrelevant). Moreover, however hard we try, we cannot make any given other, however close, think quite as we do—and this applies as well for those who feel sure that they agree with us.

The understanding of human autopoiesis as always and inevitably a historical process, Toren argues, allows for a more profound investigation and understanding of the multiplicity of what it is to be human than does the idea that there is a universal biological substrate upon which culture imposes itself in diverse and usually erroneous forms. That culture is nowadays held to manifest itself in ever more highly differentiated microforms that provide for distinctions between, say, the culture of one multinational corporation and that of another has not done away with the crude distinction between biology and culture. This is still with us, for all it is fudged by those who argue that human capacities that provide for a universal rational propensity can be isolated, as it were, from other human capacities whose artifact is social or cultural. This idea has recently gained new strength in the cognitivist paradigm that attempts to put paid to the core idea of anthropology that it is profoundly important for the human sciences to recognize that we humans, considered collectively or as particular persons, really can—and really do—live the peopled world differently from one another and find our ideas of it by and large confirmed. Thus, one of our continuing problems as anthropologists is to explain phenomena that we may think we already understand because, at least historically, they pertain to ourselves.

Having It at Least Partially Right

The persuasive analytical power of ethnography resides, in one way or another, in its demonstrable purchase on the lived world. João de Pina-Cabral argues that "there is no possible description of what actually occurs in the ethnographic encounter that does not presume some form of realism." This is not, however, an argument for positivism. Inspired by the work of Hannah Arendt and of the analytical philosopher Donald Davidson, Pina-Cabral asks us to accept that an acknowledgment of human historicity does not imply that there is no truth: "[H]istoricism runs counter to truth only [if we] confuse the existence of difference [between humans] with the absence of relevant similarity." Thus, he calls for a renewed engagement with the concept of the human condition as a precondition for anthropological thinking. This will necessarily involve a new approach to anthropology/ethnography as scientific practice.

The project of understanding what it is to be human, in other words of anthropology as science, is not and cannot be all or nothing. Pina-Cabral argues for an abandonment of the framework that presumes that we might have access to total truth. It is this kind of utopian disposition that gives rise, in the face of failure, to postmodern despondency. He calls our attention to what Davidson (2001) has described as "the fallacy of reasoning from the fact that there is nothing we might not be wrong about to the conclusion that we might be wrong about everything" (ibid.: 45). We should reject positivist notions of anthropology quite as much as contemporary, discourse-ridden dystopias. In this way, Davidson's argument meets up with the debates concerning modernity developed by Carreira da Silva and Brito Vieira.

To the contrary, Pina-Cabral argues, the anthropological endeavor has to be rooted in the awareness that it is proper to the human condition that human actions are irreversible, unpredictable, indeterminate, and underdetermined. It is precisely this recognition that makes for the "possibility of getting things at least partially right." Moreover, "[t]hese are not variables that apply solely to ethnography/anthropology; rather, they apply to all action and to all interpretation." "Anthropologists-as-ethnographers, as much as anthropologists-as-theorists," Pina-Cabral claims, are especially well positioned to understand that "we would never have been able to reach any knowledge concerning the world's plurality if we had been stuck in a solipsistic universe."

Certainly, we want to be able to capture the multiplicity of what it is to be human, but for Pina-Cabral there are serious difficulties in rejecting too briskly the notion of a single ontology. One might safely argue that ethnography reveals a plurality of ontologies, but this should not lead one to deny the existence of a single world: methodological relativism must not be allowed to collapse into ontological relativism. If alterity and identity are seen as being symmetrical—which is characteristic of the sociocentric way in which anthropology thought itself out as 'the science of difference'—then it becomes possible to contemplate the existence of all sorts of parallel ontologies placed before each other unitarily, as it were, in a row. This posture, however, would amount to a form of essentialization of the human subject or of human 'groupness'—some sort of always-already-existent 'us'—which would be even worse. It would be a form of forgetting that we all arise out of a confrontation with an other.

It follows that alterity and identity should not be seen as symmetrical, for the very possibility of identification and differentiation sits historically on the existence of an earlier form of alterity that is the constitutive ground out of which arose all identity. The possibility of human autopoiesis depends on a foundational confrontation with an anterior other. If all human beings and all superpersonal forms of identity arise out of others, this means that there is ultimately only one world. Therefore, on the one hand, we are all socio-culturally situated—and indeterminacy rules—but, on the other hand, we all share a door of entry that opens up an escape route to the situatedness of our condition. This is the door of anterior alterity.

To that extent, we can all hope to be able ultimately to make at least some sense of each other, and we must therefore live in a world that, while not necessarily unitary, is common to us all. It could be argued that this is a form of monotheistic ideological fantasy that is characteristic of 'the West'. But a monotheistic ontology is not only single, it is also unitary (and fundamentally sociocentric), so the accusation is beside the point. It could further be argued that this has little relevance for anthropology, which, being based on ethnography, has little use for such ultimate forms of determination. Pina-Cabral believes that this is not the case, for the ethical implications of ontological relativism are so tremendous that they would question the very foundations of the anthropological enterprise.

In a similar vein, Andre Gingrich concludes in his chapter that now is "the right time to envision a comparative anthropology of epistemologies," with an emphasis on "non-monotheist epistemological and philosophical traditions that are not based upon one creator." He holds that we may achieve this in part by "strengthening phenomenological elements in socio-cultural anthropology's epistemological reorientation," in order explicitly to take into account the different epistemologies of the peoples with whom we work and, by implication, to make real analytical use of them. Gingrich is particularly concerned with making possible an interdisciplinary conversation in which the ethnographer uses the fine-grained ethnographic analysis derived from primary field data toward the formulation of "medium-range conceptualizations and empirically saturated hypotheses ... related to groups of cases that we might label 'meso-evidence'." This kind of evidence will enable a "new realism" that will broaden and reinvigorate the discipline and provide the means for us to address the human condition and the problems of a globalizing world.

This emphasis on the reality that manifests itself more or less differently in each and every one of us invokes the ground of what it is to be human to which we can never gain unmediated access. Thus, Yoshinobu Ota sees the major problem as being that of "how seriously one takes the nature of cultural mediation." He holds to a position derived from Boas that "reality as it appears to the people under investigation ... is constituted through imaginings" and that because this is also the case for us as analysts, "ethnography is thus the result of double mediation." He is sympathetic to Taussig's approach which, he says, "nullifies the line of contention between reality and imagining, since it denies the existence of reality independent of consciousness and, at the same time, affirms the realness of the world created by such imagining."

Ota's is a plea for an approach that takes full account of the fact that reality mediated through imagining or consciousness cannot be "wished away." Ota's fieldwork in Guatemala makes him think in terms of "the world infused with social relations," which, in informing how imagination functions to constitute the world, informs not only the "strange tales," whose truth Guatemalan villagers at times assert and at other times contest, but also the production and writing of ethnography. Ota asks us to accept that reality cannot be independent of consciousness, and all of us would accept that human consciousness, as manifested in ideas and practices, is constitutive of the reality of the world-as-lived, even if we also know that the world continually escapes (or challenges or throws into question) human understandings of it, to the point that we (especially, perhaps, we anthropologists) are continually questioning what reality might be.

Thus, Henrietta Moore asks us to face up squarely to "the epistemological challenges inherent in recognizing that the new forms of agency and subjectification that are arising in Africa will likely … shape the future of the next stage of what we now term globalization and will also change the way that we think about and practice social science." She looks at what happens when "significant changes in culture and in ritual practices … have been the result of intensive activity on the part of churches, local NGOs, and the government." Her study of Christian Marakwet girls' rejection of circumcision and their embrace of alternative rites of passage shows that when certain practices are reified such that they come to be considered explicitly as culture and as objects of knowledge, this very process makes way for "new forms of knowledge and their explicit link to enhanced agency." Moore contends that the "hyper-agency of radical Christian belief and … the way individuals and their ideas about knowledge and action have become part of international Christian networks" make it impossible for us as anthropologists to follow the well-worn anthropological practice of rendering our informants' ideas "rational in context." Moore insists that we look at the researcher as well as the researched in an effort to understand "forms of self-description and self-objectification," so that we can attempt to meet the ethical and epistemological challenges that they present.

Inspiring Anthropology

The idea that ethnographic analysis is the primary condition for the development of anthropological knowledge is strongly asserted by 9 of our 13 contributors—most powerfully by Jadran Mimica, who argues that ethnography is best founded in an approach that marries phenomenology and psychoanalysis. The others take different theoretical perspectives and thus give a different expression to the inspiration of ethnography: for Gow, it provokes a question and suggests a means of answering; for Goldman, it is an axiom from which the analysis of other concepts can proceed; for Moore, anthropological understanding and interpretation are intimately tied to other people's local knowledge, a fact that has ethical as well as epistemological implications; for Holbraad, it is a standard from which ideas of truth can be critically assessed; for Ota, it supplies the element of surprise and wonder that is so crucial for the creation of new understandings; for Viegas, it is the key to showing how history gives rise to contemporary diversity; for Crook, it is the means for understanding epistemology as always concretely relational; for Toren, it enables the anthropologist to render analytical the categories of the people whose lived ideas and practices are the focus of study. Implicit here is an awareness that ethnography as science always has its source in an intuitive recognition of something human that at once defies understanding and demands it. The chapters by our remaining four authors provide perspectives that both oppose and complement the ethnographic chapters. Carreira da Silva and Brito Vieira want us to think about anthropological epistemology within the framework of a more general debate about the nature of modernity. The transformations in the institutional form of the academy and the state, they argue, call for a radical conceptual shift in the social science. In a related argument, Gingrich makes a plea for "new realism" and a comparative anthropology of epistemologies, while Pina-Cabral argues strongly for the scientific value of anthropological knowledge.

When we—that is, Toren and Pina-Cabral—questioned our colleagues about the epistemological conditions for anthropological knowledge, we did not expect consensus; indeed, we consciously worked at avoiding that outcome. Even so, the careful reader of this collection will see that we arrived at a kind of non-foundationalist consensus. Pina-Cabral, Ota, Gingrich, Carreira da Silva and Vieira Brito, Holbraad, and Moore are all primarily addressing long-vexed issues that they see as continuing to bedevil anthropological practice at large. They are by no means in agreement with one another as to where the answers might lie, but all are concerned with the clarity and theoretical utility of our analytical categories across disciplines and are very much alive to how good ethnography can make a real and much wanted difference to explanation in philosophy and the human sciences. The rest of us—Gow, Mimica, Crook, Goldman, Toren, and Viegas—are more inclined to push our own ethnographic analyses to their limits in an effort to demonstrate what kind of sense they can make. There is an absolute commitment here to ethnography as a profoundly radical endeavor toward achieving knowledge—one that, in going to the very roots of inquiry into what it is to be human, continues to manifest itself as inexhaustible and to constitute itself anew—and a commitment to anthropology as a comparative project that lies at the very heart of the possibility of understanding human being in the world.

Acknowledgments

Thanks are extended for the support and financial help of the Institute of Social Sciences, Lisbon, the Wenner-Gren Foundation, and the Portuguese Foundation for Science and Technology. Thanks to all those who participated in the original Lisbon workshop and the follow-up at the University of St Andrews. We are most grateful to all our contributors for the passion and seriousness that they brought to this project. Special thanks to two anonymous readers for *Social Analysis*, who will recognize where we have made use of their insights.

Christina Toren is Professor of Social Anthropology at the University of St Andrews. Her regional interests lie in Fiji, Melanesia, and the Pacific, and her anthropological interests in theories of human being, kinship, ritual, and exchange processes. She is the author of numerous articles and two monographs, *Making Sense of Hierarchy: Cognition as Social Process in Fiji* (1990) and *Mind, Materiality and History: Explorations in Fijian Ethnography* (1999).

João de Pina-Cabral is Research Coordinator at the Institute of Social Sciences of the University of Lisbon, where he was Scientific Director from 1997–2003. He was Founding President of the Portuguese Association of Anthropology (1989–1991), President of the European Association of Social Anthropologists (2003–2005), and Malinowski Memorial Lecturer in 1992. He has carried out fieldwork and published extensively on the Alto Minho (Portugal), Macau (China), and Bahia (Brazil). He has been a Visiting Professor in the UK, US, Brazil, Spain, and Mozambique.

Notes

1. For a historical overview of anthropology and epistemology, see Moore and Sanders (2006).
2. Assessing the impact of the Sahlins-Obeyesekere debate, Kapferer (2000: 183) discusses certain characteristics of anthropology's self-critique. He characterizes anthropology as a "fractious discipline" and argues that "some (but by no means all) postmodern anthropological criticism has contributed both to destructive representations of much anthropological practice and ... to an unnecessary trivialisation of central concepts and methodological requirements for anthropology" (ibid.).
3. But see Edwards, Harvey, and Wade (2007), who bring together ethnographic studies that focus on "how particular objects of science came onto the agenda as significant, what other ideas they are surrounded by and how ideas travel and have effects in the world" (ibid.: 10).
4. Compare with concurring opinions as expressed by Richard Wilson (2004) and Borneman and Hammoudi (2009).
5. Toren's formulation addresses Viveiros de Castro's (1998: 479) concern that anthropologists "persist in thinking that in order to explain a non-Western ontology, we must derive it from (or reduce it to) an epistemology"; it also acknowledges the justice of Strathern's (2005: 42) observation about "the tool science has made of the duplex 'relation' ... Positivism and its critiques ... are both ... an outcome of scientific thinking insofar as they put 'knowledge' at the forefront of relational endeavour and can imagine different approaches to it."
6. See Bruce Kapferer's (2007) illuminating discussion of the need for conjoining the humanist and the scientific heritages of anthropology. In particular, note his definition of the discipline as "a rigorous knowledge practice, by and large non-positivist in orientation, that claims the knowledge it produces has a degree of validity which, like any scientific practice, is never beyond contestation or immune from radical doubt or scepticism" (ibid.: 78).
7. See Stafford (2008) for a comparison of the significance of falsification for psychology and anthropology. With respect to studies of numerical thought, he focuses on "how much cultural evidence psychologists are prepared to take on board, and ... to what extent anthropologists are prepared—or even able—to provide psychologists with the types of (stripped-down) evidence they want or need" (ibid.: S130).
8. In anthropology, this unitary view of modernity often enough takes the unpalatable form of paternalistic and self-righteous breast-beating. Compare with Bruce M. Knauft's (2002) introduction to his wide-ranging edited collection on alternative modernities;

Knauft's call for us to rethink modernity includes a review of contributions by anthropologists. Compare with Aguilera Calderòn's (2008) ethnographic critique of the use of any idea of modernity to explain *vodou* practice in contemporary Benin.

9. The reference here is to Maurice Bloch's (1988) *How We Think They Think*.
10. With regard to how certain British children come to be who they are, Evans (2006) provides an exemplary ethnographic analysis of how the ideas of adults (parents and educationalists) structure the conditions under which these same children arrive at and make manifest their own rather different ideas of themselves and the world.

References

Aguilera Calderòn, Anna-Maija. 2008. "The *Vodou* Priest Who Lost His Spirit: Reflections on 'Modernity' and 'Tradition' in a Beninese Village." Pp. 118–132 in *How Do We Know? Evidence, Ethnography and the Making of Anthropological Knowledge*, ed. Liana Chua, Casey High, and Timm Lau. Newcastle: Cambridge Scholars Publishing.

Bloch, Maurice. 1998. *How We Think They Think: Anthropological Approaches to Cognition, Memory, and Literacy*. Boulder, CO: Westview Press.

Borneman, Jon, and Abdellah Hammoudi. 2009. "The Fieldwork Encounter, Experience, and the Making of Truth: An Introduction." Pp. 1–24 in *Being There: The Fieldwork Encounter and the Making of Truth*, ed. Jon Borneman and Abdellah Hammoudi. Berkeley: University of California Press.

Davidson, Donald. 2001. *Subjective, Intersubjective, Objective*. Oxford: Clarendon Press.

Edwards, Jeanette, Penny Harvey, and Peter Wade, eds. 2007. *Anthropology and Science: Epistemologies in Practice*. Oxford: Berg.

Evans, Gillian. 2006. *Educational Failure and Working Class White Children in Britain*. Basingstoke: Palgrave Macmillan.

Kapferer, Bruce. 2000. "Star Wars: About Anthropology, Culture and Globalisation." *Australian Journal of Anthropology* 11, no. 2: 174–198.

_____. 2007. "Anthropology and the Dialectic of Enlightenment: A Discourse on the Definition and Ideals of a Threatened Discipline." *Australian Journal of Anthropology* 18, no. 1: 72–94.

Knauft, Bruce M. 2002. "Critically Modern: An Introduction." Pp. 1–54 in *Critically Modern: Alternatives, Alterities, Anthropologies*, ed. Bruce M. Knauft. Bloomington: Indiana University Press.

Moore, Henrietta L., and Todd Sanders. 2006. "Anthropology and Epistemology." Pp. 1–21 in *Anthropology in Theory: Issues in Epistemology*, ed. Henrietta L. Moore and Todd Sanders. London: Blackwell Publishing.

Pina-Cabral, João de. 2005. "The Future of Social Anthropology." *Social Anthropology* 13, no. 2: 119–128.

Stafford, Charles. 2008. "Linguistic and Cultural Variables in the Psychology of Numeracy." *Journal of the Royal Anthropological Institute* 14, no. s1: S128–S141.

Strathern, Marilyn. 2005. *Kinship, Law and the Unexpected: Relatives Are Always a Surprise*. Cambridge: Cambridge University Press.

Toren, Christina. 2002. "Anthropology as the Whole Science of What It Is to Be Human." Pp. 105–124 in *Anthropology Beyond Culture*, ed. Richard Fox and Barbara King. Oxford: Berg.

Viveiros de Castro, Eduardo. 1998. "Cosmological Deixis and Amerindian Perspectivism." *Journal of the Royal Anthropological Institute* 4, no. 3: 469–488.

Wilson, Richard A. 2004. "The Trouble with Truth: Anthropology's Epistemological Hypochondria." *Anthropology Today* 20, no. 5: 14–17.

Chapter 1

ANSWERING DAIMÃ'S QUESTION
The Ontogeny of an Anthropological Epistemology
in Eighteenth-Century Scotland

Peter Gow

> ... since the mountain, which I little thought
> would suffer transformation,
> has now become a sheep-run,
> the world, indeed, has cheated me.
>
> — Duncan Ban MacIntyre, "Final Farewell to the Bens"

In this chapter, I want to do two things. Firstly, I want to explore the ontogenetic trajectories of two interlinked concepts from eighteenth-century Scotland. One of the concepts is *duthchas*, a notion of hereditary right of access to specific parcels of land, and the other is the 'four stages of society', an evolutionary theory of human history and societal differences that is arguably one of the foundational concepts of anthropology as a science. Secondly, and just

Notes for this chapter are located on page 38.

as importantly, I want to delineate the ontogenetic pathway whereby I came to see these two concepts as intimately related. What holds these two things together is an answer given to an ethnographic question. The ethnographic question was asked by Daimã, a Yudjá woman from the Xingú River in central Brazil, and was answered by her informant from Scotland, who was myself.

To the extent that anthropology actually needs an epistemology of its own, I think that it already has one and has known what it is for a long time. It is ethnography, what Maurice Bloch (1977) called, apropos Malinowski, the "one long conversation" and its ongoing consequences. I believe that this is a more profound definition of ethnography than Malinowski's own "participant observation," insofar as observation and participation, while valuable in themselves, are simply the preconditions for good conversations. The discovery that good conversations are of central scientific importance is by no means self-evident and, indeed, was hard-won by anthropologists. The concept continues to be regularly contested by non-anthropological scientists, who, committed to their own hard-won knowledge, are mystified that there would be anything much of value to be learned from talking to lay people who do not know what they, the scientists, know. The goal of anthropological knowledge, the object of its science, is to find out precisely what other people think. Engaging in conversations of sufficient openness and subtlety to find this out is its key method and epistemology.

This chapter reflects on what Daimã's question has made me think about my answer and where that answer came from. I have chosen to follow the actual temporal process of my analysis, and I apologize in advance for its necessarily rambling and highly autobiographical style.

Daimã's Question

My main work as an ethnographer and as an anthropologist has been my fieldwork with the Piro (Yine) and Asháninka people of the Bajo Urubamba River in Peruvian Amazonia. As a consequence of that work, I have been drawn deeply into the burgeoning project of Amazonianist ethnography and anthropology, a remarkably fertile project that, in its Brazilian, French, and British forms, to mention only a few of its national sites, can be considered as the Malinowskian realization of Lévi-Strauss's project in the monumental *Mythologiques* (Gow 2001).

In 2000, I spent a few days in the home of my friend Tânia Lima in Rio de Janeiro. I was there to visit and to talk to Tânia about my fieldwork and about her fieldwork among the Yudjá people of the Xingú River in central Brazil. My intended project of comparing notes with another Amazonianist ethnographer did not happen because I had a fellow guest in Daimã, a Yudjá woman, who had come to Tânia's house to talk for her own specific reasons. What these reasons were, I do not really know, but Daimã included me with ease in the one long conversation that she had been having with Tânia. Out of the blue, as far as I could see, Daimã asked me a question that Tânia translated from

Yudjá into Portuguese for me and which I here translate into English. Daimā asked me, "You are the white person of the Piro indigenous people, just as Tânia is the white person of the Yudjá indigenous people. I have noticed that most white people do not like us indigenous people very much. So why do *you* like indigenous people?" The question was so unexpected that Tânia whooped in amazement and told me that I had to answer it as honestly as I could. Unnerved by the question and by Tânia's rider, I was about to blurt out some sentimental nonsense. Then I remembered that indigenous Amazonian people do not expect questions to be answered quickly and do not mind prolonged pauses for reflection. Indeed, they mostly find that those whom they call 'white people' think far too little and talk far too much. So I thought for a bit and then told her what I genuinely hold to be true about my own relationship to anthropology. I said, "I don't really know, but I think it is because I believe that you indigenous people have kept something that we have lost. I don't know what this thing is, but I hope that you indigenous people know what it is and can show it to me." Daimā replied, via Tânia, that she had guessed as much.

My translation here of Daimā's *karai* and *abi* as 'white people' and 'indigenous people', respectively, is not meant to imply that for her these terms have anything to do with whiteness, indigeneity, or even people, as I might understand those words. The elucidation of concepts such as Daimā's is central to the Amazonianist project, and thinking about that conversation in the context of writing this chapter, I recently proposed to Tânia an Amazonianist explanation of Daimā's question. I suggested that her question was classically perspectivist and dealt with her attempt to assimilate what I had told her about Piro people to her own specific Yudjá perspective as a 'human being', as a woman belonging to a "people who drink manioc beer" (see Lima 2005). Tânia, who knows Daimā infinitely better than I do, was having none of it and insisted that I address the question Daimā posed to me, rather than the question raised by Daimā's question within current Amazonianist ethnography. I still believe that Daimā's question is explicable from that point of view, but here I bow to Tânia's obvious rightness and explore what that question meant, and means, to me.

The Thing That We Have Lost

Daimā's question, as I reflected on it in the pause before I responded, provoked in me a very specific and intense memory, and it was with this specific recollection in mind that I made my reply. This memory was not unconscious, for I had thought about it fairly often over the years. It was of an event that occurred when I was a child, sometime in the mid-1960s, during a family summer holiday on the Isle of Lewis in the Outer Hebrides. It occurred on the west coast of Lewis, which is about as far to the northwest as you can get in Europe. Gazing west into the Atlantic Ocean, you can sometimes see the little archipelago of St Kilda, which had been abandoned by its population in 1930. Beyond that, there is no landfall until you reach North America. Even on a quiet summer's day, it is the 'wild western ocean', as the Scottish folk songs describe it—a prospect of awesome expanse. I present this memory as I wrote it down before a recent visit to the isles of Lewis and Harris, which proved that several aspects of it were false. However, the essential core is certainly true (see the Postscript below).

On just such a quiet summer's day, my father was leading us on a walk by the sea, on the machair, the soft, sandy grazing land by the beach. At the end of the machair, there was a rocky outcrop, and in front of this was a *taigh dubh* (black house), one of the old-fashioned long and low stone-walled cottages thatched with turf that you could see all over Lewis at the time. Some, standing next to their owners' newer houses, were used as barns or storehouses, but the vast majority had been abandoned and were rapidly falling into ruin. This one was inhabited. My father started a conversation with the occupant, a woman dressed in old black clothes, who was a widow and lived in the house with her raggedly attired and tousle-haired children. These children, who were roughly the ages of my siblings and myself, looked at us with interest. I was amazed to see that they wore no shoes. Shoes and shoe-wearing were the bane of my young life, and a shoeless world seemed like paradise to me.

Then something even more amazing happened. My father, a fairly reserved man who was always very polite to strangers, asked the widow if we could look at the inside of her house. To ask to enter a stranger's house was an extremely rude thing to do, something that we children were always warned against. However, the widow happily agreed, and my father almost had to force his shocked children to go inside. We entered the low front door into the byre area, then turned right through an internal door into the single room, about which I can remember little other than that it was smoky from the peat fire and very dark. It seemed an incredibly small house for the widow and her growing children. We did not stay long, and I remember being relieved to be back out in the bright sunshine. I vaguely remember that my father explained his apparent rudeness by telling us that many people used to live like this poor widow and her children, and that it was important for us to know about these things before they disappeared completely.

Why did Daimā's question instantly and powerfully evoke that memory in me? This may seem like a slightly self-indulgent biographical question or, worse still, a self-indulgent autobiographical question, but I do not think it is. I think that it is an ethnographic question, albeit of an unfamiliar order, given that here Daimā is the ethnographer and I am the informant. What, I wondered, would happen if I were to follow the lead of Daimā's question and delve into the meaning of that memory. I knew that there had to be a powerful connection between the question and the memory. What might that connection be? And what, exactly, was the thing that we had lost?

Scientific Observation

After reading Marcel Proust, at the urging of Christina Toren, I have known that such intense memories are key aesthetic and indeed scientific problems and that they deserve closer attention. In addition, and again following Proust, rather than scrutinizing them directly, it is better to leave them be, to let them do their own slow and steady work (see Lévi-Strauss 1997). So I had Daimā's question, my reply, a childhood memory, and the certainty that they were all in some way connected, but I had nothing concrete yet. I knew I could feel something, but I did not know what it was. I was not yet aware of what my reply to Daimā's question meant.

In 2006, in a bookshop in Edinburgh, I bought a slim volume entitled *James Hutton: The Founder of Modern Geology* (McIntyre and McKirdy 2001). Motivated by this book, I found on the Internet the following quotation from the second volume of Hutton's *Theory of the Earth*:

> It is not to common observation that it belongs to see the effects of time, and the operation of physical causes, in what is to be perceived upon the surface of this earth; the shepherd thinks the mountain, on which he feeds his flock, to have been always there, or since the beginning of things; the inhabitant of the valley cultivates the soil as his father had done, and thinks that this soil is coeval with the valley or the mountain. But the man of scientific observation, who looks into the chain of physical events connected with the present state of things, sees great changes that have been made, and foresees a different state that must follow in time, from the continued operation of that which actually is in nature.[1]

I had long been interested in geology and in Hutton, but as soon as I read this passage, I felt that here was an intimation of the missing link between Daimā's question and the memory it had triggered in me.

The scene invoked by Hutton in the cited passage is clearly intended as generic, but his use of the word 'mountain' suggests that its source image is in the Highlands (a Borders image would, I think, have placed the shepherd on a hill). One of the classic places of Hutton's observations was the valley of Glen Tilt in Atholl in northern Perthshire, in the Southern Highlands of Scotland. You can read interesting things about this place in geology books, for it was here that Hutton found granite intruded into sedimentary rock. This confirmed his view that granite was not the original, primal rock, generated by currently unobservable processes, but was instead the product of ordinary vulcanism in events that succeeded processes of erosion and deposition (see, among many others, Gould 1990). This meant that the observable present could function as a reliable guide to the past, and so, as the story goes, the science of geology was born.

What you will not find in such books is what Glen Tilt meant to my great-grandfather, to my grandfather, to my father and his siblings, and hence, of course, to myself. My grandfather was born in Glen Tilt on the croft, or small rented house, held by his father at Allt Craoinidh. His father, my great-grandfather, was evicted from this croft at some point in the nineteenth century by the landowner, the Duke of Atholl, as part of the process of removing all the residents of the upper end of the glen in order to extend the deer forest and commercial stalking possibilities. This was, in the eyes of some of my great-grandfather's descendants, an example of the habitual high-handedness and disloyalty to their workers that was shown by successive dukes of Atholl.

Admittedly, my great-grandfather and his family did not actually move very far and were resettled in the lower part of the valley.

Some years after the summer holiday on Lewis, my father's older sister, my Aunt Janet, who was a schoolteacher in her home village of Blair Atholl, which lies in the mouth of Glen Tilt, took us to see the birthplace of her father, my grandfather. We walked up through the rich farmland and forests of the lower end of the valley into the increasingly bleak moorlands and mountainscapes of the upper valley. Crossing the River Tilt at the evocatively named Gow's Bridge, we soon came to Allt Craoinidh, a little group of ruined stone structures, slowly sinking into the turf. These ruins were all that remained of the house where my grandfather was born. They looked exactly like the ruins that covered Lewis and, when inhabited, must have looked pretty much like the widow's black house. This shocked me.

I have no idea when my ancestors first moved to Allt Craoinidh, and it is not clear to me that they were ever shepherds. The nature of family tradition means that I actually know more about my father's maternal grandparents from the Loch Ness area than about his paternal grandparents from Glen Tilt. One fragment of family tradition, told to me by my mother, suggests some connection between my father's paternal ancestors and shepherding. Bemused by my father's and his younger brother Ian's love of hill walking, their parents reportedly berated them as follows: "Why go up those mountains? Have you lost sheep up there?" This suggests a familiarity with my grandparents that shepherding on a mountain was onerous, unpleasant, and best to be avoided.

So when I came upon the passage from Hutton, it carried me from the memory of the black house on Lewis to much more complex, inchoate, and emotionally powerful memories. These new memories have potent meanings for me, as well as potential ongoing consequences, one of which is this chapter. Hutton's image and his opposition between scientific and common observation have implications for me in two ways: firstly, as a scientist, and, secondly, as an aggrieved descendant of those shepherds and cultivators. What would happen if I tried to put these two back together in that place and at that time?

The Scottish Enlightenment

Hutton was a thinker of the Scottish Enlightenment. The Scottish Enlightenment, like the European Enlightenment in general, was, at heart, based on an epistemology that rejected the acquisition of knowledge through authority in favor of its acquisition through reason. But the Scottish Enlightenment had certain characteristics that distinguished it from its cousin projects elsewhere in Europe. Rather than being based solely on pure reason, the Scottish Enlightenment was specifically scientific and contributed to the Age of Improvement. Rather than being pursued for its own sake, reason was to be applied to the world and to the improvement of human life. Scottish Enlightenment thinkers had a marked tendency to originate what we would now consider academic disciplines as by-products of schemes for improvement. Illustrative examples include Adam Smith's *The Wealth of Nations*, which invented economics as a by-product of thinking about how to generate prosperity in Scotland, and Hutton's own *Theory of the Earth*, which invented geology as a by-product of thinking about how landowners could improve the soil of their properties.

Hutton's evocation of the views of the shepherd, of the cultivator of the valley, and of the man of scientific observation was not fortuitous, for these three figures formed part of a series of evolutionary stages of human history in Scottish Enlightenment thought. In his *Lectures on Jurisprudence*, Adam Smith wrote: "There are four distinct stages that mankind pass thro: first, the Age of Hunters; secondly the Age of Shepherds; thirdly, the Age of Agriculture; and fourthly, the Age of Commerce" (quoted in Broadie 1997: 475). Hutton's image is thus doubly historical, for not only is his argument against the common view that mountains and valley soils have always been there and for the scientific view that such earth features have histories, but he further makes this point by evoking a history of humanity in the figures of the shepherd, the cultivator of the valley, and the man of scientific observation—a history that would have been familiar to his intended audience.

Scottish Enlightenment thinkers had a key technique for reasoning in what they called conjectural history, which has had a bad name in social anthropology since Radcliffe-Brown (1952),[2] but without which, arguably, anthropology as it exists today would be impossible. Based on the principle that like causes lead to like effects, the technique of conjectural history allowed Scottish Enlightenment thinkers to explore the history of phenomena where no documentary history existed. For Hutton, this meant that processes in the present state of the world, such as erosion and volcanic uplift, could be read as the perpetual movements of a world machine that was constantly changing, but that, in changing, was remaining constant to itself (see Gould 1990). In terms of what we would now refer to as the social sciences, the assumption that human nature was everywhere and at all times uniform provided a key to unlocking the secrets of the otherwise unknowable histories of human laws, wealth creation, aesthetics, religion, and so on. If anthropology today might be very queasy about its legacy of social and cultural evolutionism, it would probably be impossible for it to exist as a science at all without the Scottish Enlightenment's legacy of an ethnographically concrete argument for the uniformity of human nature, what Boas later called "the psychic unity of mankind."

Hutton's image occurs in a specific rhetorical context, for he appeals to the distinction between 'men of common observation' and 'men of scientific observation' at the beginning of an important argument about experience. The sorts of geological processes that Hutton was arguing for occur at such a slow rate relative to human lives that nobody could ever observe (i.e., experience) them. In the view of Scottish Enlightenment thought, Hutton's argument was against experience and thus potentially unreasonable. Here Hutton calls upon the distinction between men of common observation and men of scientific observation for primarily rhetorical reasons. He was saying, in effect, "Do not reject my argument out of hand for the same reasons that a shepherd or a tenant farmer would, because it is against received authority, nor do so because it is apparently against experience. Rather, follow me in the application of reason to the problem."

Hutton would have understood this argument to be powerful because his readership would have shared his assumption that shepherds and tenant farmers were not simply ignorant, but dangerously ignorant. As I have said, this was the Age of Improvement, and no idea was more generally accepted by the thinkers of the Scottish Enlightenment than that rural Scottish people, the men of common observation, had gotten everything wrong. It was their backwardness in knowledge that was responsible for the poverty of Scotland compared to England, and everything about their way of life needed improving. Hutton had 'improved' his own properties in Berwickshire in the south of Scotland by enclosing the land, by employing the new Suffolk plow and a Suffolk plowman, and, as far as I can see, by proletarianizing his existing tenants (Jones 1985). For the 'improvers', 'improvement' meant the capitalization of agricultural land, the bourgeoisification of the landowners, and the proletarianization of the tenantry.

Unreason and Ignorance

A good example of such improvement is Glen Tilt itself. Eleven years before Hutton visited Glen Tilt in 1785, his host, John Murray, the 4th Duke of Atholl, commissioned a report on his lands north of Killiecrankie. The report concluded that valleys like Glen Tilt were inappropriate for agriculture.

> No Hill grasings were let independent of Farms, except the grasing of Fealar, and the other Hill grounds were a kind of general commonty among the Tenantry—in some places even common with other Heritors. Particular spots indeed were marked out on which Sheals were built, and around these somewhat of an exclusive grasing maintained by Tenantry of Districts in the summer months. Even what was denominated Forest was studded with such Sheals, and the grasing of the deer and numbers quite reduced—scarcely more than 100 Hinds left of stock—Harts rarely in the Forest except in the Summer and rutting season, and a few in Benyglow. Implements of husbandry on the worst construction … No attempt at sown grass, Fallow, Green crop, or any kind of fit rotation. The only system, ploughing the outfield so that it would yield even a double of the seed, then leaving it to recover, and saying it was laid down to grass. The Infield in constant tillage, mostly manured from the roofs of the Houses or the Flaughter spade—not a Farmhouse slated, or with any adequate offices—with the average of nine years to run of leases. (quoted in Atholl 1908)

As Devine (2006) has pointed out, such attacks on the backwardness of existing agricultural practices were both general to the thinkers of the Scottish Enlightenment and highly stereotypical. Arguably, the 4th Duke of Atholl was simply repeating, in an aristocratic manner, the standard bourgeois view of what was wrong with rural, and especially rural Highland, Scotland.

It should be noted that when Murray speaks here of the "Tenantry," he is not referring to crofters as we might think of them today. His tenants would have been men who considered themselves to be gentlemen[3] and, in turn, rented their tenancies to sub-tenants, men who, along with landless cottars, did the actual work. Notionally, between the duke and his tenants, and between their sub-tenants and cottars in turn, there was a relationship that was called, in Scots, 'kindness'—a form of kinship that eclipsed strict commercial transactions. Tenancies and sub-tenancies flowed downward through kindness, and rents and loyalty flowed upward in reciprocation. In the particular case of the dukes of Atholl, it is likely that many of Murray's tenants felt that they had a better title to their tenancies than he did to his lands, since his claims rested on a female ancestor, while theirs rested on their male ancestors, for this was a society in which unbroken patrilineal descent mattered (see Allan Cameron's account from 1711, quoted in Stevenson 2004).

Writers of Murray's era persistently represented standard agricultural practices as irrational, that is, as contrary to reason. I say 'standard' practices advisedly, because it is very tempting to say 'traditional' practices, which would simply replicate the Enlightenment's key opposition of authority and reason. What the duke was describing in the passage just quoted was, as far as I can tell from my reading in the literature, a perfectly rational economy based on a complexly orchestrated combination of cereal cultivation and animal husbandry. As Dodgshon (2006: 206) has put it for the very similar agricultural systems of the Western Highlands: "Arguably, the key organizing feature of such systems is how they used manure." The 'infield' was the best local land constantly tilled for barley or oats, and manured with the soot-encrusted thatch of the houses in spring and the dung of the animals overwintered indoors. The 'outfield' was poorer land, cultivated in some years but left to grass in others. The 'sheals' were high mountain pastures, where women and children would take the flocks to graze on the new grass of summer, which fattened the animals and simultaneously prevented them from getting into the ripening crops growing in the infields, and allowing the uncultivated outfield to grow grass important for autumn and winter fodder. This economy provided barley, oats, milk, butter, cheese, meat and blood, those foods that formed the staple diet of those people. It gave those people, my ancestors, a living and a sustenance.

If Murray, the 4th Duke of Atholl, could envision more rational uses for Glen Tilt, later writers were able to retrospectively pathologize local life in the late eighteenth century. In 1838, the Reverend John Stewart, the then minister of Blair Atholl, wrote of Glen Tilt in *The New Statistical Account of Scotland*: "In former times, the highgrounds were inhabited by numerous tenants. Their possessions were small and their supply of farinaceous foods precarious and in the best season offered only a scanty subsistence. They had no potatos and their principal aliment was animal food. A system of more beneficial management had converted these dreary and comfortless habitations into sheepwalks."[4] There is no reason to believe that this "system of more beneficial management" was to the advantage of the valley's former inhabitants rather than to the advantage of the valley's owner.

As James Hunter (1999: 239–240) has pointed out, there was a fundamental incompatibility between the existing agricultural system and the introduction of commercial sheep rearing:

> [A] newly established sheep farm ... tended to spell the end of alternative forms of agriculture in its neighbourhood. This is because sheep production, as it began to be practiced in the Highlands and Islands during the 1760s, was incompatible with land-use patterns of the sort characteristic of the cereals-cattle mix on which the region's rural economy has traditionally depended. In summer, to be sure, a blackface or a cheviot flock could be kept on hills where cattle had formerly grazed. In autumn, winter and spring, however, that same flock—especially the younger, more vulnerable portion of it—needed access to more sheltered, low-level pastures. These could be made available only if the rigs [fields] which had hitherto been given over to grain were put permanently under grass.

From the Duke of Atholl's point of view, the eviction of the tenants and their replacement by sheep was rational, since it increased the rental value of his lands in Glen Tilt. The viewpoint of his tenants did not much matter, because the land was his, not theirs.

It is thus clear that Hutton's division between the shepherd, the cultivator of the valley, and the man of scientific observation was not the one, familiar to us, between the uneducated and the educated. It was instead a division tied very specifically to the land: who owned it and who did not; who would use it rationally and who would not. The man of scientific observation did not signify a generic individual, educated or not, but rather a class relation based on the ownership of land. This class relation held, as its other term, the man of common observation.

Duthchas

The recent historical and other literature on the Highland Clearances and their aftermath has highlighted a Gaelic word, *duthchas*, and its meanings. In his dictionary, Dwelly (2001: 375) defines this word as follows: "Place of one's birth. 2 Heredity, native or hereditary temper, spirit or blood ... 4 Hereditary right." These are definitions from the early twentieth century, but it seems that the word had a stronger earlier form. Hunter (1999: 172) writes as follows: "During the sixteenth century and subsequently, the importance of [the] link between tenant and land was reflected in the concept of *duthchas*—an almost untranslatable Gaelic term which encapsulated a pervasive belief that clansfolk were entitled to a permanent stake in the territories pertaining to their clan. Although its precise implications are difficult to pin down, this entitlement was thought to extend to all grades of landholder; to the occupant of a few scattered rigs [field strips], at one extreme; to tacksmen [major tenants], at the other." Hunter is clearly pointing toward a generally unrecognized conception of right of access to land in Highland Scotland—an idea that was, and perhaps still is, important. However, I think that he is doing so in terms that must strike anthropologists as epistemologically inadequate.

Firstly, as an anthropologist, I am wary of describing other people's ideas as 'beliefs', whether 'pervasive' or otherwise. In our own modernist folk epistemology, 'to believe' is the opposite of 'to know'. In this modernist epistemology, 'they believe' corresponds not to 'we believe' but to 'we know'. To attribute beliefs to others is intrinsically to assert knowledge for ourselves. For anthropologists, it is both meaningless and dangerous to style other people's ideas as beliefs except when those other people explicitly acknowledge the epistemically uncertain (i.e., belief-like) status of their own ideas. As Christians, Highland Gaelic speakers in the past would have had a rich vocabulary and a frequent need to explore what belief meant to them, but it seems very unlikely that they attributed intrinsic (belief-like) epistemic uncertainty to their notions of place of birth, heredity, hereditary temper, and hereditary rights.

Secondly, and also as an anthropologist, I know that to describe any human concept as 'almost untranslatable' would render my science impossible. If Malinowski could provide a satisfying account of the Kiriwinan word *kula*, surely we can, potentially, provide a satisfactory translation of what *duthchas* might have meant to eighteenth-century Gaelic speakers. Admittedly, as the historians know well and the anthropologists must recognize, we have little access to the rich meanings of eighteenth-century Gaelic lexicalized concepts of the sort available, say, to Malinowski in Kiriwina or to other ethnographers elsewhere. I fully accept that neither Hunter nor myself could possibly do participant observation among, or have the 'one long conversation' with, eighteenth-century Gaelic speakers, but there are historical sources available. Indeed, Hunter (2005: 124–125) himself quotes the contemporary account of the Earl of Selkirk, who certainly recorded a powerful sense of what *duthchas* might have meant when he wrote of the dispossessed Highland people: "They know well of how little avail was a piece of parchment and lump of wax under the old system of the Highlands; they reproach their landlord with ingratitude, and remind him that, but for [the military service rendered by] their fathers, he would now have no property. The permanent possession which they [previously] retained of their paternal farms, they consider only as their just right, from the share their predecessors had borne in the general defence, and [they] can see no difference between the title of their chief and their own."

Selkirk's account lucidly contrasts two Highland concepts of rights over land. In Gaelic, the parchment was the *oighreachd*, or 'royally sanctioned title', while the permanent possession of paternal farms was *duthchas*, or 'heredity, nature, ancestral land' (see Macinnes 1996). Aristocrats such as the dukes of Atholl were not simply landowners but chiefs. The people were not simply tenants but also their landowners' fighting force in war, and their loyalty was primarily to the land, as in the phrase 'the Atholl Men'.[5] The *oighreachd* (title) lay with the landlord/chief, but the *duthchas* (hereditary possession) was shared equally with the people.

The concept of written title deeds to individual property is familiar enough to us today, but the idea of claiming hereditary rights over land owned by other people necessarily strikes us foreign, something that belongs either in the distant past or in ethnographies of faraway societies. As such, it would have seemed perfectly reasonable for such a knowledgeable historian as Hunter to describe the concept of *duthchas* as a Gaelic or Highland belief. I know of no recent accounts where *oighreachd* (written title) is described as a Gaelic or Highland belief, presumably because it fits so well with what 'we know' about how the world is. The social historiography of Scotland seems in need of an anthropological perspective that would counterpoise what 'we know' with what 'they knew'—and what they might continue to know.[6]

The Reverend Alexander MacLagan, the minister of the parish of Blair Atholl, wrote the following pithy and careful statement in the 1790s for John Sinclair's *The Statistical Account of Scotland, 1791–1799* (1983: 12:101):

> When … men of landed property could not make their tenants fight their battles, they became less careful of having clever fellows about them, and so began to consider how they might make the most of that class of men in another way. Then the rents began to be raised, the farms to be enlarged, much land to be taken into the landlord's domain, and the shepherd and his dog to be the inhabitants of the farms, that formerly maintained many families; though this last particular is not, as yet, so much the case here, as it is in many other places. In consequence of these changes, some of the tenants are become cottagers [landless or almost landless laborers]; some have migrated to towns, to gain a livelihood by labour; and a few have emigrated to America, though that spirit is not become very common here as yet.

This statement is a lucid account of the nationalization of military force by the British state following the Jacobite uprising of 1745; the transformation of the local aristocracy into capitalist landowners; and the immiseration and harsh choices of their tenantry and dependents. A popular local Gaelic poem, "Salute to Atholl," collected in 1781 by this same Reverend MacLagan (and quoted in Leneman 1986: 67), praises the land and its attendant social relations, but notes a disturbing possibility:

> Your new generation are promising to give pleasure,
> Both to their good king and to their land,
> May he not have heirs who value them less,
> Than the sheep which come from the Lowlands.

Out of Glen Tilt

In this sort of historical context, a social concept like *duthchas* was simply ignored or ridiculed by those who could prove ownership of land in southern courts through written records and thus, with state backing, could treat the relation that *duthchas* asserts as unreal, unreasonable, and backward. The people, the other term in the relation that the concept generates, could not so lightly give it up, because they knew it to be both real and reasonable. Of course, they had to consider it 'backward' precisely because it pertained to how the past, their ancestors, and their work on the land—this specific land—had brought them, their ancestors' descendants, into being. Those ancestors and their descendants could not unknow the concept; they could only continue to nurse it in traditions that denounced the heinous perfidy of their former landlords and their increasingly *sassenach/southron/*southern ways.

The former tenants and their descendants could not, however, maintain a concept like *duthchas* in untransformed ways, since its other term, the landlords or aristocracy, had repudiated it. They had to find another term to relate to, and I think that this other term increasingly became simply the past itself and a sense of violent dislocation from it, a highly personalized and kin-mediated sense of loss and betrayal. I look on the opinions of my aunts Elizabeth and Janet about the eviction of their grandfather and their father from Allt Crao-inidh, and from Glen Tilt itself, which I heard about in my youth, as a late-twentieth-century transformation of *duthchas*. They would certainly have known, from their mother Anne MacMillan, a native Gaelic speaker from Glen Urquhart by Loch Ness, what that Gaelic word meant. Both of my aunts were educated professional women who had little enough to fear from the then Duke of Atholl, but who retained a bitter—and in the case of my Aunt Janet, a politically articulated—hostility toward his family and their deeds. In my father's case, this hostility was much more muted, but I suspect that his love of hill walking was his own personal transformation of *duthchas*, for he had a very well-developed sense of his right to go wherever he wanted in the Highlands of Scotland.

Social Space

Thus, in the late eighteenth century, my paternal ancestors were experiencing dramatic transformations of the material and social underpinnings of their lived worlds. Meanwhile, the thinkers of the Scottish Enlightenment were engaged in a cult of the practical application of reason to the world, which was, simultaneously, the ideological justification for those dramatic transformations. I want to show how my approach here has a certain fertility for anthropology and its epistemology. While obviously nobody can now do ethnographic fieldwork in the Highlands of the late eighteenth century, it is possible for an experienced ethnographer to look back over materials from that period and note some interesting new connections.

Hutton visited Glen Tilt to make his observations in 1785, the very year in which the Duke of Atholl began the evictions that transformed the valley from a landscape of mixed farming of cereals and cattle into a sheep farm, and so his image is one of nascent 'improvement', from the duke's perspective, and of nascent 'clearance', from the people's perspective. His image of the shepherd and the cultivator of the valley, and the consequent opposition of common and scientific observation, as I have noted, appealed to Smith's four stages of society, but it also appealed to two other forms of transforming social landscape in eighteenth-century Scotland.

Firstly, it appealed to pre-improvement agriculture. This was based on an intricate orchestration of a complex spatio-temporal system founded on an iterated structure of what were known in Scots as 'inby'/'outby' (i.e., inside/outside) relations (see Grant 1924, 1995). Houses, like that of the widow on Lewis, had an 'inner inside', where the people lived, and an 'outer inside', where the cattle overwintered. Beyond the houses were the fields, divided between manured and intensively cultivated infields, and non-fertilized and less intensively cropped outfields. Houses and fields together were surrounded by a 'head dyke', which kept the animals off the crops in between planting and harvest and divided the inside of the town from the rough hillside grazing beyond. In summer, furthermore, cattle and other livestock were herded up into mountain valleys to fatten on the new grass around the shielings, the outside dwellings. All this human space was opposed to the wilderness of the deer forests.

This pre-improved landscape was also the social geography of Scotland. Especially when viewed from the perspective of the professional bourgeoisie of Edinburgh, the nation's capital and the 'Athens of the North', as it was called, these inside/outside relations provided a basic map of Scotland as it then existed and were associated with specific economic zones. Looking out from Edinburgh, they would have seen the agricultural districts of the Lowlands. Beyond these, lay the pastoral zones of the Highlands to the north, the source of much of the beef cattle sold in the Edinburgh market. Beyond the Highlands lay the islands of the Hebrides, which were too remote to transport beef cattle easily to market and whose residents were notorious for the role of wild animal foods in their diets and their use of wild animal products in rent payments in kind (see Martin 2003).

And what is this if not a sequence of commerce, agriculture, pastoralism, and hunting? Invert it and temporalize it, and a journey from the Outer Hebrides to Edinburgh becomes a journey through Smith's four stages of society. I suggest, therefore, that the key model of Smith's historical stages lay in Scotland. For Smith, Hutton, and their Scottish readers, the temporal sequence running from hunters to commerce would have been instantly recognizable as a sketch map of Scotland as it existed prior to their own age, during which they were assiduously attempting to destroy it through the application of reason to improvement.

We tend to imagine that evolutionary theories of human societies were born in the colonial encounter and reflected a theorization of colonial racial hierarchies. That the Scottish Enlightenment's scheme of the four stages of society derives directly from the transforming spatial forms of Scottish life is made clear by the following ethnographic note by Smith: "The whole of the savage nations which subsist by flocks have no notion of cultivating the ground. The only case that has an appearance of an objection to this rule is the state of the North American Indians. They, tho they have no conception of flocks and herds, have nevertheless some notion of agriculture. Their women plant a few stalks of Indian corn at the back of their huts. But this can hardly be called agriculture" (quoted in Broadie 1997: 479–480). It is clear that, for Smith, Native American exceptionalism was distinctly secondary. More important for Smith and his audience would have been the pragmatic obviousness of the fourfold stages of society as instantiated in everyday life around them.

The four stages of society in Scotland would have had a powerful meaning for Enlightenment thinkers such as Smith and Hutton. It is possible that Smith had already formulated his 'four stage' theory in lectures he gave in Edinburgh during the winter of 1750–1751 (Stocking 1987). If so, that would have been within four years of the end of the prolonged military occupation of that same city by his 'Hunters' and 'Pastoralists', the Highland supporters of the Jacobite rising of 1745—closer in time, that is, than the events of 9/11 are to us. The Select Society, a debating society and one of the crucibles of the Scottish Enlightenment, allowed discussion of any topic bar two: revealed religion and anything that might give occasion to vent any of the principles of Jacobitism (Broadie 2001). The application of reason, even for Scottish Enlightenment thinkers, had its strict limits.

In this context, Smith's conception of the four stages of society reads more like a pious hope for the growth of a society based on peaceful commerce than as a given fact about the world. It was also a distinctively bourgeois hope, for the traditional political elite of Scotland, its aristocracy, suffered badly in the aftermath of the 1746 Battle of Culloden, the last major military engagement of the Jacobite rising, which led to the defeat of the cause. The then Duke of Atholl had remained loyal to the House of Hanover, but his younger brother was Bonnie Prince Charlie's main general and was joined by many of the duke's tenantry. Like the rest of the Highland aristocracy, the Duke of Atholl lost many of his feudal powers over his tenants and, consequently, his interest in retaining them. This is the rhetorical force of the minister of Blair Atholl, quoted above, as he wrote in the 1790s, "When the jurisdiction act took place, and men of landed property could not make their tenants fight their battles, they became less careful of having clever fellows about them." This process could conveniently be called 'improvement' and got the assiduous ideological support of the Scottish Enlightenment thinkers. And that, of course, is the other side of my own relationship to Glen Tilt. What counts as commercial improvement to the aristocracy and the bourgeoisie is seen as vile expediency by those who lost access to their lands in the process.

The Thing That Got Lost

Daimā's question had evoked in me an intense memory of my childhood and then the answer about my sense that my ancestors had lost something that her people might yet retain. At the time, I had told Daimā that I did not know what that thing was. Here I want to look at what it probably is and its implications for the epistemology of anthropology—or at least of my anthropology.

The nature of the thing that got lost was identified in the very beginnings of anthropology as an ethnographic science, that is, a practical science, by James Mooney in his classic monograph, *The Ghost-Dance Religion and the Sioux Outbreak of 1890*. There he makes clear that the thing that got lost is youth. Mooney (1896: 657) wrote: "The wise men tell us that the world is growing happier—that we live longer than did our fathers, have more of comfort and less of toil, fewer wars and discords, and higher hopes and aspirations. So say the wise men; but deep in our own hearts we know they are wrong. For were not we, too, born in Arcadia ...? ... The lost paradise is the world's dreamland of youth." Mooney is a significant figure here, since he began his anthropological life as a committed Morganian social evolutionist but became increasingly drawn into political activism on behalf of the Native American peoples whom he had studied and had come to know, in particular, supporting their right to practice their own religions without government interference. This move toward a sense of human sympathy with the Native American peoples was undoubtedly mediated by his lifelong devotion to the cause of Irish republicanism (Moses 1984).

Mooney's view that "[t]he lost paradise is the world's dreamland of youth" seems to me to be an almost perfect account of a romantic take on the epistemology of Smith's four stages of society and of all subsequent social evolutionary theories in anthropology. Such theories inevitably present the 'hunters' or the 'savages' or the 'primitives' as the possibility of re-encountering the younger, more innocent, and more vivid days both of humankind and of oneself. Of course, such romanticism has been largely shunned by professional academic anthropology, but it is almost certainly personally central to much ethnographic fieldwork. As Janet Siskind (1973: 18) put it in her remarkable and profound book, *To Hunt in the Morning*: "Romance is a form of insanity in which one projects onto another a response to needs unmet and ignores the reality of the other person. The romance of fieldwork is no exception ... Just as the delusions of romance may be the only way in which it is possible for two people to justify the attempt to get to know one another, the romantic view of the field throws the anthropologist into an interaction with his people." The strongest possibility for a distinctive anthropological epistemology is when that which is initially only sensed and felt is transformed into that which is clearly known, but without ever losing sight of its irrational origins.

Conclusion

The Highlands of Scotland constituted a key transitional object in the move between the Scottish Enlightenment and the development of nineteenth-century evolutionary anthropology. Words such as 'savages', 'barbarians', and 'tribal', which were regularly used of Highland people in the seventeenth and eighteenth centuries by southern writers, whether Scottish or otherwise, went on to provide the conceptual vocabulary of that anthropology. The Gaelic word for progeny, *clann*, joined the Ojibwe *dodem*, the Polynesian *mana*, and many other non-English words as names for un-English concepts that were suddenly of interest to thinkers of scientific bent. For a concept like *clann* to become an anthropological category, it would seem that it was necessary for it to be first evacuated of its instrumental efficacy, its reasonableness, and then invested with its scientific curiosity, its irrationality. Lévi-Strauss was correct when he said, "How did anthropology come into being? It has made itself out of all kinds of refuse and left-overs from other fields … Trying to do what we can with the 'garbage' of other disciplines is still the task of anthropology, and it is extremely important that all of us should be trained as ragpickers. This is the main and first thought of our work and should never be forgotten" (quoted in Tax et al. 1953: 349). The Gaelic concepts of progeny and birthright were, until the mid-eighteenth century, unproblematically connected. Then they were violently disconnected: *duthchas* (birthright) was violently repressed, and *oighreachd* (written title) was violently asserted. This left the mediating term *clann* (progeny) as a sort of conceptual orphan, a 'garbage' concept that anthropology could pick up and work over.

In *The Savage Mind*, Claude Lévi-Strauss (1966: 15) makes the key anthropological point that common and scientific observation are the same thing. So when I read the passage in Hutton's work that set up the opposition between common and scientific observation, I already knew this—but as an anthropologist, not through personal and social history. And of course the ethnographer in me notes that Hutton's account of what the shepherd thinks about the mountain is effectively worthless, for there is no evidence that Hutton ever bothered to ask a shepherd for his opinions or would have thought it might be interesting to do so. That sort of curiosity came only much later, although my epigraph from Hutton's contemporary, the gamekeeper and poet Duncan Ban MacIntyre, suggests that the men of common observation had much to say.

Finally, none of what I have written here could have been thought about by me in this way but for Daimā's question. Her question evoked in me the memory of the widow's black house, which in turn allowed me to grasp the personal significance of that passage by Hutton on what the shepherd thinks about the mountain, and hence to search out its historical meaning. Daimā's question was directly ethnographic, for it was about the internal differentiation of an important Yudjá social category, white people, a category to which I belong. As such, it posed my personal and social history back to me as an anthropological, and hence ethnographic, question. The ethnographic question, "Who are you?" carries within itself, by the nature of conversation, the reciprocal question, "Who, then, am I?"

Postscript

Since originally writing this chapter, I have engaged in two kinds of search that suggest that the personal memories on which it is based are, if not exactly false, powerful condensations of much more complex events. While writing the piece, I was conscious of my debt to Stephen Jay Gould's remarkable exposition of Hutton's *Theory of the Earth* in *Time's Arrow, Time's Cycle* (Gould 1990). I had completely forgotten a much shorter essay by Gould on a connected theme, very pertinent to the present chapter, until reminded of it by Marcio Goldman. This essay, "Muller Bros. Moving and Storage," is about the nature of memory, its fallibility, and our responsibility toward the truth of what actually happened in the past and how we can possibly know this.

Gould (1993: 205) writes in conclusion to that essay, "Of course we must treat the human mind with respect, for nature has fashioned no more admirable instrument. But we must also struggle to stand back and scrutinize our own mental certainties. This last line poses an obvious paradox, if not an outright contradiction, and I have no resolution to offer. Yes, step back and scrutinize your own mind. But with what?"

Shortly after writing the section on the widow's black house, I went on holiday to Lewis with my old friend Michael Bowles, and, with a lot of generous local help, we found that house. It is in Na Geàrannann/Garenin. It is not located at the end of a long stretch of machair, the woman was not a widow, she was not dressed in black, and she had no children. Those aspects of the memory were generated from specifiable other sources, such as a beach on the west coast of Harris to the south and widowed Highland women I knew as a boy. The house was real enough, the rocky outcrop was real enough, and the woman who lived there was real enough, too. Her name was Effie Macleod. The shoeless tousle-haired children are more of a problem. They were most certainly not Miss Macleod's children, as my local interlocutors at the Gearrannan Blackhouse Village visitors' center made very clear to me (in my obtuseness, it took a while for me to realize the local implication of my false memory, and I hope that they forgive me for it). Nor do they appear in either of the photographs that my father took that day and that still remain in my possession. It is possible that Miss Macleod was simply looking after them for the day, or even that they were completely unconnected to her and were simply there at the same time. It was a different world then and a much safer one for children who were free during the long summer holidays. Certainly, even as an urban Scottish boy, I was trusted to look after myself, whether alone or with other children, very much more than would be considered reasonable today.

The existence of the Gearrannan Blackhouse Village as a very interesting and engaging heritage/tourist site attests to my father's prescience and, retrospectively, excuses his apparent rudeness back then. He was right, for these things were about to disappear forever, and to have known them face to face was an extraordinary personal privilege that he could give to his children.

So that was one kind of search, my personal search for lost time. The second kind of search was very different in its emotional register. This was genealogical research. This research is still in its infancy, so to speak, and consists of a few hours logged on to the excellent ScotlandsPeople Web site.[7] As I wrote the chapter, I was conscious of certain doubts that had arisen within me, as regard to the precision of my memories and their lack of accord with the historical sources I was reading in order to write this account. For example, the popular historian John Kerr (1984–1986: 410), in his account of the Atholl Forests, records the following: "In 1785, the leases of four tenancies on the west side—Dail Mhoraisd, Clachglass, Craig Dhearg and Dalarie ran out and were not retaken by their former tenants. They were therefore granted to Ralph Hall who turned the whole area into a large sheep run." Dail Mhoraisd is the name of the tenancy of which Allt Craoinidh was a part, so it cannot have been my grandfather, however young, who was evicted from there. The genealogical research confirmed these doubts with the awesome rapidity of electronic media. My grandfather was certainly born in Glen Tilt, but not in Allt Craoinidh, nor was his father evicted from that place. I must have misunderstood what my Aunt Janet had told me. It was not my grandfather who was evicted as a boy from Allt Craoinidh, I now believe, but his grandfather. The evicted boy would have been my great-great-grandfather. This discovery was, in one way, much less surprising to me than it should have been and, in another way, much more mysterious.

Genealogical telescoping was a classic feature of structural-functionalist understandings of non-Western societies, and especially of African ones. One of the most beautiful features of these accounts was the way in which they managed to show how things that existentially mattered to specific people, such as specific places or specific feuds, were elegantly mapped back onto the past as concise stories about it. To find that what my memory had done exactly replicates what the structural-functionalists said that African people habitually do pleases me, and restores to me the more generous vision that I had of them both before a more mean-spirited agenda took over.

What is genuinely mysterious to me is that the story of my grandfather's eviction as a boy from Allt Craoinidh probably refers to an actual event that took place around 1785, when the then 4th Duke of Atholl began to evict his tenantry from Glen Tilt. My great-great-grandfather, and not my grandfather, must have been that boy. The memory of that event has been handed down through five generations of my family, including myself. This is now a span of well over two hundred years. Furthermore, it is has been handed down with such adamantine clarity that, in 2007, I could point to a specific set of ruins, in a valley full of pretty much indistinguishable ruins, and tell my friend, visiting from England, "This is the spot where my forefathers dwelt." Not Scotland, not the Highlands, not Perthshire, not Atholl, not even Glen Tilt, but this specific place, these ruins here. This little place is *mo duthchas*, "the spot where my forefathers dwelt." Now, how on earth do I know that?

Acknowledgments

The origins of this chapter are with the Piro (Yine) and Asháninka people of the Bajo Urubamba river in Peruvian Amazonia. I thank Daimā for listening to me and for asking the question, and Tânia Stolze Lima and Marcio Goldman for providing the other long conversations in which the original conversation could begin to make sense. I thank Tadesse Wolde for first showing me, in his own ancestral lands in Gamo, that thinking respectfully of my ancestors as an anthropologist might be a good thing to do. I thank João Pina Cabral and Christina Toren for inviting me to think these thoughts; Gillian Evans, Jadran Mimica, and Jeanette Edwards for their lucid comments on them; and Michael Bowles for help with the research. I thank Sue Lewis for first alerting me to the mystery about what Malinowski famously never said, and Maurice Bloch for resolving it. I thank my late mother Helen Gow, my sister Vivien Young, and my brother Ian Gow for their support and for key conversations.

Peter Gow is Professor of Social Anthropology at the University of St Andrews. He has been conducting long-term ethnographic research in southwestern Amazonia since 1978, primarily with the Piro (Yine), Asháninka, and other people of the Bajo Urubamba River in Peru. He is the author of numerous articles and two monographs: *Of Mixed Blood: Kinship and History in Peruvian Amazonia* (1991) and *An Amazonian Myth and its History* (2001). He is also engaged in a project on social transformation since the eighteenth century in Atholl in the Southern Highlands of Scotland.

Notes

1. See http://www.gutenberg.org/etext/14179 at the Web site of Project Gutenberg, the first and largest individual collection of electronic books.
2. Radcliffe-Brown (1952: 50) wrote, "My objection to conjectural history is not that it is historical, but that it is conjectural."
3. Most of the tenants were men, although a few were widows (see Leneman 1986).
4. Published in 1835–1845 in Edinburgh and London by William Blackwood and Sons, *The New Statistical Account of Scotland* is composed of reports, written by parish ministers under the superintendence of a Committee of the Society for the Benefit of the Sons and Daughters of the Clergy, that contain descriptions of each parish (see http://edina.ac.uk/stat-acc-scot/). This particular citation is from vol. 10, for the county of Perth, published in 1845.
5. The people of Atholl were notorious for their frequent refusal to accept the legitimacy of their Murray landlords' claims on their loyalty and obedience.
6. In conversational response to an earlier version of this chapter, both Jeanette Edwards and Gillian Evans have told me that the notion of asserting hereditary rights over land owned by others is also held by people in their respective fieldwork sites of Bacup (north Lancashire) and Bermondsey (south London), neither of which have any strong historical connections to Highland Scotland. It seems likely that many of the recent anthropological studies of what is slackly called 'identity' in Britain are actually describing unrecognized concepts such as multiple ownership of place and existential territories.
7. See http://www.scotlandspeople.gov.uk/.

References

Atholl, John, Duke of. 1908. *Chronicles of the Atholl and Tullibardine Families*. Privately printed.

Bloch, Maurice. 1977. "The Past and the Present in the Present." *Man* 12: 278–292.

Broadie, Alexander, ed. 1997. *The Scottish Enlightenment: An Anthology*. Edinburgh: Canongate Books.

_____. 2001. *The Scottish Enlightenment: The Historical Age of the Historical Nation*. Edinburgh: Birlinn.

Devine, T. M. 2006. *Clearance and Improvement: Land, Power and People in Scotland 1700–1900*. Edinburgh: John Donald.

Dodgshon, Robert A. 2006. *From Chiefs to Landlords: Social and Economic Change in the Western Highlands and Islands, c. 1493–1820*. Edinburgh: Edinburgh University Press.

Dwelly, Edward. 2001. *The Illustrated Gaelic-English Dictionary*. Edinburgh: Birlinn. [First published in Glasgow in 1901–1911.]

Gould, Stephen Jay. 1990. *Time's Arrow, Time's Cycle: Myth and Metaphor in the Discovery of Geological Time*. London: Penguin.

_____. 1993. *Eight Little Piggies: Reflections in Natural History*. London: Jonathan Cape.

Gow, Peter. 2001. *An Amazonian Myth and its History*. Oxford: Oxford University Press.

Grant, Isabel F. 1924. *Every-Day Life on an Old Highland Farm, 1769–1782*. London: Longmans, Green & Co.

_____. 1995. *Highland Folk Ways*. Edinburgh: Birlinn.

Hunter, James. 1999. *Last of the Free: A Millennial History of the Highlands and Islands of Scotland*. Edinburgh: Mainstream Publishing.

_____. 2005. *Scottish Exodus: Travels among a Worldwide Clan*. Edinburgh: Mainstream Publishing.

Jones, Jean. 1985. "James Hutton's Agricultural Research and His Life as a Farmer." *Annals of Science* 42: 573–601.

Kerr, John. 1984–1986. "East by Tilt." *Transactions of the Gaelic Society of Inverness* 54: 376–410.

Leneman, Leah. 1986. *Living in Atholl: A Social History of the Estates, 1685–1785*. Edinburgh: Edinburgh University Press.

Lévi-Strauss, Claude. 1966. *The Savage Mind*. London: Weidenfield and Nicholson.

_____. 1997. *Look. Listen, Read*. New York: BasicBooks.

Lima, Tânia Stolze. 2005. *Um peixe olhou para mim: O povo Yudjá e a perspectiva*. São Paulo: Editora UNESP.

Macinnes, Allan I. 1996. *Clanship, Commerce and the House of Stewart, 1603–1788*. East Linton: Tuckwell Press.

Martin, Martin. 2003. *Curiosities of Art and Nature: The New Annotated and Illustrated Edition of Martin Martin's Classic "A Description of the Western Islands of Scotland."* Ed. Michael Robson. Port of Ness: Island Book Trust.

McIntyre, Donald B., and Alan McKirdy. 2001. *James Hutton: The Founder of Modern Geology*. Edinburgh: National Museums of Scotland Publishing.

Mooney, James. 1896. *The Ghost-Dance Religion and the Sioux Outbreak of 1890*. Pp. 645–1136 in *Fourteenth Annual Report (Part 2) of the Bureau of Ethnology to the Smithsonian Institution, 1892–93*. Washington, DC: Government Printing Office.]

Moses, L. G. 1984. *The Indian Man: A Biography of James Mooney*. Urbana: University of Illinois Press.

Radcliffe-Brown, Alfred R. 1952. *Structure and Function in Primitive Society*. London: Routledge and Kegan Paul.

Sinclair, John, ed. 1983. *The Statistical Account of Scotland, 1791–1799*. Wakefield: EP Publishing.

Siskind, Janet. 1973. *To Hunt in the Morning*. New York: Oxford University Press.

Stevenson, David. 2004. *The Hunt for Rob Roy: The Man and the Myths*. Edinburgh: Birlinn Press.

Stocking, George W., Jr. 1987. *Victorian Anthropology*. New York: Free Press.

Tax, Sol, Loren C. Eiseley, Irving Rouse, and Carl F. Voegelin, eds. 1953. *An Appraisal of Anthropology Today*. Chicago, IL: University of Chicago Press.

Chapter 2

PHENOMENOLOGICAL PSYCHOANALYSIS
The Epistemology of Ethnographic Field Research

Jadran Mimica

I

For the purpose of this presentation, I will define myself as an ethnographer whose quest is for an accurate interpretation of the Yagwoia life-world (Papua New Guinea) in terms of these people's own cosmo-ontological categories and concrete practices. From the very beginnings of my ethnographic project (my first long-term fieldwork having started in 1977), I accepted the common view that anthropological understanding is bedeviled by the practitioners' own cultural biases and uncritical use of a range of concepts specific to Occidental cultural, especially academic, frameworks of knowledge—from the scientific to the commonsensical. These are constituted as a personal egoic synthesis of understanding, affectivity, and cognitive practice. This perspective has been and still is a basic step toward a standard exercise of anthropological self-critique. Indeed, through ethnographic practice anthropology inherently calls for a radical, critical reflection on itself as a project of critical knowledge *of* human beings *by* human beings. I also regard this perspective as a sort of shared normative value among anthropologists. Therefore, one can assume it to be a trademark

Notes for this chapter begin on page 55.

characteristic of any anthropologist working as an ethnographer. However, describing concretely the practice of critical knowledge and understanding in the case of any particular ethnographer is an open problem. Correlative to this indeterminate reality of the actual process of anthropological knowledge making are the overt epistemological self-presentations by specific practitioners. These too have to be critically considered. It is the practitioner's ethnography and concrete interpretations that will be the primary basis for judging his/her self-accomplishment as the epistemic subject, understood as an ongoing personal dynamic synthesis of his/her knowledge-and-ignorance.

It is important to be mindful of this dialectical determination of knowledge, namely, that there is no knowing without an N number of correlative modes of unknowing, the most important ones being determined by the un/conscious[1] structures of the personality and the narcissistic dynamics of its egoity, both of which shape and co-determine volitional cogitation and objectification, the latter usually through the activity of writing. Thus, conterminous with the positive will to knowledge, there is a negative will that generates a myriad of intentional modifications of what is seemingly a positive self-projection. Accordingly, the epistemic subject, apart from knowing that which s/he endeavors to know, is also the one who always knows less than what is knowable about his/her chosen subject matter. This is the horizon of positive, factical ignorance, which is inexhaustible. But in addition, s/he also is the subject of his/her own ignorance because s/he does not *want* to know. To be sure, s/he actively suppresses this self-determination qua negative will from within his/her volitionally sustained self-consciousness. Of the two modalities of ignorance, it is this latter negativity that is of critical importance, since it shapes the subject's relation to the project of knowledge as a dynamic totality, most importantly, its immanent horizon of truth, which is determined by the subject's own activity as the author of his/her knowledge and its veracity.

As for the object of his/her knowledge and understanding, for the moment I will not prioritize some alien cultural life-world that the ethnographer strives to interpret as best as s/he can and preferably in its own terms, but rather the ethnographer's own native intellectual tradition, which enables him/her to carry out his/her project as a project of knowledge. And since I will take the Western anthropologist as my prototypical ethnographer, it is the Western intellectual tradition that is in question. Having delimited the epistemic situation within this particular cultural-historical horizon, I will provide a few additional specifications of the epistemic subject.

Thus, to the extent that the anthropologist experiences, explores, and cogitates any specific life-world (e.g., myself in relation to the Yagwoia), s/he does so relative to his/her own cultural life-world, specifically, its intellectual tradition. Now, it is an open question as to whether this knowing subject is in any credible way knowledgeable of his/her Occidental cultural life-world and its intellectual tradition, or whether s/he would have a mindful and open orientation toward it, which is to say that this life-world, too, has to be understood in its own terms.

In this regard, the following will have to suffice as a fairly realistic characterization. Anthropologists differ from each other in terms of their knowledge of anthropology and their ability to transform this knowledge, obtained through undergraduate and postgraduate studies, into an ethnographic project. Equally so, they mutually differ with respect to their relation to the wider horizon of critical knowledge and intellectual tradition to which anthropology belongs as a body of Occidental cultural knowledge. Bluntly stated, some ethnographers are more knowledgeable 'all around', as it were, than others. Nonetheless, any ethnographer in relation to his/her cultural intellectual tradition is its conduit, and in this determination (by no means absolute and unalterable) s/he is making some other (alien) life-world intelligible, as best as s/he can, through a mixture of knowledge and ignorance of primarily his/her own cultural frameworks of knowledge.

This I take to be the plight of every anthropologist and ethnographer. This is why, I hasten to say, anthropological self-critique and epistemological self-reflection should not be viewed solely as self-gratifying rhetorical bravado and expostulation about Western culture and its 'metaphysics', examples of which abound in current academic 'discourses'. Instead, they would have to be more concretely informed and thoughtful explorations of Western cultural life-worlds and, especially, the vicissitudes of the Western tradition of critical thought.

To the extent that a viable ethnographic understanding and interpretation of other human beings and their life-world presupposes the practice of critical self-knowledge,[2] it is not an exaggeration to point out that anthropology qua the ethnographic project is one of the most radical and demanding undertakings in the quest for knowledge and understanding.

II

Consider the contrast between Lévi-Strauss's and Malinowski's self-testimonies about their respective field experience. Fundamentally, Lévi-Strauss's *Tristes Tropiques* (1973) is an intellectual-aesthetic testimony of a limited ethnographic project, although it can also be seen as a failure.[3] But if he failed to achieve recognition as an ethnographer, Lévi-Strauss did become a truly great anthropologist. Defeated and overwhelmed by the flesh-and-blood concreteness of specific modes of Amerindian existence, he reconstituted himself through the universality of anthropological perspective, which freed him "from doubt, since it examines those differences and changes in mankind which have a meaning for all men, and excludes those peculiar to a single civilization, which dissolve into nothingness under the gaze of the outside observer. Lastly, it appeases that restless and destructive appetite I have already referred to, by ensuring me a virtually inexhaustible supply of material, thanks to the diversity of manners, customs and institutions. It allows me to reconcile my character with my life" (ibid.: 58–59). In his case, the narcissistic wound (well attested to in the chapter "The Apotheosis of Augustus") (ibid.: 373–382) and character were transmuted through a magnificent intellectual self-synthesis and a matching illustrious academic career. One's character is assuaged by one's life.

The last sentence in Malinowski's *A Diary in the Strict Sense of the Term* (1967: 298) is "Truly I lack real character." The inner, un/conscious horizon of Malinowski's fieldwork situation was determined by the archetypal dimension of his primordial condition. Enwombed by pre-Oedipal symbiotic (incorporative) identifications with his Mother, Malinowski was struggling with his narcissistic-symbiotic character. As he recounts: "In the evening the devil persuaded me to call on Dr Simpson. I went in a bad humor and completely torpid, and climbed slowly up the hill ... At moments was assailed by blackest depression. Today, Monday, 9.20.14, I had a strange dream; homosex., with my own double as partner. Strangely autoerotic feelings; the impression that I'd like to have a mouth just like mine to kiss, a neck that curves just like mine, a forehead just like mine (seen from the side). I got up tired and collected myself slowly" (ibid.: 12–13). A split soul, Malinowski was living internally as an adhesive syzygy of his inner Mother, craving a narcissistic ideality of his primordial monadic unity: "My whole ethics is based on the fundamental instinct of unified personality" (ibid.: 296). This "fundamental instinct" is his intra-psychic umbilicus, which he never severed. This is why his monadic instinct revealed to him the only place in which he could experience self-unity: "At times I see Mother still alive, in a soft grey hat and a grey dress, or in a house dress, or in a black dress, with a round black hat.—Again frightening thoughts: death, a skeleton, naturalistic thoughts interwoven with pain in the heart. My own death is becoming something infinitely more real to me.—Strong feeling—to join her in nothingness. I recall things Mother used to say about death. I recall the countless occasions when I deliberately cut myself off from Mother, so as to be alone, independent—not to have the feeling that I am part of a whole—furious regrets and guilt feelings" (ibid.: 297).

Correlative to this interior situation, in the exteriority of two Melanesian life-worlds (Mailu and the Trobriands), Malinowski conducted fieldwork that produced a magisterial ethnographic corpus and laid the foundations for the project of ethnography and, relative to it, anthropological theory building. To top it off, he left a profound document of his own inner being, handwritten in his Mother tongue, with no plan to publish it in order to make self-gratifying epistemological and moral capital out of it.

To conduct a systematic psychoanalysis as an ethnographer in relation to individual (local) co-workers facilitates a better management and understanding of the personally very demanding and self-alienating experiences that commonly characterize ethnographic research and are constitutive of its results (see Devereux 1967). Furthermore, I hold that insofar as it purports to be a productive science of human existence, anthropology has to be founded upon phenomenology and psychoanalysis. Castoriadis's (1987) theoretical work provides one particular lead that may be used to implement, through concrete work, the unsurpassed horizons of psychoanalytic anthropology developed by Freud, Jung, Rank, and Roheim.[4] What I advocate is a self-critical ethnographic psychoanalysis that is shaped by self-transformative transferential-countertransferential relations between the ethnographer and the specific individuals (informants) who mediate for the ethnographer their life-world and its constitutive imaginary (see, e.g., Mimica 2006, 2007a; Weiss and Stanek 2007). In trying to reach the depths of a culture that he/she is exploring, the very foundations of the ethnographer's egoity are in question. What is challenged is the most cherished and deeply ingrained sense of humanness as the function of one's own egoity. In this regard, Devereux's (1967) insights are as vital as ever.

In doing ethnography, one's character and personality structure are both the limiting and facilitating conditions of the ethnographic project itself. Here, a self-reflective exercise has to be carried out in a Malinowskian mode. The ethnographer has to work through his/her own egoic self-erosion, defenses, and projections, and, equally so, through the defenses and projections of the informants (Mimica 2003a, 2003b, 2007a). Through this process, the ethnographer is genuinely creating a critical understanding that is grounded in the depths of his/her and other people's psychic being. Unless one is willing to work self-critically at this level, ethnographic understanding will not break out of the limitations of the ethnographer's self-idealizations that are rooted in his/her inner archaic-narcissistic position.[5] Only through the modification of this self-deceiving yet vital threshold of the ethnographer's subjectivity will a self-reflective and critical method produce a more acute and objective mode of ethnographic understanding. In this sense, the theoretical basis of an empirically validated *verstehen* method (Weber) must necessarily be developed through phenomenology and psychoanalysis. No formulaic application or supervision is a viable solution; every practitioner has to discover the objective possibilities of subjective understanding in the first person and through empirical practice.

If one aspires to perfectibility in the field of indefinite knowledge shaped by omnipresent ignorance, that is, if the ethnographer aspires to an ever more accurate ethnographic knowledge and its synthesis into theoretical understanding, the only way is through intensive and, in principle, endless concrete work, a permanent self-modification that can be characterized as an intra-psychic surgery by one's own hand—and without an anesthetic. One can learn it all from Freud, Jung, Klein, Fairbarn, Winnicott, and Guntrip, or from Husserl and Sartre. And, of course, in the process one is making errors. The only remedy is that one should be willing to endeavor to detect and duly correct them, which in turn requires more fieldwork, more self-exercise of authentic relations with one's own fieldwork experience and labor, more thinking, more suffering. All in all, it is worthwhile, but not because, as the ethnographer Herdt (2001: 28) recently put it, "anthropology may be an impossible dream (which may die, if not nurtured)." This is an idealization, and hence the rhetorical incantation of anthropology as "an impossible dream"—as if the 25 years of Herdt's own professional life as a prominent figure in American institutions and as the recipient of numerous grants were not enough to convince him that (at least as an academic profession) anthropology is a wholly socio-economically and politically realized practice that allows him and numerous other anthropologists to pursue it as a self-project, which they actualize every which way. And when it is practiced as a self-critical and self-responsible activity, at its best it may be humanizing in the sense that one may choose to make the best possibilities out of one's own far from perfect, and perfected, being.

An ethnographer neither lives the life nor dies the death of the people s/he is working with. And yet it is the interrelations between the two and the dynamics of human passions and radical imagination that constitute the ontological nexus of any given life-world. To be sure, human facticity does not exist outside of its own human self-constitution. Intrinsic to every society, being the field generated as the dynamic structure of egoic bodily intersubjectivity, is the internal self-defense against itself, its own weaknesses, vulnerability, and sham, along with the amplification of its own ideality and omnipotence. The constitution of every human society primordially includes a synthesis of its own ambivalence and the concomitant schizoid dynamics that generate its totalization. Power, exploitation, violence, and distortions, vulnerability and sham—these should not be approached as primarily the symptoms of failure at the synthesis, but the very reality of every human social synthesis. Therefore, for every anthropologist the preparatory task is to open him/herself up to a mood that discloses this very situation of total humanness, and this demands a creative effort—the effort to create a new horizon of intelligibility that correlates with a particular ethnographic encounter. To descend into the pleroma of total humanness and to behold with understanding its expression in each particular human situation, one has also to recognize it in oneself and as such to acknowledge this transpersonal ontological horizon of the psychic being over and against one's own social-cultural-historical, moral, and intellectual finality. Herein is the permanent relevance of psychoanalysis and anthropology in the conquest of human ignorance and the creation of knowledge, truth, and human freedom.

The acuteness of ethnographic understanding depends on a will to enter into this pleromatic matrix of existence, which psychoanalysis and phenomenology can clarify and deepen like no other framework of critical reflection, providing that it is practiced with a total commitment to the project of ethnography for which "one's character in relation to one's life" (Lévi-Strauss 1973) is in need of self-critical transformation rather than self-reconciliation. One can reconcile oneself with oneself, but one can still misunderstand both oneself and other humans. Ignorance, self-deception, and false consciousness are not taken care of by any techniques of reconciliation. Rather, the latter requires the former. In this view, anthropology is far from being an impossible dream. Its self-transcending actualization is effected through each individual practitioner's will to achieve true self-recognition and the will to choose to act accordingly as an epistemic subject.

Critical in psychoanalytic practice are the vicissitudes of the narcissistic depths of the human egoic self (its archaic core), the ethnographer's no less than that of the individuals s/he is working with. There is no possibility of escaping the archaic narcissistic dynamism of the egoic un/consciousness, but one can learn how to contend with it and avoid being defeated in the process. As a bonus, one can use it more constructively, such as in the service of the creation of a more realistically viable self-grounded and self-accountable knowledge of oneself and others.

Many anthropologists with what I shall call 'refle-x-tionist' sensibilities do not seem to appreciate sufficiently that a critical self-reflection is not the same as a narcissistic theatre of selective self-disclosure, a pseudo-drama of idealized balance of the 'truth' of one's own limitations and actualizations, but rather a means of creating more accurate knowledge. To be lucid about one's own limitations is a basic step. There is no epistemological and concrete empirical gain to be derived from it. The immediate step is to do something constructively about one's defects. A person with a healthy narcissistic equilibrium will know what to do: swallow his/her self-idealization, suspend his/her delusory desire for omnipotence and omniscience, and proceed to do work on his/her deficiencies and see how far he/she will get in that regard. Concrete work is more likely to transform one's narcissistic desires, and in fact it does yield far more gratifying objects, since the project of ethnography is about concrete knowledge. And because narcissistic desire is inexhaustible, one will be able to draw on it to propel oneself into more action, whose aim is to conquer the problematic, resisting, and titillating object. It is better to make the limitations real than to make them a narcissistic object of one's own idealized self-representations, which is what, more often than not, is managed in so many would-be self-reflexive ethnographies.

This is but a glossy metaphoric prop for the stage of self-representation. The 'critical' hyper-reflexivity evidenced in such writings is nothing else but the investigators' defensive self-consolidation within the shield of narcissistic self-mirroring, which systematically occludes the real flaws, that is, deficiencies, and the limitations in the dimension of concrete knowledge. The former purports to be the icing for the latter. An authentic, psychoanalytically guided reflective turn is an altogether different operation. In taking up psychoanalysis and phenomenology, one stands and falls by it, although not primarily through its application to others, but, firstly and recurrently, to oneself. What abounds in the purportedly self-reflective anthropological liturgy is an egoic circuity that I call 'reflexivity', with the x inflection, to emphasize the fixed, blind, or routinized character of egoic self-regard, which, precisely because of its automatism and routinized 'strategic' (i.e., opportunistic) modes of being oneself, brings into the scope of consciousness only those aspects that cancel and/or inhibit further need for self-understanding or critical self-modification.

Reflexivity is a closed-off circuit of the egoic self-regard determined by its own unpunctured narcissistic auto-scotoma. Two of its main qualities, cowardice and defensiveness, are projected as a higher (grandiose) morality. Reflection, on the other hand, is a penetrating and critical self-regard that, with each current of the inward turning, spreads deeper and deeper into the realms of the egoic self and attempts to comprehend its internal constitution. Relative to the intensity and depth of self-reflection, such circuity is bound to destabilize, at some stage, the egoic dimension of the self. Among other effects, this will cause depression, for it becomes evident that one is not exactly the kind of being that one aspired, and assumed oneself, to be. The narcissistic dynamics of these and other modes of the circuity of egoic self-regard, which now amounts to a struggle with the death instinct and a transformation of knowledge (Bion [1962] 1994, [1970] 1995) through the transformation of the capacity to love self and object in relation to the truth-driven will to knowledge, cannot be dealt with here. My point, however, is that as an 'epistemophilic pursuit',[6] the practice of self-reflectivity has to engender and to sustain systematically a genuine depressive position, which alone will transform the practitioner into a mature epistemic—or, more accurately, gnostic—subject. To be sure, this practice of anthropological understanding through love and knowledge of humanity, the result of authentic ethnographic encounters, has nothing to do with the degradation of anthropology and critical knowledge at large that is characteristic of current academic enterprise. Here, the managerial-performative online packaging of information deemed to be competitive and marketable has effectively reduced research to participation in seasonal grant applications, while the purpose of lecture courses is seen primarily as a means for the fee-paying students to get their degrees, that is, 'value' for money. The increasing effect is that institutional academic performance thinking makes both ignorance and knowledge approximate an equal degree of non-sense, fraudulence, and lack of accountability.[7] Fueled by envy and arrogance, the currently dominant styles of performative thinking in anthropology have turned into a narcissistic mutilation of the extant diversity of human cultural life-worlds, as well as of knowledge and values created by past generations of scholars and thinkers, a veritable expression of the self-seeking global 'subjectivities'. Appropriately, these egoities advocate 'multi-sited field research' and write 'non-evidentiary' ethnographies.

III

Henri Michaux once remarked: "Rare indeed are madmen equal to madness." Similarly, it can be said: "Rare indeed are ethnographers equal to the human realities of the cultures they study." With respect to the ouroboric and related ontological underpinnings of New Guinea (and other) life-worlds (Mimica 1981, 1991), even the most sagacious ethnographers miss their significance, despite long periods of field research and the use of powerful conceptual frameworks, including psychoanalysis. This has to do with the fact that their use of psychoanalysis lacks ontological grounding in the life-worlds that these ethnographers purport to interpret.

For all Melanesian cultures, the cultural life-worlds are shaped to the positive realizations of the ontological phantasy of the psychic being, not just for its control, sublimation, attenuation, rationalization, or, say, transcendence. The Yagwoia life-world (or, for example, the Gimi of the Eastern Highlands) is not, to use Gillison's (1993) characterization, "between culture and fantasy." It is the life-made-culture, made so by the plenitude of desires of the human embodied un/conscious psyche, whose primordial project is its own self-projection into and actualization as phantasy-which-is-the-world. In this sense, culture is the fulfillment and affirmation of phantasy. These life-worlds articulate radical passions of the soul, not a middle position on existence, a neurotic self-compromise. Therefore, not being a collective existential mediocrity, New Guinea life-worlds demand from the ethnographer a total commitment to their truth, which is both phantasy and culture-as-reality. There is no 'between' for these people precisely because their phantasy is constitutive of their vital, sexual-appetitive-aggressive cathexes of the world. Their libido is inseparable from their mortido. And as any New Guinea ethnographic corpus clearly shows, these life-worlds histori-cally have had an absolutely total self-commitment to themselves, as a totality of life-and-death. Indeed, nothing less is to be expected from a humanness that practiced, among so many other formidable modes of autopoietic self-consum-mation, exo- and endo-cannibalism, institutionalized male homosexuality, and headhunting, to mention only a few.

In other words, all psychoanalytic (and ethnographic) interpretations are in need of a more thorough grounding in the given life-world subjectivities. There is always a problem of the choice of the psychoanalytic framework of understanding, the depth of the ethnographer's/psychoanalyst's self-reflection, and, correlatively, his/her ability and will to project him/herself imaginatively into the life-world of a particular people, who, most importantly, are neither good citizens nor citizen-subjects. The tacit and diverse ontologies of the Mela-nesian egoity and sociality require that the ethnographer reflect critically on the cultural ontology of the human subject embedded in all psychoanalytic metapsychologies. Such a precaution will not only enhance the hermeneutic potential of psychoanalytic theories (Freudian, Kleinian, Lacanian, Kohut's self-psychology, Jungian, etc.), but also facilitate the construction of a cultur-ally more adequate representation of a New Guinea (or any other) subjectivity and its life-world. This, in turn, will also appropriately modify a metapsycho-logical scheme of understanding.

The need for this kind of culturally specific hermeneutic grounding of psy-choanalysis becomes evident when one tries to grasp the psycho-cultural logics of incest and their articulations in different life-worlds. One deals here with radically different constitutions and self-problematizations of 'family' or, better yet, societal complexes and the bisexual matrix of the human psychic being. From these follow all other ontological differences between the 'subject' as constructed by psychoanalytic metapsychologies, developed in concrete Occi-dental social-cultural conditions of existence, and a particular constellation of New Guinea subjectivity and its cultural life-world. Let me expand on this by drawing on my work among the Yagwoia, since among them, as elsewhere in New Guinea (and in so many other life-worlds on this globe), the sphere of human egoity is constituted as that entity which is commonly rendered in ethnographic literature as the 'soul' (see Mimica 2003a). But here, it is deter-mined consubstantially with human embodiment as a microcosmic realm that is intrinsically dependent on the macrocosmic world-body, the luno-solar ener-gies, and other powers existing therein.

In the Yagwoia life-world, all modalities of human experience and action belong to this macrocosmic existential totality. Here, the realm of the 'social' has no ontological privilege of being the arbiter of what is 'real' or 'socialized' and thus acceptable as such. The horizon of human experience in all its depths, heterogeneity, and intensity is conterminous with everything that there is—past, present, and future. Accordingly, the Yagwoia un/conscious is macrocosmic, and the realm of the 'social' is but the microcosmic, part = whole self-expression of the macrocosmos.[8] And qua dreaming, due to the wanderings of the human soul-component, which detaches when a person falls asleep (Mimica 2006), the physical exteriority of the Yagwoia world has a permanent constitutive determination in and of their living un/conscious, which, reciprocally, is continuously objectified in and qua the exteriority of the world. In the same process, the living un/conscious is continuously open to somatization and socialization.

Parenthetically, given the intensity of the Yagwoia cathexis of their world-body and the ubiquity of its immanence in the un/conscious body-images of concrete individuals, it can be firmly said that their coenaestheses are saturated with the quiddity of the world-body as much as with their primary maternal embodiment. The two define one and the same primordial habitus of motility and sensibility. I am true to the facticity of the Yagwoia embodiment when I say that in their life-world insanity, which is a condition induced by spirits (not infrequently of the deceased maternal relatives), is as much a rupture of the somatized psyche as of the coenaesthetic image of its world. As for the 'social', it lives the life borrowed from the powers/energies of the psycho-soma, its imaginary, and the world, which is the immediate realm of the sensuous. It is more to the point to say that for so many modern and postmodern Westerners (but not for the Yagwoia), insanity is the unpalatable truth of the limitations and idealizations of the parameters that define their sense of the normal human socius. By and large, the Western civic socius is at ease with neuroses of all sorts (they are the stuff of 'socialized emotion' and of egos well equipped with 'social skills'), but it cannot tolerate psychotic leakages and ruptures. In a life-world where spirits are as much a part of the 'natural' order of the day as pigs, marsupials, and humans themselves, 'psychoses' are nothing more than a commonly encountered 'social fact'.[9]

This brief sketch of the facticity of the Yagwoia life-world, with the accent on the oneiric mode of experience, makes it clear that, for the Yagwoia, their life-world is no less real in their dreaming than in their wakefulness. Correspondingly, to know the Yagwoia life-world and themselves, as they are qua their experience and action, requires exploration of every mode of their experience and its articulations. Only through this total perspective can one come to understand the Yagwoia sense of reality and their modes of reality-appraisal and validation. Dreaming and dreams constitute the existential domain that can be entered into relatively easily. Through a long-term, systematic ethnographic-psychoanalytic exploration, dreams will disclose the concrete dynamic configurations and cultural specificity of the un/conscious imaginary matrix of the Yagwoia life-world, at once personal and transpersonal. Every dream is an expression of this totalizing synthesis of the dreamer and his/her life-situation, the life-world immanent in it as a whole, and identical to its living part = whole, the dreamer.[10] The radical imaginary invoked here is, literally, the ontological source of all human reality (Castoriadis 1984, 1987),[11] the creative matrix by virtue of which there is any given human cultural life-world.

Furthermore, by studying the practice and intersubjective dynamics of mourning (Mimica 2006), the ethnographer comes to experience it as a process that, with singular force, realizes the Yagwoia life-world as an indissoluble socius of the living and the dead. It is in this context that the ethnographer also comes to experience and appreciate the palpability of spirits as the real denizens of the Yagwoia world and, by the same token, is moved to explore more cogently the horizonal differentiation and delimitations of their experiential field, specifically in terms of the topographical implications of the notion of the un/conscious.

In the life-world dimension of dream experience, the egoic self's noetic activity articulates itself without the willful interference of the wakeful self-conscious and critical self-regard. To the extent that all Yagwoia dreams were reported to me (as they are among the Yagwoia) ex post facto, they still were the products of their sleeping egos and their internal objects. As such, they are the work of what I delineate as their un/conscious. I put it so precisely because the relation between consciousness and the un/conscious is subject to diverse articulations in different life-worlds. Experientially, their mutual articulation does not conform to a universal dimensional topography, principally in terms of a distinction between psychic interiority and exteriority. My use of the slash in 'un/conscious' indicates that there is no a priori assumption made as to how and in what mode, if at all, something is unconscious in a given field of experience.[12] This calibration varies between individuals and life-worlds, and between different periods within one and the same life-world. In terms of the Yagwoia life-world-specific ontological underpinnings of their experiences and existence, the basic dimensionality of their 'I-ness', such as interiority/exteriority and all its derivatives, is a radically different inner/outer field. Spirits no less than the soul, or any other presences experienced, for instance, in dreams, are not for the Yagwoia 'internal objects' composed of life-memories or archetypal images. These entities are either entirely autonomous (e.g., spirits) and external to a given 'I' (ego) or in a semi-detachable incorporative/excorporative relation with the body and 'I-ness', as, for instance, one's dream-soul component (see Mimica 2003a, 2006, 2007a).

The ego and its derivations, egoic, egoity, stress the primary, irreducible bodily sphere of the human experiential field and its constitution qua the dialectics of the body ego (Fliess 1956, 1961) and its maternal envelopment (Klein [1932] 1988; Lacan 1977; Mahler, Pine, and Bergman [1975] 1985; Neumann 1954; Stern 1985). By a somewhat cumbersome phrase, 'egoic self', I specify the figure-ground dynamics within the embodied sphere of experience. Selfhood is the total dynamic ground of the psycho-soma vis-à-vis which the ego/I-ness is the figure subject to a myriad of fluctuating modalities of auto^allo-morphic dynamics (including auto^allo-centricity, auto^allo-recognition) and always in reciprocal formative relation to its total ground. When I write 'Self' with a capital S, I am referring to the realm of the radical, archetypal schemata of experience (Jung 1968a, 1968b), which in the Yagwoia life-world is objectified as the ouroboric Cosmic Self. This transpersonal Self is immanent in the egoic selfhood of every living and dead Yagwoia. This, in short, is the framework within which the Yagwoia sense of 'agency' can be adequately explored and interpreted. My published work provides ample ethnographic demonstration of this formulation,[13] and, accordingly, I can say that my psychoanalysis is phenomenologically grounded in the Yagwoia life-world. Their psychic being is accounted for with a maximal fidelity to its life-world constitution. So although my use of notions such as 'un/conscious', 'egoic self', and 'internal objects' is within the frame work of psychoanalytic metapsychological conceptualization, this is done as an interpretive exercise that both maintains and amplifies the ontological original-ity and existential integrity of the Yagwoia selfhood and life-world.

More significantly, this approach also brings us most immediately into the sphere of the primary, constitutive somatic imagination of the Yagwoia embodiment, whereby its 'material' composition and quiddity of substance (that which we readily know and identify as flesh, tissue, organs, skin, bone, blood, and semen, or, more recently, as cells, genes, etc.) acquire their primary objectification.[14] Organismic articulation of experience and cognition takes place in the mediation of bodily interiority and exteriority and the total trajec-tory of bodily composition, growth, transformations (injuries, regrowth, etc.), and eventual disintegration (corpse fluids, disincarnation, etc.). This is the realm of concrete experience of some such categorical quiddity as 'substantial-ity' of the human embodied self (its 'materiality', 'animatedness', etc.) and its concrete world (earth, stones, trees, mountains, sky, sun, moon, rain, rivers, etc.). Fundamentally, numerous modes of quiddity, haecceity, and seity of the world's 'matter' are shaped by the primary imaginary matrix of the synthesis of experience through which human embodiment, at once intersubjective and cosmicized, achieves and sustains its living objectivity.

I should also add that this set of reflections on the macro/microcosmic dialectics of subjectivity and articulation of experience is one way of concret-izing Leenhardt's (1979: 61) cosmo-poetic pronouncement that because "the native is filled with the world's pulse, he does not distinguish the world from his body." As for his view that the Melanesian is "unaware that the body is an element which he himself possesses" (ibid.: 32), all I can say is that, at its best, this would-be cosmo-ontological pronouncement is a piece of misleading rhetoric, exemplary of how one can go astray in an effort to do cosmo-poetic ethnography. One would have to ask how the Canaques perform such a hum-ble, practical action as transporting themselves through their concrete world. If one takes Leenhardt at his word, it would follow that falling into a fire, hitting a stone, or getting injured would make no difference to the Canaques. If this were so, I do not think that any of them would live for too long. Leenhardt's concept of 'cosmomorphism', as opposed to 'anthropomorphism', is on closer scrutiny unsustainable, specifically in reference to the Canaques, although it has a reasonable coefficient of propaedeutic usefulness. More important, how-ever, is to recognize that his ideas concerning the Melanesian experiential field are motivated by his own sublimated phantasies about the immanent depths of the human (or rather, Christian) psychic being.[15] He had used naive psy-chological theories whose empirical experiential content (be that imagination, perception, affectivity) was minimal. Accordingly, his intellectual constructions could proceed unobstructed, but at the price of unnecessary absurdities.[16]

Leenhardt's flaws are at once too fundamental and too serious to be com-pounded with uncritical appreciation (e.g., Strathern 1988). Rather, one has to learn from his and Lévy-Bruhl's errors by familiarizing oneself with thinkers such as Cassirer, Freud, Jung, Melanie Klein, and Schilder, to name a few.[17] They are also necessary for a critical appreciation of Heidegger's 'primordial understanding' and 'Dasein analysis', which some New Guinea ethnographers like to draw on.[18]

IV

For a psychoanalytically grounded anthropologist, it is critical to conduct field-work with a psychoanalytic self-application. But to be sure, exposure to analytic experience does not necessarily ensure a better grasp of psychoanalysis or human reality. The crucial problem is that very few anthropologists who use psychoanalysis do have an adequate understanding of the radical reality of the human psyche. (Nota bene: This is also a deficiency of Castoriadis, who vacillates in his conceptual apprehension of radical imagination or instituting imaginary. In this regard, Jung's analytics of the transpersonal, archetypal sphere of the human psyche is of critical relevance for the further development of psychoanalytic anthropology.)

With or without a personal experience of psychoanalysis, there is often a pronounced and tedious dissonance between the ethnographic material and the ethnographer's interpretative commentaries. Every human life-world is a testimony to the radical reality and generativity of the human psyche—the ontological condition of the human existential matrix determined at once as the intersubjective social-cultural-historical realm and as the intra-subjective interiority and individuality. Anthropological interpretations, on the other hand, first and last reproduce unreflected-upon (mis-)conceptions of the ontological regions that are readily referred to by a battery of labels, such as 'social', 'cul tural', 'psychic', 'material', 'real', 'imaginary', 'symbolic', etc., all of which are usually welded into a very basic functionalist framework of understanding,[19] but are masked by any number of coatings liberally splashed from the cans of the 'currently topical' theoretical discourses. Even in the most committed pursuits of psychoanalytic anthropology, psychoanalysis figures as a veneer rather than as the encompassing horizon of intelligibility and the uncompromisingly penetrating illumination of human existence. Take, for instance, Juillerat's ([1986] 1996) uneasiness about his use of psychoanalysis;[20] he appeals to Bastide as a support rather than, more appropriately, as a footnote to a critical construction and demonstration. Thus, Bastide (but not Juillerat) is reported to have "shown that psychoanalysing a culture is in no way tantamount to reducing the social to the psychic, but requires identifying 'transformation rules' which have enabled the psychic structure to reproduce itself in the sociocultural structure and conversely the latter to produce meaning in individual thought" (ibid.: 546).

This rhetorical proclamation itself attests to the fact that Bastide himself is rather suspect as to achieving a lucid understanding of both the social and psychic, this being clearly indicated by the invocation of some such notions as 'transformational rules'. I am sure that he never identified any such rules, although he might have posited many of them, probably because he would not know any better how to deal with either the psychic or the social. Which is to say that in the hands of such a thinker, psychoanalysis has not come into its own as the basis of the interpretation of the psyche, intersubjectivity, and the creation of the specifically human reality circumscribed by Western notions such as social-cultural-historical. In short, like any framework of understanding, psychoanalysis can be predominantly a gloss in a shaky edifice of concepts that primarily affirm the interpreter's worldview as an ideological form. Thus, psychoanalysis is brought in to consolidate the interpreter's defenses, self-valuation, false self-idealizations, and unattended-to deficiencies, rather than to explore the psychic depths and qua them the self-formations of human life-worlds. Reciprocally, this would enrich and transform the ethnographer's quest for the understanding of a specific life-world and for the reconstruction of anthropology, especially in the present moment of its institutional (academic) disintegration in which thinking is dominated by a lethal atrophy of human spirit, as evinced by the overwhelming conformism and 'omn/i/mpotence'[21] of thought among those who practice it primarily as a vehicle for their career-bound self-realization in the context of that social institution whose object was creation and cultivation of critical knowledge and, by means of such knowledge, action in the social world. Needless to say, this institution (the university) has collapsed, primarily due to the cowardice and opportunism of those who make a living out of it.

Psychoanalysis is as old as the last century, and so virtually is its pursuit in anthropology. The fundamental entailments of psychoanalytic ethnography and the rigors it demands were explicated a long time ago by Devereux (1967), but primordially they were set forth by that great Pythian dictum, 'know thyself'. It applies to the pursuit of the ethnographic project regardless of one's acceptance or rejection of psychoanalysis. Crucial to the integrity of the ethnographic project, with or without psychoanalysis, is the construction and practice of anthropological understanding. This is the medium of increasingly conceptually deficient but conceited discourses spun by the professional fraternities/sororities who inhabit Western metropolitan academic institutions. In regard to this terminal station, one has to be aware that these discourses themselves are the products of the Western civic un/conscious and its culturally and historically specific modes of objectifications, in the form of 'critical' knowledge and moral-aesthetic styles of self-presentation. What starts off as a local fieldwork situation, determined by an alien existential milieu and un/conscious matrix, becomes refracted and metabolized in a psychic medium and sphere of critical-theoretical understanding that caters to and is driven and determined by egoities external to this or that originary life-world, which is also their transpersonal, cultural-historical objectified psyche.

The accomplishments of ethnography as an epistemic project always balance precariously on the relations between some such two (or more) life-worlds, coalescing in the egoity and the un/conscious, at once personal and transpersonal, of the ethnographer. In this perspective, most ethnographers' ethnographic scales tilt heavily on the side of their academic sphere of self-synthesis qua understanding, rather than on the side of the life-worlds that they write about.

To achieve the latter does not mean that the ethnographer would have to become 'one of them'—that is, the people s/he has worked with—or to abandon the perspective of a critical-theoretical self-un/consciousness. Rather, it is a matter of a self-critical and self-reflective exercise for which the basic tenets of classical ethnography and psychoanalysis are more than enough to serve the purpose of methodical guidance. There is no need for the hyper-reflexive bravado that has been in vogue since the inception of postmodern anthropological styles of self-presentation. Every productive ethnographic interpretive process hinges critically on the psychoanalytical self-regard of the interpreter him/herself (Devereux 1967; Mimica 2001) and is not carried out for the sake of reproducing a conceptual framework that quickly calcifies into a formulaic application exercise, determined by his/her own situation, external to the life-world under scrutiny. The second-order formulaic amplifications are at best that—auxiliary amplifications. They cannot carry the crucial work of self-critical analysis, being a work in the service of elucidating an alien cultural life-world in its own terms.

Echoing the dramaturgical perspective, for an ethnographer, the perennial task is to seek the truth of his/her characters in the facticity of their own self-creation and self-interpretation. In this regard, the characters have to be bespoken, refracted, and resynthesized from inside themselves, in their own terms. The ethnographer is the medium of their maximally actualized self-semblance. Neither the ethnographer-dramatist nor the characters themselves may like the emergent self-semblance. But then, who is ready to claim as their own the whole of their own self, sired by critical self-knowledge, rather than glimpsed in that primordial twinkle of maternal eyes that intimate the promise of infinite bliss and perfection, but at the price of narcissistic misrecognition and self-ignorance? Psychoanalytic ethnographers, I expect.

Acknowledgments

This is an extract from a longer work on anthropology and epistemological issues. It comprises three parts, of which the first will appear as a separate article. The bulk of the present chapter comprises the second part of the original, in combination with several sections from the other two. Much-abridged versions of the first and the second parts were presented at the Lisbon and St Andrews symposia on anthropology and epistemology held in late September 2007. I am grateful to the participants for their comments, especially Christina Toren, Peter Gow, and Marcio Goldman.

Jadran Mimica is a Senior Lecturer in Anthropology at the University of Sydney. He has carried out long-term field research among the Yagwoia-Angan people of Papua New Guinea over a period of three decades. His most recent publications include "Descended from the Celestial Rope: From the Father to the Son, and from the Ego to the Cosmic Self" (2007) and "Mother's Umbilicus and Father's Spirit: The Dialectics of Selfhood of a Yagwoia Transgendered Person" (2008).

Notes

1. I explain below the reason for writing 'un/conscious' with a slash.
2. Here, self-knowledge is extended to include one's own cultural life-world, especially within the historical horizon of its own critical self-interpretation.
3. In order to get a better picture of Lévi-Strauss as an ethnographer, one should read his 1936 essay, "Contribution à l'étude de l'organisation sociale des Indiens Bororo" and his 1948 monograph, *La vie familiale et sociale des Indiens Nambikwara*. His English-language contributions in the famous *Handbook of South American Indians* (vol. 3, 1948) on the Nambikuara, Tupi-Cawahib, the tribes of the upper Xingu River, and on the use of wild plants in tropical South America, as well as two papers (one on the social use of kinship terms among Brazilian Indians, the other on Nambikwara chieftainship) supplement his strictly ethnographic writings. According to Peter Gow (personal communication, St Andrews, September 2007), when the famous German-Brazilian ethnographer Curt Nimuendaju was asked to recommend an able anthropologist for the job of a full-time ethnographer of Brazilian Indians (which is what he himself did), his choice was Lévi-Strauss. Nimuendaju characterized him "as an outstanding young French anthropologist, eminently suitable for the task." Many years later, Lévi-Strauss made the following assessment of himself as an ethnographer: "Finally, why not admit it? I realized early on that I was a library man, not a fieldworker. I don't mean this disparagingly, quite the contrary, but fieldwork is a kind of 'women's work' (which is probably why women are successful at it). Myself, I had neither the interest nor the patience for it" (in Eribon 1991: 44).
4. Castoriadis's views have to be clarified with respect to his specific philosophical and psychoanalytic synthesis of understanding (i.e., his ideas and their conceptual articulation). He is a thinker who indeed thinks for himself within the Western philosophical tradition, which he knows very well. But precisely as such he has to be critically elucidated in relation to that tradition, and especially in relation to the field of psychoanalytic and ethnographic evidence.
5. In my formulations, narcissistic dynamics is not separable from the dynamics of instinctual drives. The archaic nucleus of the latter is what I call 'oral-ocular', indicating the immanent synthesis of narcissistic dynamics and the primordial sucking-digestive-groping instinctual self-circuitry. This is the core of the primal ideal-ego and the super-ego (well illustrated by Malinowski's self-account cited above).
6. The Kleinian concept 'epistemophilic pursuit' (Klein [1932] 1988) refers to 'love of knowledge', echoing directly the notion of 'desire for knowledge'. Although a commonplace expression belonging to the classical matrix of Western philosophy, this determination of knowing as driven by desire requires that it be explored and elucidated psychoanalytically. My brief discussion draws on Klein (ibid.) and Bion ([1962] 1994, [1970] 1995), whose work enriches the understanding of the psychic realities implied by this commonplace notion.
7. I am drawing primarily, although not exclusively, on my experience of Australian universities. However, I should stress that the antipodean academe is in the avant-garde of the managerialization of universities and the concomitant degradation of research and critical thought that is traditionally associated with these institutions.
8. On the phenomenological problematics of ontological differentiation of the world, including the realm of the 'social', see James ([1890] 1950: 2:21), Schutz (1962), Gurwitsch (1964: pt. 6), and Luckmann (1970). Wallace's (1959) paper is a classical positing of the same problematics from within the conceptual parameters of anthropological inquiry. With regard to the part = whole relation, it is the dominant mode of part > < whole dynamics in the Yagwoia universe (see, e.g., Mimica 1988), which is to say that, in their realm, the world is a holographic totality. For an elaboration of holographic worldviews as characteristic of New Guinea life-worlds, see Wagner (2001).
9. For the aesthesiological structuration of embodiment, see Husserl (1989), Schilder (1950, 1951), and Merleau-Ponty (1962). See also Scott (1948), Winnicott (1958), and McDougall (1989).

10. I take this as the universally valid perspective. An excellent illustration of this can be found in Beradt (1968). See also Binswanger (1963).

11. The radical imaginary discussed here is not to be mistaken for Lacan's imaginary, despite the fact that the condition for the latter is the matrix of the radical imaginary. See Castoriadis (1984: 46–115) for a critique of Lacan and his concept of imaginary. Although an astute discussion, Castoriadis's critique does not diminish the general importance of Lacan's concept for the elucidation of the psychic being and human reality. Corbin's (1969, 1972) concept of *mundus imaginalis*, or the 'imaginal', is also relevant in this context; however, given the brevity of this discussion, I will refrain from carrying out a more sustained critical clarification. The same holds true of Durand's ([1964] 1999, 1971) great work.

12. This fundamental caution was stressed a long time ago by Leach (1958). Similarly, Lienhardt (1961) observed about the Dinka that they "have no conception which at all closely corresponds to our popular modern conception of the 'mind' as mediating and, as it were, storing up the experiences of the self " (ibid.: 149). In an accompanying note, Lienhardt stated further: "*And still less of conscious and unconscious elements, of course*" (ibid.: 149n1; emphasis added). The reader would profit from reading the rest of the paragraph from this great ethnography.

13. For concrete ethnographic demonstrations, see Mimica (2006, 2007a, forthcoming).

14. For further elaboration on the problematics of ontological categories such as 'matter', 'bodily substances', 'spirit', and 'soul', see Mimica (2003a: 262–265, 274–277).

15. In order to elucidate critically, that is, psychoanalytically, the transferential-countertransferential context of Leenhardt's interpretations of the Canaques' life-world, I would have to examine in some detail his relation with his informants, principally his eldest convert Boesoou Erijisi. Leenhardt wrote about him: "(His) Christianity is no way an imitation of the white; it is lived, and it is the Christianity of a pure Canaque ... Everything that I have been permitted to clarify in the obscurity of native questions I owe to Boesoou" (cited in Clifford 1981: 141–142).

16. I should say that this also applies to more recent anthropological importations into Melanesian life-worlds of concepts (and their concomitant absurdities) such as Strathern's (1988, via McKim Marriott), notion of 'dividual' and Gell's (1998) 'distributed person'. Never mind for a moment the theory of 'agency', these concepts are supposed to capture an authentic sense of Melanesian personhood, as opposed to Western notions such as 'individual' or, indeed, the psychoanalytic 'ego' or 'egoic self', all of which are assumed to be supposedly a-relational entities. By the same token, these authors and their numerous followers have nothing to say about whether their constructions do in any way have some basis in the constitutive-constructive dynamics of the human psyche and lived embodiment, be that in the experiences of the alleged Melanesian (or Indian) 'dividuals' or Western self-centered 'individuals'. It is worthwhile pointing out that a version of the idea of a 'dividual' was presented by von Bertalanffy ([1952] 1960: 48–50) in his remarkable comments on what constitutes an individual in unicellular organisms and primitive animals such as hydra and turbellarian worm. See also Koestler (1967: 59–70, who had expanded on and popularized von Bertalanffy's discussion. Contemplating such primitive life forms and their life cycles stimulates theories about the ontology of individuality and multiplicity and the dialectics of one-and-the-many. It also prompts reflections on the dynamics of human egoity and its social matrix in any life-world, past or present.

17. To this list of thinkers should be added Heinz Werner, Bernard Kaplan, and Silvano Arieti.

18. For a critical perspective on Heidegger in anthropology, see Mimica (1993) and Weiner (2001).

19. Now more than ever, it is evident that most anthropologists never mastered Lévi-Strauss's structuralist thought, let alone tried to emulate his power of imagination to feel and literally discern generative, pattern-creating dynamics in human life-worlds.

20. It should be acknowledged that this was an earlier work on the Yafar translated into English 10 years after the original French edition. Subsequently, Juillerat published two

other psychoanalytic ethnographies of the Yafar (1991, 1995) and a volume of essays on psychoanalytic anthropology (2001).
21. I use the term 'omn/i/mpotence' to designate the economy of the archaic narcissistic equilibrium in which, due to its extreme mirror-schizoid bivalency, symbiotic omnipotence and impotence are equipollent and conterminous (see Mimica 2003b: 27).

References

Beradt, Charlotte. 1968. *The Third Reich of Dreams*. Trans. Adriane Gottwald. Chicago, IL: Quadrangle Books.
Binswanger, Ludwig. 1963. "Dream and Existence." Pp. 222–248 in *Being-in-the-World: The Selected Papers of Ludwig Binswanger*. Ed. and trans. Jacob Needleman. New York: Basic Books.
Bion, Wilfred. [1962] 1994. *Learning from Experience*. Northvale, NJ: Jason Aronson.
_____. [1970] 1995. *Attention and Interpretation*. Northvale, NJ: Jason Aronson.
Castoriadis, Cornelis. 1984. *Crossroads in the Labyrinth*. Brighton: Harvester Press.
_____. 1987. *Imaginary Institution of Society*. London: Polity.
Clifford, James. 1981. *Person and Myth: Maurice Leenhardt in the Melanesian World*. Berkeley: University of California Press.
Corbin, Henri. 1969. *Creative Imagination in the Sufism of Ibn 'Arabi*. Trans. Ralph Mannheim. Princeton, NJ: Princeton University Press.
_____. 1972. "Mundus Imaginalis: Or the Imaginary and the Imaginal." *Spring: An Annual of Archetypal Psychology and Jungian Thought*: 1–19.
Devereux, George. 1967. *From Anxiety to Method in Behavioral Sciences*. The Hague: Mouton.
Durand, Gilbert. [1964] 1999. *The Anthropological Structures of the Imaginary*. Brisbane: Boombana Publications.
_____. 1971. "Exploration of the Imaginal." *Spring: An Annual of Archetypal Psychology and Jungian Thought*: 84–100.
Eribon, Didier. 1991. *Conversations with Claude Lévi-Strauss*. Chicago, IL: University of Chicago Press.
Fliess, Robert. 1956. *Erogeneity and Libido*. New York: International Universities Press.
_____. 1961. *Ego and Body Ego: Contributions to Their Psychoanalytic Psychology*. New York: Schulte Publishing.
Gell, Alfred. 1998. *Art and Agency: An Anthropological Theory*. Oxford: Clarendon Press.
Gillison, Gillian. 1993. *Between Culture and Fantasy: A New Guinea Highlands Mythology*. Chicago, IL: University of Chicago Press.
Gurwitsch, Aron. 1964. *The Field of Consciousness*. Pittsburgh, PA: Duquesne University Press.
Herdt, Gilbert. 2001. *Sambia Sexual Culture: Essays from the Field*. Chicago, IL: University of Chicago Press.
Husserl, Edmund. 1989. *Ideas Pertaining to a Pure Phenomenology and to Phenomenological Philosophy*, Book 2. London: Kluwer Academic Publishers.
James, William. [1890] 1950. *The Principles of Psychology*. 2 vols. New York: Dover.
Juillerat, Bernard. [1986] 1996. *Children of the Blood: Society, Reproduction and Cosmology in New Guinea*. Trans. Nora Scott. Oxford: Berg.
_____. 1991. *Oedipe chasseur: Un mythologie du sujet en Nouvelle-Guinee*. Preface by A. Green. Paris: Presses Universitaires de France.
_____. 1995. *L'avenement du père: Rite, représentation, fantasme dans un culte mélanésien*. Paris: Editions de la Maison des Sciences de l'Homme.
_____. 2001. *Penser l'imaginaire: Essais d'anthropologie psychanalytique*. Lausanne: Editions Payot Lausanne.

Jung, Carl G. 1968a. *Aion: Researches into the Phenomenology of the Self* (*Collected Works of C. G. Jung*, vol. 9, pt. 2). Trans. R. F. C. Hull. London: Routledge & Kegan Paul.

_____. 1968b. *The Archetypes and the Collective Unconscious* (*Collected Works of C. G. Jung*, vol. 9, pt. 1). Trans. R. F. C. Hull. 2nd ed. Princeton, NJ: Princeton University Press.

Klein, Melanie. [1932] 1988. *The Psycho-Analysis of Children*. London: Virago.

Koestler, Arthur. 1967. *The Ghost in the Machine*. London: Hutchinson.

Lacan, Jacques. 1977. *Ecrits: A Selection*. Trans. Alan Sheridan. New York: Norton.

Leach, Edmund. 1958. "Magical Hair." *Journal of the Royal Anthropological Institute* 88: 147–164.

Leenhardt, Maurice. 1979. *Do Kamo: Person and Myth in the Melanesian World*. Trans. Basia Miller Gulati. Chicago, IL: University of Chicago Press.

Lévi-Strauss, Claude. 1973. *Tristes Tropiques*. Trans. John and Doreen Weightman. London: Jonathan Cape.

Lienhardt, Godfrey. 1961. *Divinity and Experience: The Religion of the Dinka*. Oxford: Oxford University Press.

Luckmann, Thomas. 1970. "On the Boundaries of the Social World." Pp. 73–100 in *Phenomenology and Social Reality*, ed. M. Natanson. The Hague: Nijhoff.

Mahler, Margaret, Fred Pine, and Anni Bergman, eds. [1975] 1985. *The Psychological Birth of the Human Infant: Symbiosis and Individuation*. London: Karnac Books.

Malinowski, Bronislaw. 1967. *A Diary in the Strict Sense of the Term*. London: Routledge & Kegan Paul.

McDougall, Joyce. 1989. *Theatres of the Body: A Psychoanalytical Approach to Psychosomatic Illness*. London: Free Association Books.

Merleau-Ponty, Maurice. 1962. *The Phenomenology of Perception*. London: Routledge & Kegan Paul.

Mimica, Jadran. 1981. "Omalyce: An Ethnography of the Iqwqaye View of the Cosmos." PhD diss., Australian National University.

_____. 1988. *Intimations of Infinity: The Mythopoeia of the Iqwaye Counting System and Number*. Oxford: Berg.

_____. 1991. "The Incest Passions: An Outline of the Logic of the Iqwaye Social Organisation." *Oceania* 62, no. 1: 34–58; no. 2: 81–113.

_____. 1993. "The Foi and Heidegger: Western Philosophical Poetics and a New Guinea Life-World (a critical review of James Weiner's *The Empty Place: Poetry, Space, and Being among the Foi of Papua New Guinea*)." *Australian Journal of Anthropology* 4, no. 2: 79–95.

_____. 2001. "A Review from the Field (a critical review of Gilbert Herdt's *Sambia Sexual Culture: Essays from the Field*)." *Australian Journal of Anthropology* 12, no. 2: 225–237.

_____. 2003a. "The Death of a Strong, Great, Bad Man: An Ethnography of Soul Incorporation." *Oceania* 73, no. 4: 260–286.

_____. 2003b. "Out of the Depths of Saurian Waters: On Psycho-Bakhtinianism, Ethnographic Countertransference and Naven." *Anthropological Notebooks* 9, no. 1: 50–47

_____. 2006. "Dreams, Laki, and Mourning: A Psychoanalytic Ethnography of the Yagwoia (PNG) 'Inner Feminine.'" *Oceania* 74, no. 1: 27–60; no. 2: 113–129; no. 3: 265–284.

_____. 2007a. "Descended from the Celestial Rope: From the Father to the Son, and from the Ego to the Cosmic Self." Pp. 77–105 in Mimica 2007b.

_____, ed. 2007b. *Explorations in Psychoanalytic Ethnography*. New York: Berghahn Books. First published as the 2006 special issue of *Social Analysis* 50, no. 2.

_____. Forthcoming. "Flying Away Like a Bird: An Instance of Severance from the Parental Abode (Iwolaqamalycaane, Yagwoia, Papua New Guinea)." *Journal de la Société des Océanistes* (commemorative special issue for Bernard Juillerat).

Neumann, Erich. 1954. *The Origin and History of Consciousness*. Princeton, NJ: Princeton University Press.

Schilder, Paul. 1950. *The Image and Appearance of the Human Body*. New York: International Universities Press

_____. 1951. *Brain and Personality*. New York: International Universities Press.

Schutz, Alfred. 1962. "On Multiple Realities." In *Collected Papers*, vol. 1. The Hague: Nijhoff.
Scott, W. Clifford M. 1948. "Some Embryological, Neurological, Psychiatric and Psycho-
    Analytic Implications of the Body-Scheme." *International Journal of Psycho-Analysis* 29,
    no. 30: 141–155.
Stern, Daniel. 1985. *The Interpersonal World of the Infant*. New York: Basic Books.
Strathern, Marilyn. 1988. *The Gender of the Gift*. Berkeley: University of California Press.
von Bertalanffy, Ludwig. [1952] 1960. *Problems of Life: An Evaluation of Modern Biological
    and Scientific Thought*. New York: Harper & Brothers.
Wagner, Roy. 2001. *An Anthropology of the Subject*. Berkeley: University of California Press.
Wallace, Anthony F. 1959. "Cultural Determinants of Response to Hallucinatory Experience."
    American Medical Association: Archives of General Psychiatry 1: 58–69.
Weiner, James F. 2001. *Tree Leaf Talk: A Heideggerian Anthropology*. Oxford: Berg.
Weiss, Florence, and Milan Stanek. 2007. "Aspects of the *Naven* Ritual: Conversations with
    an Iatmul Woman of Papua New Guinea." Pp. 45–76 in Mimica 2007b.
Winnicott, Donald W. 1958. "Mind and Its Relation to the Psyche-Soma." Pp. 243–254 in
    Collected Papers: Through Pediatrics to Psychoanalysis. New York: Basic Books.

Chapter 3

PLURAL MODERNITY
Changing Modern Institutional Forms—Disciplines
and Nation-States

Filipe Carreira da Silva and Mónica Brito Vieira

Like our predecessors, we are faced today with a central challenge. This challenge or problematic can be experienced on at least two different levels. At an epistemological level, we join our voices to those claiming that we are living in a post-disciplinary age. Science today is increasingly organized and performed through inter- and sometimes transdisciplinary projects and networks (Nowotny, Scott, and Gibbons 2001). At a political level, a similar trend away from the modern institutional political form par excellence, the territorial nation-state, has been subject to detailed analysis for at least a generation. The challenge confronting us today is that these two modern institutional forms, academic disciplines and nation-states, no longer enjoy the overwhelming dominance that they possessed for most of the last two centuries, especially in Western Europe and the United States. The reason is that modernity is currently undergoing a dramatic and radical shift. This presents a particularly daunting challenge for sociology, a discipline born out of modernity whose conceptual apparatus is inextricably associated with the territorial nation-state. In the terminology of the discipline, 'societies' refer to national communities, 'social classes' to segments of those national communities, and 'social actors' to modern individual selves. How is sociology, itself a product of modernity, to cope with this epochal change?[1]

Our response to this challenge acknowledges the institutional resilience of these two modern forms while insisting on the need to account for new organizational structures and dynamics in both realms. Such emerging organizational forms and patterns require both theoretical and empirical analysis. In what follows, we try to provide the first steps toward the theoretical treatment of this problem. Before doing so, some words on the organization of this chapter, which is arranged in four parts, are in order. The first part frames our epistemological discussion within the larger debate on modernity. In particular, we identify three major problematics that are said to be constitutive of the modern condition. In the second part, we emphasize the need to avoid a monist and excessively coherent conception of modernity. The tendency in that direction can be found more often among sociologists, who often conceive of sociology and modernity as twin projects. The third part is devoted to a brief presentation and discussion of Axel Honneth's theory of recognition, one of the most influential critical theoretical proposals available today. Honneth's non-foundationalist orientation will be used to exemplify our meta-theoretical thesis on an epistemological level. The fourth and final part turns to the political realm and briefly illustrates our thesis with a performative conception of citizenship. Both examples ('problem solving on the move' and 'performative citizenship') hinge upon the notion of performance. This concept is more familiar among anthropologists than sociologists or political scientists, but it is one that we believe can be productively articulated with a 'dialogical pluralist' meta-theoretical framework.

What is meant by that? Briefly, 'dialogical pluralism' refers to a meta-theoretical strategy that sees the history of theory and theory building as different sides of the same coin. In particular, the plurality of theoretical contributions from the past (recent and distant) is to be integrated within theory building as if current practitioners and their predecessors were partners in an imaginary conversation with the goal of solving common problems, or at least problems that share some common features.[2] Two intellectual traditions can be identified as the sources of inspiration for this thesis. First is the historicist methodological orientation of the so-called Cambridge School, whose main figures include Quentin Skinner, John Dunn, and J. G. A. Pocock. Both authors of this chapter began their careers with doctoral dissertations in which this methodological orientation was applied, even though not uncritically (see Silva 2009a, 2009b; Vieira 2009). Second, the influence of classical American philosophical pragmatism is worth noting, especially John Dewey's conception of science as a problem-solving activity (shared to a large extent by George Herbert Mead). As developed elsewhere, dialogical pluralism has a number of theoretical and methodological implications (Silva 2006). In our work we have explored two main theoretical proposals (one sociological, the other political) as deriving from this meta-theoretical position: a social theory of the self and a deliberative conception of democracy (see Silva 2002, 2007). Methodologically, our position in the historicism versus presentism debate is closer to the former pole. In particular, we tend to reject the latter's quasi-naturalism and disembodied rationalism in favor of processual and more culturally sensitive approaches. Furthermore, we locate our theoretical reflection squarely within the horizon of modernity. In other words, modernity provides the general background for our work and is one of our chief objects of study (see Silva 2001a, 2001b, 2004).

In this sense, the recent debate on 'multiple modernities' constitutes an important frame of reference for our dialogical pluralism.[3] As will be seen, our position in this debate differs from the claim of Eisenstadt and his followers that there are different modernities, and from neo-modernization theorists, like Volker Schmidt (2006, 2007), for whom the process of functional differentiation (as analyzed by Parsons and Luhmann) still constitutes the best analytical reference to explain the diffusion of modernity. Although we subscribe to Schmidt's notion of 'varieties of modernity', we reject his reliance upon functional differentiation as the dominant pattern of societal development in modern times. As the last two parts of this chapter will demonstrate, other patterns besides differentiation can be seen operating in the realms of science and democratic politics. The modern institutional forms in these two realms, academic disciplines and nation-states, were developed over the course of several centuries as responses to the functional requirements of modernity. Our claim is that the current stage of modernity's development entails a profound redefinition of these responses. Beginning with the epistemological realm, our main claim is straightforward. Social sciences have to respond to the challenges of global modernity. Foundationalist strategies are increasingly less convincing, given the post-disciplinary nature of our epoch. As a result, theory building can no longer rely upon that sort of strategy and must instead seek alternative forms of justification. 'Problem solving on the move', to paraphrase Michael Gibbons (1994), seems to be a promising solution for this difficulty.

On Modernity: Provisional Answers to Inescapable Questions

We would like to begin by questioning the widespread assumption that social and human sciences require an epistemological foundation. In our view, such foundationalism is misleading. One should not ask, "What are the moral, social, or rational principles upon which human societies are founded?" The later philosophy of Wittgenstein provides ample evidence of why this is so. A word, as Wittgenstein ([1953] 2003) explains in his *Philosophical Investigations*, does not derive its meaning from its link to some unmediated external reality as opposed to its use within a stream of life. If this is true, it follows that philosophical reflection on language cannot take place in a vacuum; rather, we have to be concerned with those traditions, practices, language games, and contexts in which words have a home. If we are interested in the concepts of justification, of right, of truth, then we must understand them in this contextual, non-foundationalist way.

Instead of recognizing the multifaceted nature of language and its relation to social practices, which inevitably means a good deal of particularity, the craving for generality behind foundationalist proposals leads one to develop complex metaphysical theories in which, as Wittgenstein ([1953] 2003: § 38) puts it, "language goes on holiday." That is to say, language is detached from the contexts in which it naturally functions and becomes part of a complex theory, which, precisely because it abstracts from particularity, fails to shed light on that particularity. The point is that objectivity, too, is internal to context. There is no context-free standpoint from which we can evaluate the world and social practices. There are no a priori reasons for action, nor any universal epistemological foundations that can be identified independently of the particularities of the context and practice of scientific activity.

The point at issue here is what might be seen as Wittgenstein's commitment to the view that there is a non-contingent link between the self and the social context of which the self is a part. Derived in part from William James's influence, Wittgenstein's insistence on the link between self and society relates centrally to one of the themes we wish to discuss in this chapter, namely, the extent to which the self in liberal theory is seen as atomized, asocial, and solitary. Central to liberalism is the attempt to solve the problem that arises when 'essentially solitary individuals' come together in society. If Wittgenstein's contention that there can be no logical separation of self from context is true, it follows that a central element of the liberal position is defective. But, it might be asked, why contrast liberal rationalism and the contextualist and non-foundationalist insights of both Wittgenstein and classical American pragmatism?

We would like to suggest that the debate on 'an epistemology for anthropology' is clarified once it is framed within the more general debate on the nature of modernity, in which, from its very inception, liberal rationalism has always played a pivotal role. Within what can be called the 'Western variety of modernity' (discussed further below), the liberal rationalistic paradigm has been the quasi-hegemonic voice in the debate on science and rationality, selfhood, and democratic politics. In all these broad problematics, liberal rationalism has played a central role. Consider Descartes' paradigmatic statement that self and context can indeed be separated. In his *Meditations*, Descartes suggests that one can doubt the existence of the external world, the existence of other human beings and even the existence of one's own body—but not the existence and the contents of one's own mind. The argument for the denial of this position is found in Wittgenstein's (]1953] 2003) *Philosophical Investigations* and can be phrased as follows: is it really conceivable to possess the whole range of mental concepts *in the absence* of other people and relationships? This question must be answered negatively, as language is inseparable from rule following, and one cannot follow a private rule because it is not possible discriminate in a purely private way as to whether a rule is being followed or not.

The point we are trying to make is that one can reconstruct common problem areas faced by different generations of social and political theorists (see

Silva 2008: 15). At a fundamental level, the problematics that we struggle with today are the same as those that Wittgenstein coped with half a century ago and that, three centuries before him, Descartes had already tried to come to grips with. It is in this specific sense that one should interpret Habermas's ([1985] 1998: 43) observation that Hegel "is not the first philosopher who belongs to modern times, but he is the first for whom modernity became a problem." What, then, are the basic components of this problem? An attempt to answer this question should start by distinguishing between the basic components of modernity as a problem (what we, following Wagner, may call the 'modern problematics').[4]

The Western variety of modernity can be understood as a discursive field comprehending at least three general problematics, which are as unavoidable as the attempts to answer them are provisional. To understand what it is to be modern entails an explanation of (1) the processes of production of knowledge and control of nature (science), (2) human autonomy (selfhood), and (3) democratic self-rule (politics). Since the end of the eighteenth century, the most successful answers to these central problematics have been developed within a paradigm that one may designate as liberal, rationalist, and individualistic. From this viewpoint, the clear-cut separation between the objective world and the subjective mind of positivism, the disembodied and instrumental self of neo-classical economics and rational choice theories, and the abstract rights-endowed individual of political liberalism are but different aspects of one and the same conception of human beings and their place in the world.

A few words on each one of these problematics are now in order (see Silva 2008: 19–25). Admittedly, the backbone of the modern project relies on science and the principles of the experimental method and on faith in the rational resolution of the problems that have afflicted humankind since times immemorial. This confidence in the combined powers of human reason and the principles of the experimental method—exemplarily illustrated by figures such as Galileo, Bacon, and Newton—is a fundamental component of what it is to be modern. Tradition was to be discarded as an element of a bygone era, something that modern individuals could well do without. The belief that every single aspect of reality was amenable to a scientific explanation—a belief that Weber termed 'rationalization'—distinguishes the modern era. Thus, a tradition of sociological analysis was inaugurated that still today occupies a dominant position in the discipline's discourse on modernity.

In which sense is the second problematic, selfhood, distinctively modern? The relation between identity and modernity is clarified once one bears in mind Claude Lefort's (1988) thesis that the latter entailed, on the one hand, the loss of "markers of certainty" and, on the other, the continual attempts at their recovery. What is at stake here is the fact that the human self acquires a modern configuration or character insofar as it is faced with the constant and unavoidable questioning of its place in the world. This specific modern problematic has been recently scrutinized in a magisterial way by Jerrold Seigel (2005).

Finally, moving to the third fundamental modern problematic, democratic politics, one finds the human effort to reconcile the notions of individual autonomy and liberty counter-balanced by predictability and certainty. Contrary to what is usually assumed, constitutionalism and the rule of law are not distinctively modern, although they both have developed new forms over the past couple of centuries. What is distinctively modern is the assertion of individual rights and, to a certain extent, the demand for universal social equality. What makes one more modern than the other is the time orientation: while constitutionalism is fundamentally backward looking (one has to refer back to the founding text of the polity, even if one wishes to interpret it in light of current problems), individual rights-based perspectives tend to be future oriented and are therefore distinctively modern.[5] The Grotian-Lockean theory of moral order, from which the doctrine of universal human rights stems, is thus the dominant discursive resource of political modernity, in opposition to which all alternatives define themselves.

Modernity: One, Many, or a Plurality?

Of course, to refer to a phenomenon as complex as modernity is not without problems. The term 'modernity' (in the singular) is one of the best illustrations of Gallie's (1964) theory of 'essentially contested concepts'. The plurality of meanings encompassed by the expression 'modernity' includes, without any pretension to exhaustiveness, an empirical reality amenable to scientific analysis, an epistemological condition, and a temporal framework. In fact, there are good reasons to abandon a singular, monolithic conception of modernity. As Bernard Yack (1997) has recently argued, treating modernity as a coherent and fully integrated unit tends to "fetishize modern thought and experience," which "once tended to broaden and deepen rebellious and revolutionary sentiments," while today, "with the collapse of hopes for such a revolution, the fetishism of modernities is much more likely to promote an exaggerated passivity" (ibid.: 130). Moreover, to fetishize modernity is to misrepresent it. Far from acknowledging its huge internal variety and contradictions, to conceive of modernity as a single phenomenon results in a fatally flawed understanding of it.

The risk of fetishizing modernity is particularly acute among sociologists. Ever since Karl Mannheim's ([1936] 1972: 222) observation that "out of the investigation into the social determination of history arises sociology," sociologists have been accustomed to conceive of sociology and modernity as twin projects. The foundational narrative of the discipline taught to sociology undergraduates reinforces this idea, year after year. With the emergence of modernity, the scientific conditions for a science of society were made available. In turn, the central object of this new social science was the manifold expressions of the societal shift toward modernization, from mass urbanization and industrialization to the emergence of specifically modern forms of sociability. We are not suggesting, of course, that every sociological analysis of modernity can be criticized for fetishizing it. Most do not. The sociological study of the new forms of association that emerge in modern societies is often nuanced and sensitive enough to the fact that the mutually constitutive entanglement of 'modern' and 'traditional' elements is many times a central feature of individual trajectories, the collective action of groups and associations and even of national societies. Yet some of the most influential contemporary sociological reflections on modernity do tend to conceive of modernity in an excessively coherent way, as if it constitutes an integrated whole with little or no space for diversity, plurality, and internal divergence and dissent. A case in point is Habermas's conception of modernity as an 'unfinished project'.

In works like *The Theory of Communicative Action* ([1981] 1986) and *The Philosophical Discourse of Modernity* ([1985] 1998), Habermas suggests the outline of a theory of modernity that aims at reconciling the positive (or affirmative) proposals of Talcott Parsons with the critical understanding of modernity of Marx, Horkheimer, and Adorno, as well as with Weber's simultaneously positivistic and critical analysis of this phenomenon. To begin with, it is important to bear in mind that Habermas distinguishes two ways of conceiving of modern societies. On the one hand, one can adopt the perspective of an external observer. The material and institutional reproduction of society is guaranteed by the economy and the bureaucratic state, two social sub-systems that tend to be differentiated under modern conditions and that are governed by the steering media 'money' and 'power', respectively. Habermas uses the concept of 'system' to designate this perspective and associates it with specific types of rationality, namely, strategic and instrumental. On the other hand, this systemic perspective of modern social formations can be complemented with a participant's point of view. Habermas uses the concept of 'life-world' to express this perspective. The largely unquestioned shared experience of all social participants, which includes traditions, culture, and language, becomes increasingly autonomized in modern conditions into three different sub-systems: culture, society, and personality. In these realms, communicative rationality allows for a coordination of human conduct according to the uncoerced force of the best argument.

At this point, it is relevant to emphasize that the system–life-world distinction is itself a modern product. This distinction emerges as the processes of societal rationalization and cultural rationalization gradually take place. Whereas the former process refers to the internal differentiation of the 'system' in the sub-systems of economy and the state, a process of rationalization that led to the hegemony of instrumental rationality in these realms, cultural rationalization designates processes first of differentiation and then of autonomization within the life-world, in particular, in the cultural sub-system. Habermas ([1981] 1986) explains this latter process in the following way: "With science and technology, with autonomous art and the values of expressive self-presentation, with universal legal and moral representations, there emerges a differentiation of *three value spheres, each of which follows its own logic*" (ibid.: 163–164; italics in the original). In other words, what Habermas is suggesting is that when science, art, and politics come to be practiced according to their "own logic," the project of modernity will be completed. In this light, the incoherence between these value spheres is not analyzed as such but rather is viewed as a sign of the incompleteness of the project of modernity. It is not hard to see the limitations of Habermas's perspective. By presupposing a general movement toward ever greater harmonious coherence, Habermas precludes the possibility that modernity is ultimately compatible with, or might even be defined by, the incoherence between those value spheres (see Yack 1997: 37). There are simply no strong reasons to believe that greater internal coherence might occur as modernity unfolds.

What is at stake here is Habermas's attempt at overcoming the dichotomy that separates contextualism and anti-foundationalism, on the one hand, and transcendentalism, on the other. He does that by means of his theory of communicative action, a simultaneously descriptive-explanatory and normative-critical theory, which is to say that it not only serves as a framework for the systematic integrating of existing and new research programs in sociology and other human sciences, but also is able to account for the pathologies of post-industrial Western societies in such a way as to suggest a redirection rather than an abandonment of the emancipatory project of the Enlightenment (see Knodt 1994: 78). These two facets of Habermas's theoretical project manifest themselves in his distinction between the perspectives of the system and the life-world, between the instrumental and communicative types of action and rationality, and so on. To conceive of modernity in this way signifies an endorsement of a monological perspective that is contradictory to Habermas's own fundamental intentions. It is 'autopoietic' in the sense that it is a self-creating referential system that evades the principle of 'performative contradiction', which he so often uses against his adversaries. As a self-referential system, Habermas's theory of communicative action appears as an effort to control, restrict, and domesticate the irreducible heterogeneity of language games in the name of a single game called 'rational argumentation' whose rules are defined by Habermas himself. From this perspective, the force of Habermas's discourse lies in its ability to reduce complexity by neutralizing potential disturbances. As Knodt (1994: 94) aptly remarks, "In the name of communication and tolerance, Habermas can thus dispense with entire intellectual traditions—the mere presence of self-referential paradox in Nietzsche, Adorno, or Foucault is enough to disqualify them—while at the same time, Habermas's own research programme keeps expanding in its attempt to integrate ever more areas of interdisciplinary inquiry into a coherent whole."

In sum, not only is Habermas's fetishizing conception of an 'unfinished project of modernity' insensitive to the internal diversity of that project (the very usage of the notion of 'project' to refer to modernity being problematic), but it is a particularly inadequate framework in the context of our globalized world. If anything, what we have been experiencing since the last decades of the twentieth century provides ample evidence of the limitations of self-centric cultural conceptions, 'Eurocentrism' being one of the most influent and pervasive. Instead of the monologue suggested by Habermas, we propose a dialogical approach to the history of ideas so that we can learn from all the other partners in dialogue how to respond to the combined challenges of the modern problematics of science, selfhood, and democratic politics. Before moving on to the illustration of this claim, a few words on the recent sociological debate on modernity are in order.

Contrary to Habermas's unfinished project of modernity, and also differently from the postmodernist narrative of the end of modernity (hence ultimately self-defeating), Shmuel Eisenstadt and others have argued that to conceive of multiple modernities is the best way of coping with the irreducible differences between different civilizational interpretations of the modern program. As stated elsewhere, we believe that the plurality of interpretations of modernity suggested by this paradigm is a refreshing and important corrective to the only too common equation of Europeanization with modernization (Silva 2008). Still, the multiple modernities proposal is itself open to criticism. In particular, authors working within this paradigm tend not only to privilege transnational or inter-civilizational comparisons, thus ignoring the regional and local levels of analysis, but also to assume that the differences separating modern societies or civilizations are larger and more significant than those distinguishing modern from traditional ones. As Volker Schmidt (2006: 88) rightly points out, the conception of "multiple modernities suggests homogeneity within civilizations; at least more so than across civilizations." It seems that the multiple modernities paradigm tends to change one kind of fetishizing for another. Whereas the theories of modernization of the 1950s and 1960s are accused of fetishizing Western modernity (more specifically, the variety of modernity developed in the United States after the end of World War II), the multiple modernities alternative can be charged with fetishizing civilizational and national interpretations of modernity at the expense of both smaller analytical levels and previous developmental stages. Schmidt's (2007) neo-modernization alternative presents one important advantage in this regard. It shows great sensitiveness to the empirical confirmation of the theoretical claims on the nature of the processes of modernization. In his view, one could speak of 'varieties of modernity' insofar as one could empirically demonstrate the existence of "coherent patterns of institutional co-variation that systematically separate not only the economies or polities or educational systems etc. of one group of countries from those of others, but the *whole institutional make-up of society across the board* and according to a common, overarching logic that visibly shapes all (important) sub-systems" (ibid.: 224; italics in the original).

The problem with neo-modernization theorists is that they, like their predecessors from the 1950s, still rely on a reductionist analytical framework, and Schmidt is no exception. In his view, functional differentiation is still the dominant and primary pattern of societal development. Although it is laudable, Schmidt's (2007: 210) openness to the possibility that modernity is compatible with a plethora of institutional forms (see also Therborn 2003) is not sufficient to make him sensitive to other patterns of societal development besides functional differentiation. Classic modernization theories and their contemporary neo-modernization followers can thus be said to epitomize what Wagner (2001: 4) has aptly called "modernist" modes of thinking, that is, analytical schemes that confuse possibility with necessity. Even though certain societal developments were made possible by modernity, they are not to be confused with functional requirements of modern societies.

In short, we view both the multiple modernities proposal and the neo-modernization theories as unsatisfactory responses to the question of how to conceive of modernity today. Our alternative, drawing upon a dialogical pluralist meta-theoretical framework, points instead to a plural modernity, with several organizing societal patterns operating in different institutional realms organized in different regional sub-units that may (following Peter A. Hall's 'varieties of capitalism' approach) be designated as varieties of modernity (Hall and Soskice 2001). As hinted above, within each variety of modernity, institutional realms are associated with general problematics, even though they do not necessarily overlap (e.g., the selfhood problematic cuts across several institutional domains, from schooling to the economic realm). In the case of the two we discuss next, however, they do. In what follows, we focus on the epistemological and scientific realm in order to make two claims: first, that a successful theoretical strategy today is necessarily non-foundationalist, and, second, that such theory-building endeavors take place in an increasingly post-disciplinary context. Let us now see how one can justify these claims.

Dialogical Pluralism in Science: The Case of Critical Theory

How does this work? To help clarify what is in mind, we refer to an example that brings together several generations of critical responses to the liberal rationalistic paradigm, from Hegel to the current generation of Frankfurt's critical theorists. In particular, we refer to Axel Honneth's ([1992] 1996) appropriation of G. H. Mead to supplement and correct Hegel's model of the struggle for recognition. This is not to say that there are no reservations concerning Honneth's interpretation. What we wish to underline here is that the use Honneth, a former student of Habermas and the most recent 'leader' of the Frankfurt School (see Baert and Silva 2009), made of Mead's ideas is an excellent example of the extent to which contemporary social and political theorists can still benefit from a meaningful dialogue with Mead. The conditions for such a dialogue were laid down above: our own research problems will benefit the most from such a dialogue if we complement a non-presentist study of Mead's words with the general problematics they were concerned with.

Honneth's project seems to be consistent with this thesis. His starting question is simple: what explains the emergence of social conflicts? The usual answer, based upon the 'socio-ontological premise' of 'individual self-preservation' shared by the utilitarian rationalistic doctrine founded by Hobbes and Machiavelli and still pursued today by mainstream rational choice theorists, points to self-interested motives: conflicts arise because individuals have conflicting interests—a too 'thin' explanation for the 'thick' issues of identity, allegiance, and citizenship. Honneth's route is different. He follows Hegel and, most importantly for our purposes, Mead's intersubjectivist conception of the self. Drawing on these authors' critical responses to the problematics of modernity, Honneth is able to devise an alternative to the utilitarian perspective, according to which social conflicts arise to a large extent from experiences of disrespect on the part of the individuals in question. How do people come to experience such types of disrespect and enter into conflict with each other because of them? In Honneth's view, this happens because individuals can have undistorted relations with themselves only if three forms of recognition occur: love, rights, and esteem. If these forms of recognition are not respected, then a feeling of disrespect emerges, potentially leading to social strife. This is the chief insight of one of the latest and most promising normative social theories oriented to the challenges of the politics of identity raised by our increasingly multicultural societies, at least outside the atomistic tradition that goes back to Descartes, Hobbes, and Machiavelli.

Although Honneth's deeply original reconstruction of Hegel's model of the struggle for recognition and his innovative appropriation of Mead's social psychology triggered a lively debate that deserves attention (see Silva 2006), what we wish to call attention to at this point is the extent to which Honneth's project seems to illustrate our argument. Making use of the crucial responses of Hegel and Mead to the central problematics of the Western variety of modernity, Honneth proposes his own *critical* response to the dominant utilitarian tradition of modern social philosophy. Unlike that of Habermas, Honneth's critical proposal does not rely upon a fetishizing conception of modernity and a subsequent modernist interpretive framework. In our view, Honneth's perspective possesses a genuine transcultural character. We refer specifically to his insight that the struggles for recognition that have dominated the political agenda in the last few decades should not be seen as motivated by self-interest (as suggested by the Hobbesian state of nature), but instead regarded as attempts on the part of social actors to establish patterns of reciprocal recognition. In addition, Honneth avoids a foundationalist strategy. His aim is not to uncover general principles upon which human conflict is founded. Instead, Honneth ([2000] 2007) rightly wishes to reconstruct the inner logic of the concrete forms that human conflict assumes in different social spheres, from the private/intimate domain to the realm of work relations (see also Markell 2007).

We would thus like to emphasize the need to complement a historically minded reconstruction of our predecessors with a theoretically sustained examination of the inescapable questions they sought to answer. These are the questions that Simmel ([1900] 1978: 53) seminally described as those that "we have so far been unable either to answer or to dismiss." That these very same questions still motivate much of our work today shows that it is both possible and desirable to learn from those who preceded us, as partners in an imaginary conversation, the best ways to respond to the central problematics of our own times. At the heart of our proposed dialogical pluralism is the insight that theory building and the history of theory are closely related intellectual modes. Faced with the 'inescapable questions' that our condition as moderns imposes on us, we should strive to reconcile the most accomplished responses provided by our predecessors with our own responses to common yet ever-shifting problematics. Such would amount to a meaningful dialogue with all those in similar circumstances, including those who are no longer with us.

Such a meta-theoretical strategy seems particularly suited for the current conditions of the academic system. As several authors have pointed out, after an initial phase in which interdisciplinarity marked the beginning of the end of the hegemonic reign of disciplines as self-enclosed organizational units, scientific practice today is increasingly dominated by transdisciplinary endeavors (Klein 1990). From research projects that bring together numerous practitioners in different fields to work side by side solving a given problem to large international networks of scientists collaborating in postgraduate programs and research and development initiatives, the scientific landscape today is no longer dominated by academic disciplines. In our view, however, one should be careful in dismissing too readily the organizational function performed by disciplines. Ours might no longer be a 'disciplinary age' per se, but the emerging 'post-disciplinary' era certainly does not preclude a central role for this specific institutional form. As we see it, disciplines still constitute the backbone of scientific practice, and there is no reason to believe they will cease to do so in the future. In order to understand why we believe this to be so, a few comments on the chief organizational patterns of the academic system might be useful.

There are two main methodological and theoretical orientations that can be observed in modern academia (Heilbron 2004). First, there are those who favor a systems theoretical perspective. Their main influence is Reinhart Koselleck, for whom a major societal break occurred between 1750 and 1850. The modern understanding of the word 'discipline' was born in this epoch and expressed a structural transformation of higher learning. These authors claim that the modern academic system is but a sub-system of the more general social system and is subject to the very same functional requirements and organizational patterns. Rudolf Stichweh is a case in point. According to Stichweh's model of functional differentiation, the passage from the old regime to modern society marked the beginning of a process of differentiation in European scholarly institutions. Disciplines are, from this viewpoint, the main institutional form brought about by modernity—an institutional form that came to replace the older, less professionalized clubs, salons, and learned societies. Second, the work of Michel Foucault provides an alternative perspective to the systems theory. Drawing on the French tradition of historical epistemology (in particular, the work of Bachelard and Canguilhem), Foucault (1966) identifies an epistemological break marking the emergence of the modern era. But this epistemological break was not a purely discursive phenomenon: a new institutional form emerged as a correlate of this rupture. Disciplines were born, and through them modern science acquired an extremely efficient institutional structure that enabled the pursuit of the modern project of control to previously unimaginable levels (Foucault 1975).

In recent years, both of these perspectives have been subject to severe criticism. In particular, the image of a sudden break at the end of the eighteenth century, inaugurating an ever more homogeneous yet differentiated modernity, lacks empirical sustainability. As we have seen above, the image of modernity as an ever more coherent monolith underlying the work of both Foucault and the system theorists can be criticized for its fetishized character. In particular, and contrary to what the latter suggest, there is simply no empirical indication that the European academic system was institutionally less heterogeneous before 1800 than afterward—if anything, the opposite seems to be true (Heilbron 2004:

28–29). Furthermore, the history of modern science has plenty of examples of disciplines that evolved according to developmental patterns other than differentiation. Biology is a well-known example of a discipline formed with the logic of synthesis, integrating a number of previously separated domains (botany, zoology, medicine, etc.) into a new and more general science of life. Chemistry, on the other hand, exemplifies how a craft-like practice was upgraded into a fully fledged academic discipline by applying principles of the established sciences (ibid.: 36). In short, the logic of differentiation is but one of the operating logics under modern conditions.

Furthermore, as these modern conditions have been rapidly changing in the past few decades, one wonders what might be the most adequate diagnosis of the present situation. There is a growing consensus among sociologists of science that we are living in a post-disciplinary age (Abbott 2001). The general trend of erosion of disciplines as the predominant mode of organization in scientific work, deemed too bureaucratic and rigid to cope with the flexibility requirements of our globalized era, is said to be the chief trait of science at the dawn of the twenty-first century. We subscribe to most aspects of this diagnosis. Specifically, we find very plausible the claim by Michael Gibbons that transdisciplinarity is the emerging disciplinary mode: the production of knowledge is increasingly "oriented towards and driven by problem-solving" (Gibbons et al. 1994: 24; see also Klein et al. 2004). Such a new mode of knowledge production is inherently performative, presupposing a permanent movement back and forth between the fundamental and the applied. In addition, transdisciplinarity expresses a logic not of differentiation but of *de*-differentiation: communicative networks between researchers are increasingly denser, bringing together different actors, modes of doing, and value orientations. Nonetheless, academic disciplines remain the most important institutional form of scientific activity. The problem-solving capability envisaged by Gibbons is simply unthinkable without the training, conceptual and methodological tools, and intellectual traditions that only disciplines are able to provide and guarantee. In order to collaborate in an interdisciplinary or transdisciplinary project, one must be a practitioner of a certain discipline.

Dialogical Pluralism in Democratic Politics: The Case of Citizenship

If, in the scientific domain, academic disciplines are the modern institutional form, very much the same can be said of the territorial nation-state for the political realm. It should thus not come as a surprise that strikingly similar claims are being made in these two different debates. While in debates on science we are told that we are now living in a post-disciplinary era, an increasing number of political theorists claim that the nation-state is an institutional form of a bygone era. Lurking behind these claims yet again is the work of Foucault. As he showed in the 1970s, the process of state consolidation from the seventeenth to the nineteenth centuries took place not only at the level of institutions but also, and fundamentally, in the realm of political thought. The state appeared then, for the first time, as an object with measurable properties, such as its wealth and power, to be studied by political arithmetic, statistics, and political economy. By contrast, medieval and early modern political thought was primarily occupied with cities and their troubled relationship with rising states (Isin 1999: 166). This historical legacy has now been reappropriated by much urban literature. However, trying to draw lessons for post-Westphalian experiences of urban citizenship from pre-Westphalian ones is unwarranted. Underlying this comparative exercise is the belief that our rapidly changing postmodern reality demands conceptual tools that have not been contaminated by modern, state-centered categories. In this light, having recourse to pre-modern conceptual grids appears to be a more promising theoretical strategy.

There are, however, several familiar problems with this sort of strategy. Much as we may feel reassured by historical continuities, the work of the true historian is to be open to the unfamiliarity of the past (Skinner 1969). Looking into the past in search of answers for our problems makes us turn a blind eye to what these problems really are. For instance, the present effects of global corporate capital upon the changing, fluid, and essentially de-territorialized nature of power is unprecedented and lives in a new tension with the 'placedeness' of city politics. This tension explains some current tendencies to urban disengagement and urban de-politicization (Bauman 2003; Castells 1989).

Another point of contention is the dismissal of the state that these proposals presuppose. Very much like the dismissal of academic disciplines, it is unwarranted and premature. States continue to wield important mechanisms that contribute to the shaping of social and economic contexts within their borders. Non-state actors (such as multinational corporations or NGOs) on a par with bodies politic (such as cities, regions, and federations) cannot operate or operate procedurally with a certain degree of fairness without states. Despite all the claims pointing to the growing influence of corporations over world affairs and the life of global cities, the fact remains that corporations have not taken over from states. Corporations need money to be printed and interest rates to be set, while at the same time they need to be regulated. In fact, they need far more regulation than is commonly assumed in order to prevent them from lapsing into sheer criminality or recklessness (Stråth and Skinner 2003: 1–2). If in doubt, just think of the 2008 financial crisis, responsible for the worst economic downturn since the Great Depression.

In insisting that states still matter, we are not denying that the urban scale of governance has grown in importance in the course of the past couple of decades (Vieira 2008). That much is undoubted. Cities are political arenas where important struggles for citizenship rights are to be fought—first and foremost, the right to the city itself—in the face of observed tendencies of polarization and inequality between social groups, the privatization of public space, and housing market price distortions, to give but a few examples. This right that is owed to city dwellers gives rise to obligations both on their part and on that of the municipal structures governing them (e.g., participatory budgets). However, the literature on the revival of the urban scale of governance suffers from a recurrent limitation. Although it is written against the scalar mode of thinking that underpins Western modernity, the rescaling alternative it proposes, on the whole, expands rather than moves beyond it. Scalar thought is characterized by assuming exclusive, hierarchical, and ahistorical relationships among different bodies politic, such as those mentioned above, and by concealing their fluid, multiple, and overlapping forms of existence. By suggesting that citizenship rights can be neatly disaggregated in different scales of governance, if possible eliminating the middle layer (i.e., the state), rescaling alternatives reproduce the same logic but now at multiple levels.

Reality is not a neatly stratified set of layers—local, national, global—in which human action acquires a sort of independent character. If one wishes to understand citizenship rights, one cannot simply disaggregate the various types of rights of the modern conception of citizenship and redistribute them according to different levels of governance. While it might be the case that the liberal paradigm privileged one particular level of governance, that is, the state, at the expense of all the others, the alternative is not to disaggregate them into different levels and privilege a new one in turn (e.g., Cohen 1999). That would amount to the subscription of the scalar logic concealed behind the liberal paradigm that one sought to go beyond.

The crux of the matter is that the notion of scale itself is a human construct: it is we who set the boundaries; it is we who define where a city ends and the countryside begins; it is we who distinguish between local, regional, national, and global levels of governance. Those who propose to associate certain levels of governance with the exercise of certain rights seem to forget this. There is no necessary relation between this particular scale and that specific type of right. Our perception of the world as divided into multiple layers is one thing, but to believe that such a perception is the only possible viewpoint, and the only one that represents the world as it is, is another. A better alternative is to conceive of the city as a context for action in which the citizen, the rights that she or he enjoys, the socio-economic background conditions and institutions that guarantee them, the economy that enhances and questions many of them, and the consumer and political culture that transforms them all contribute to define one another. Determining the relative weight of each contribution is an empirical question. But the reach of each particular 'act of citizenship' can be fully captured only if one abandons a rigidly stratified logic and sees it as the outcome of a plurality of intersecting factors and as, at the same time, using and traversing, in their concrete embodiments, the inflexible constitution of scales. By rejecting scalar thought, we discard the dominant liberal, rationalistic discursive paradigm on the grounds of its unwarranted abstract and atomistic nature. As stated elsewhere, the rights-endowed individual suggested by liberal political theories, the reductionist self of behaviorism, and the purely instrumental self of Cartesian rationalism are all to be criticized for not paying justice to the worldly and social nature of the self in modern times (Silva 2008). From this perspective, a performative conception of citizenship seems a consistent alternative to the rigid and juridical, liberal rationalist conception.

An example might help us explain what we have in mind. Imagine a young woman protesting in Trafalgar Square against the invasion of Iraq in 2003. The exercise of that particular citizenship right in that public rally in that city at that specific moment in time can be understood only if one conceives it as one such complex interface of factors and scales, in which the performance of that particular act of citizenship incorporates elements from all other dimensions of reality: the woman's right to demonstrate against a decision of her government is state given; her exercise of that right is spatially local, dependent on previous authorization of the local authorities and on her capacity to buy herself out of work (even if only for a couple of hours). Yet the object of the act, as well as its intended reach, is transnational (i.e., to prevent a war elsewhere), as well as national (i.e., to object to a decision of her government: "Not in my name," was the slogan of many of the demonstrators, which implies the sending of British troops). The political values that motivate the woman's action can be more or less global in scope, but, as she incorporates them, they are self-appropriated, and, as she acts, they are being redefined and redefining her. Such a process of incorporation, performance, and redefinition can be grasped only if one supersedes the common trichotomy—citizenship as a legal status; citizenship as identity, belonging, and social status; and citizenship as practice—and avoids placing different rights on different spatial levels. In particular, the performance of any act of citizenship always uses and overflows neat categories, or scales, and what is critical is how these overflows reconstitute citizenship through the struggles of different social groups. It is through the body of the citizen that the citizenship which unites them into a body of citizens (struggling to define the contours of their common fate) comes to life.

Conclusion

A few words on the implications of the foregoing discussion are now in order. We have distanced ourselves from the Luhmannian functionalist orthodoxy, according to which functional differentiation is the primary and dominant mode of societal development in modern conditions. Empirical analyses show that this is not the case in either the scientific realm or the political domain. We have also rejected the multiple modernities proposal. Again, there are simply not enough theoretical or empirical reasons to support the thesis that modernity should be equated with the nation-state. A plural modernity, with several historically entangled varieties, seems a more convincing portrait. Such a plural modernity encompasses a number of institutional forms, of which we discussed here academic disciplines and territorial nation-states. Contrary to what is suggested by modernization and neo-modernization theorists, however, the process of development of these institutional forms was often guided by a logic other than that of functional differentiation.

We are living today, in science as in democratic politics, in an epoch of profound and rapid redefinition in which modern institutional forms co-exist with new dynamics. Democratic politics today is increasingly post-national politics. International bodies such as the UN, multinational companies, NGOs, and cities are openly contesting the hegemonic status of the nation-state as the sole bearer of the principle of sovereignty. Likewise, the future of science is more and more associated with transdisciplinary endeavors. In both cases, however, disciplines and nation-states co-exist with novel institutional forms, and patterns of differentiation unfold side by side with patterns of de-differentiation and synthesis. Furthermore, if the notion of performance seems to be useful for conceiving of a notion of citizenship that avoids the pitfalls of scalar thought, it is no less helpful to explain the transdisciplinary flow between disciplines, methods, and theories that characterizes the cutting edge of science today (Alexander, Giesen, and Mast 2006).

In order to make sense of these developments, the best solution would be to engage the plurality of scientific resources in a productive dialogue, that is, to subscribe to dialogical pluralism.[6] Such a meta-theoretical position can be of use to both sociologists and anthropologists. Hence our answer to the debate that triggered this volume is that 'an epistemology for anthropology' should avoid the search for universal epistemological foundations, a search that is associated with the quasi-naturalistic agenda of liberal rationalism. Joining other social scientists in transdisciplinary projects (like the study of post-national acts of citizenship, as suggested above), anthropologists should focus instead on responding to the central problematics of our time in such a way that, paraphrasing Wittgenstein, the 'thick' fabric of culture, sociality, and history does not 'go on holiday'.

Filipe Carreira da Silva is a Research Fellow at the Institute of Social Sciences, University of Lisbon, and a Senior Member of Wolfson College, Cambridge. His current research interests revolve around sociological theory and citizenship studies. In particular, he maintains an interest in social and political theories, namely, the 'multiple modernities' approach, the model of deliberative democracy, and the 'historicism vs. presentism' methodological debate. He has written several articles and books on classical and contemporary sociological theories, including *G. H. Mead: A Critical Introduction* (2007) and *Mead and Modernity: Science, Selfhood, and Democratic Politics* (2008).

Mónica Brito Vieira is a Research Fellow at the Institute for Social Sciences, University of Lisbon, and Visiting Scholar at Murray Edwards College, Cambridge. Her research currently focuses on three main areas: intellectual history, the history of political thought, and contemporary political theory. She is above all interested in the history of early modern and modern political thought. Her work in this area revolves around seventeenth-century political philosophy, in particular that of Thomas Hobbes. Her most recent publications include (with David Runciman) *Representation* (2008) and *The Elements of Representation in Hobbes* (2009).

Notes

1. A similar question has been posed by Connell (2007). See also Wimmer and Kössler (2006).
2. The rules of engagement in such an imaginary dialogue are laid out in Silva (2008).
3. For discussion on multiple modernities, see, for example, Eisenstadt (2002, 2003), Roniger and Waisman (2002), Therborn (2003), and Yack (1997).
4. Peter Wagner (1994, 2001) distinguishes several modern problematics, including those of science and democratic politics.
5. For a development of this insight, see Yack (1997: 88-109).
6. For a similar viewpoint, see Levine (1995).

References

Abbott, Andrew. 2001. *Chaos of Disciplines*. Chicago, IL: University of Chicago Press.
Alexander, Jeffrey C., Bernhard Giesen, and Jason L. Mast, eds. 2006. *Social Performance: Symbolic Action, Cultural Pragmatics, and Ritual*. Cambridge: Cambridge University Press.
Baert, Patrick, and Filipe Carreira da Silva. 2009. *Social Theory in the Twentieth Century and Beyond*. Cambridge: Polity Press
Bauman, Zygmunt. 2003. *City of Fears, City of Hopes*. London: Goldsmith's College, University of London.
Castells, Manuel. 1989. *The Informational City. Information Technology, Economic Restructuring, and the Urban-Regional Process*. Oxford: Basil Blackwell.
Cohen, Jean. 1999. "Changing Paradigms of Citizenship and the Exclusiveness of the Demos." *International Sociology* 14, no. 3: 245-268.
Connell, Raewyn. 2007. *Southern Theory: Social Science and the Global Dynamics of Knowledge*. Cambridge: Polity Press.
Eisenstadt, Shmuel N., ed. 2002. *Multiple Modernities*. New Brunswick, NJ: Transaction Publishers.
_____, ed. 2003. *Comparative Civilizations and Multiple Modernities, Part II*. Leiden: Brill.
Foucault, Michel. 1966. *Les mots et les choses: Une archéologie des sciences humaines*. Paris: Gallimard.
_____. 1975. *Surveiller et punir: Naissance de la prison*. Paris: Gallimard.
Gallie, Walter B. 1964. "Essentially Contested Concepts." Pp. 157-191 in *Philosophy and the Historical Understanding*, ed. W. B. Gallie. London: Chatto & Windus.
Gibbons, Michael, Camille Limoges, Helga Nowotny, Simon Schwartzman, Peter Scott, and Martin Trow. 1994. *The New Production of Knowledge: The Dynamics of Science and Research in Contemporary Societies*. London: Sage.
Habermas, Jürgen. [1981] 1986. *Reason and Rationalization of Society*. Vol. 1 of *The Theory of Communicative Action*. Trans. Thomas McCarthy. Cambridge: Polity Press.
_____. [1985] 1998. *The Philosophical Discourse of Modernity*. Cambridge, MA: MIT Press.
Hall, Peter, and David Soskice. 2001. *Varieties of Capitalism: The Institutional Foundations of Comparative Advantage*. Oxford: Oxford University Press.
Heilbron, Johan. 2004. "A Regime of Disciplines: Toward a Historical Sociology of Disciplinary Knowledge." Pp. 23-42 in *The Dialogical Turn: New Roles for Sociology in the Postdisciplinary Age*, ed. Charles Camic and Hans Joas. Lanham, MD: Rowman & Littlefield.
Honneth, Axel. [1992] 1996. *The Struggle for Recognition. The Moral Grammar of Social Conflicts*. Cambridge, MA: MIT Press.
_____. [2000] 2007. *Disrespect: The Normative Foundations of Critical Theory*. Cambridge: Polity Press.
Isin, Engin. 1999. "Introduction: Cities and Citizenship in a Global Age." *Citizenship Studies* 3, no. 2: 165-171.

Klein, Julie. 1990. *Interdisciplinarity: History, Theory and Practice*. Detroit, MI: Wayne State University Press.

Klein, Julie T., Walter Grossenbacher-Mansuy, Rudolf Häberli, Alain Bill, Roland W. Scholz, and Myrtha Welti, eds. 2004. *Transdisciplinarity: Joint Problem Solving among Science, Technology, and Society—An Effective Way for Managing Complexity*. Basel: Birkhäuser.

Knodt, Eva. 1994. "Toward a Non-Foundationalist Epistemology: The Habermas/Luhmann Controversy Revisited." *New German Critique* 61: 77–100.

Lefort, Claude. 1988. *Democracy and Political Theory*. Cambridge: Polity Press.

Levine, Donald N. 1995. *Visions of the Sociological Tradition*. Chicago, IL: Chicago University Press.

Mannheim, Karl. [1936] 1972. *Ideology and Utopia: An Introduction to the Sociology of Knowledge*. London: Routledge.

Markell, Patchen. 2007. "The Potential and the Actual: Mead, Honneth, and the 'I.'" Pp. 100–132 in *Recognition and Power: Axel Honneth and the Tradition of Critical Social Theory*, ed. B. van den Brink and D. Owen. Cambridge: Cambridge University Press.

Nowotny, Helga, Peter Scott, and Michael Gibbons. 2001. *Re-thinking Science: Knowledge in an Age of Uncertainty*. Cambridge: Polity Press.

Roniger, Luis, and Carlos H. Waisman, eds. 2002. *Globality and Multiple Modernities: Comparative North American and Latin American Perspectives*. Brighton: Sussex Academic Press.

Schmidt, Volker. 2006. "Multiple Modernities or Varieties of Modernity?" *Current Sociology* 54, no. 1: 77–97. doi: 10.1177/0011392106058835.

_____. 2007. "One World, One modernity." Pp. 205–228 in *Modernity at the Beginning of the 21st Century*, ed. Volker Schmidt. Newcastle: Cambridge Scholars Press.

Seigel, Jerrold. 2005. *The Idea of the Self*. Cambridge: Cambridge University Press.

Silva, Filipe C. 2001a. "Espaço Público e Democracia: O Papel da Esfera Pública no Pensamento Político de Habermas." *Análise Social* 36, nos. 158–159: 435–459.

_____. 2001b. "Habermas e a Esfera Pública: Reconstruindo a História de uma Ideia." *Sociologia – Problemas e Práticas* 35: 117–138.

_____. 2002. *Espaço Público em Habermas*. Lisbon: Imprensa de Ciências Sociais.

_____. 2004. *Virtude e Democracia: Um Ensaio sobre Ideias Republicanas*. Lisbon: Imprensa de Ciências Sociais.

_____. 2006. "G. H. Mead in the History of Sociological Ideas." *Journal of the History of the Behavioral Sciences* 42, no. 1: 19–39.

_____. 2007. *G. H. Mead. A Critical Introduction*. Cambridge: Polity Press.

_____. 2008. *Mead and Modernity: Science, Selfhood, and Democratic Politics*. Lanham, MD: Lexington Books.

_____. 2009a. *Em Diálogo com os Tempos Modernos: O Pensamento Social e Político de G.H. Mead*. Rio de Janeiro: Tempo Brasileiro.

_____. 2009b. "Bringing Republican Ideas Back Home: The Dewey-Laski Connection." *History of European Ideas* 35, no. 3: 360–368.

Simmel, Georg. [1900] 1978. *The Philosophy of Money*. London: Routledge.

Skinner, Quentin. 1969. "Meaning and Understanding in the History of Ideas." *History and Theory* 8, no. 1: 3–53.

Stråth, Bo, and Quentin Skinner. 2003. "Introduction." Pp. 1–8 in *States and Citizens: History, Theory, Prospects*, ed. Quentin Skinner and Bo Stråth. Cambridge: Cambridge University Press.

Therborn, Göran. 2003. "Entangled Modernities," *European Journal of Social Theory* 6, no. 3: 293–305. doi: 10.1177/13684310030063002.

Vieira, Mónica B. 2008. "O Espaço Urbano e a Arquitectura da Cidadania." Pp. 79–106 in *Cidade e Cidadania: Governança urbana e participação cidadã em perspectivas comparadas*, ed. Manuel Villaverde Cabral, Filipe Carreira da Silva, and Tiago Saraiva. Lisbon: Imprensa de Ciências Sociais.

_____. 2009. *The Elements of Representation in Hobbes: Aesthetics, Theatre and Law in the Construction of Hobbes's Theory of the State*. Leiden: Brill.

Wagner, Peter. 1994. *A Sociology of Modernity: Liberty and Discipline*. London: Routledge.

_____. 2001. *Theorizing Modernity: Inescapability and Attainability in Social Theory*. London: Sage.

Wimmer, Andreas, and Reinhart Kössler, eds. 2006. *Understanding Change: Models, Methodologies, and Metaphors*. Basingstoke: Palgrave Macmillan.

Wittgenstein, Ludwig. [1953] 2003. *Philosophical Investigations*. Blackwell.

Yack, Bernard. 1997. *The Fetishism of Modernities: Epochal Self-Consciousness in Contemporary Social and Political Thought*. Notre Dame, IN: University of Notre Dame Press.

Chapter 4

ONTOGRAPHY AND ALTERITY
Defining Anthropological Truth

Martin Holbraad

The call for 'an epistemology for anthropology' seems justified—laudable, even—at a time when the discipline may appear somewhat to have lost its way under the pressure of successive self-critical reorientations and due to its success in terms of sheer growth. As Pina-Cabral argues in his contribution to this book, one of the effects of anthropology's numerous critical turns in recent decades (e.g., the feminist and Marxist critiques in the 1970s, the reflexivism of the 'writing culture' in the 1980s, and the discovery of 'globalization' and even 'professional ethics' since then) is that the discipline has tended to retreat into a theoretical timidity of sorts. The problem is not necessarily that most anthropologists have come to eschew generalizations about 'the human' (Bloch 2005) or systematic attempts at regional comparison (Gingrich, this book), and that ethnographic 'particularism' has become a habit—even the recent insistence on doing ethnography, often 'multi-sited', of 'globalized', 'diasporic',

Notes for this chapter are located on page 92.

'transnational', or other putatively infra-cultural phenomena, seems just to draw the premise of particularism on a larger canvas (cf. Tsing 2004). The problem is more that the sedimentation of self-critique—more an attitude now than a task—has contributed to a situation that could best be characterized as theoretical idiosyncrasy. While still tracing loose allegiances to national 'styles' of anthropology (US, UK, France) and more firm ties to influential individuals (the 'star-system' and other forms of patronage), anthropological arguments nowadays tend to be elaborated without much reference to overall analytical frameworks or paradigms. Worse, when such references are made at all, it is habitually through 'in' catchphrases—'Foucauldian' this, 'phenomenological' that, 'post-' the other—that take the place of substantiated and developed arguments. So anthropological debates continue to rage, while their premises and their wider analytical significance to the discipline are left opaque. One might say that compared to previous generations of students, the main challenge for those entering the discipline today is not so much to take a position with respect to existing models of anthropological work, but rather to try to determine what the apparently available models actually are. And since this is an almost impossible task in the cacophony of contemporary debate, the confusion seems set to be perpetuated.

In this atmosphere, an image conjured by this book's call to epistemological appraisal is that of rolled-up shirtsleeves. Is there scope for sorting out this mess, or at least for achieving some clarity about what is at stake in the pursuit of the knowledge we call anthropological? Indeed, the very notion of epistemology has the promise of such clarity built into it. If anthropology, by analogy to other disciplines, is imagined as the pursuit of a certain type of knowledge (if, in other words, it is assumed to be an 'episteme'), then any serious attempt at disciplinary housekeeping must, it seems, be 'epistemological' in nature. It was, after all, primarily by virtue of its epistemological branch that philosophy was once called the 'queen of sciences'. So just as mathematicians, economists, or literary critics might wonder about their own disciplines, we too, as anthropologists, may ponder the following: For what kind of knowledge might anthropology strive? What are the conditions of possibility of such knowledge? What is its object? And so on. Such questions are epistemological through and through, and asking them seems not just reasonable but downright imperative at the present juncture of the discipline.

Nevertheless, the main premise of this chapter is that such questions are in a crucial sense inappropriate for anthropology. In particular, I want to show that the notion that the clarity for which anthropologists ought to strive must be epistemological contradicts what is arguably the most distinctive characteristic of anthropological thought, namely, that it is oriented toward difference—what used sometimes to be called 'the Other' (e.g., Fabian 1983) and is now often designated as 'alterity' (e.g., Evens 2008; Kapferer 2007; Povinelli 2001; Taussig 1993; see also Holbraad 2007a). My central argument turns on the idea that alterity proper must be construed in ontological rather than epistemological terms. The questions that alterity poses to us anthropologists pertain to what exists rather than what can be known. They pertain, if you like, to differences between 'worlds' rather than 'worldviews' (see Henare, Holbraad, and Wastell 2007; Latour 2002; Viveiros de Castro 1998). So the syllogism is that since anthropology is centrally concerned with alterity and since alterity is a matter of ontological rather than epistemological differences, it follows that anthropology must reflect upon its modus operandi in ontological rather than epistemological terms.

In the main body of this chapter I pursue this approach with reference to an issue that may be assumed to fall most naturally under the remit of epistemology—the notion of truth. In particular, I seek to align two concerns: the methodological question of what may count as truth in anthropology, and the substantive ethnographic question of what counts as truth for practitioners of Ifá divination in contemporary Cuba. In doing so, I argue that thinking of truth in epistemological terms, as a property of one's knowledge about the world, inhibits the attempt to make sense of the role of truth in Ifá divination. In fact, as I show, epistemological assumptions about truth would render Ifá diviners' claims to wield it quite absurd. This analytical predicament places the onus on us as anthropological analysts to come up with an alternative conceptualization of truth—one that does not make nonsense of diviners' own claims. Hence, with reference to the ethnography of Ifá, I formulate a concept of divinatory truth that avoids the epistemological assumption that truth must be a property of representations that make claims about the world. Rather, I argue, diviners' claims to pronounce truth turn on an essentially ontological operation. The role of the truths that diviners pronounce is not to make a claim about the world but rather to change it—to interfere, in other words, in its ontological constitution. As I explain, diviners are able to do this by effectively redefining the entities 'about' which they appear to speak in divination, with speaking 'about' things being the mark of an epistemological frame (see Henare, Holbraad, and Wastell 2007). So pertaining to the definition of concepts (what counts as 'x') rather than their application (what does x say about the word), divinatory truths have ontological effects. This is meant literally. Inasmuch as it invents new concepts through acts of redefinition, divination brings novel entities forth into existence.

But if divination populates the world, in this sense, so does anthropology (see Holbraad 2009). Thus, the strategy of the argument that follows may best be described as recursive: my attempt to redefine truth as an act of redefinition must, by its own measure, count as an act of truth (see Holbraad 2007a: 218; Henare, Holbraad, and Wastell 2007: 20–22). In other words, the aim of this chapter is to offer an argument about the need to redefine the notion of truth for anthropological purposes in a recursive manner, in the sense that the argument is also made by its own performance. As will be shown in the final sections of this chapter, the upshot of this exercise is an ontologically revamped conceptualization of truth as, precisely, conceptual revamping. Elsewhere I have called this approach to anthropological analysis 'ontographic', to indicate that what is at stake in it is the attempt to chart out the ontological presuppositions required to make sense of a given body of ethnographic material (see Holbraad 2003, 2009).

Truth in Anthropology

Anthropologists do all sorts of different things, and the truth stakes are not necessarily the same in each case. For example, my argument about redefining anthropological truth is in no way meant to cover ordinary data collection, without which anthropological analysis could most likely not get off the ground. Thus, when we say that a certain group are horticulturalists, or that suicide rates are going up, or that a particular informant is ill, or any other such statement of fact, we may assume that we are doing our job as anthropologists properly insofar as those statements are accurate representations of the phenomena that they are about, that is, that they are true in a straightforward sense. But what makes this admission relatively uninteresting in the context of this discussion is that this kind of data collection is one we share with other social sciences.

As already indicated, however, the guiding intuition of this chapter is that what most distinguishes anthropologists from even their most immediate disciplinary neighbors is that they tend to deal also in questions of alterity (although clearly some of our neighbors, such as historians, can learn from us in this respect, and some apparently have). An easy way to tag alterity would be to say that it comprises data that resist collection, with the word 'collection' being used in the ordinary sense of accurate description. Why might some data resist collection in this sense? The answer I am arguing for here is that this is because the concepts available to anthropologists for describing them are inadequate. In order to get to that argument, however, we may begin with a weaker criterion of resistance by saying simply that what makes certain data 'alter' (as in the opposite of 'ego') is that the peculiar difficulty they present to the researcher is precisely that of determining how best to describe them, that is, how best to find concepts that distort them as little as possible. So if fieldwork is our trademark method, description (and its cognitive corollary, comprehension) is our trademark difficulty. And let there be no misunderstanding. Of course, all scientists struggle to find the right concepts to describe what they study. But the problem in our case is compounded by the fact that the data we seek to conceptualize are themselves concepts (for 'practices' too are determined conceptually). Moreover, we are typically working with concepts that are initially alien to us.

Thus, the question to determine is how alterity relates to truth. The answer is intimately. For what is the most obvious index of alterity as we have defined it? With regard to data that we find difficult to describe, the one thing that they all have in common is that they appear to be a form of negation of what we are used to describing, and negation (the 'not', as it were) is what is ordinarily taken to be the opposite of truth. In other words, the 'difference' of alterity initially takes the form of negation. So to take our example, divination appears 'alter' (and therefore anthropologically interesting) to the extent that it negates a number of key notions that I—not as a person but as an analyst—would assume to be obvious: that deities do not really exist; that even if they do, they probably will not be inclined to tell me whether I should stay with my partner (as they are often purported to do in Cuba); that the palm nuts that Cuban Ifá diviners use to divine with are not really imbued with sacred substance; that their casting by the diviner is a random matter rather than one of divine necessity, and so on. Cuban divination seems 'alter' just because it negates what I assume to be true when writing anthropologically.[1] The same could be said not only of other classic anthropological exoticisms (cross-cousin marriage, say), but also of the more 'right on' topics of contemporary anthropology, such as the power of identity, the cosmology of technologies, or the workings of post-industrial institutions. All of these become anthropologically compelling only after having been shown to be more surprising than they might initially appear—that is, only after they have been 'othered', as people used to say.

Appeals to negation are the most efficient and obvious heuristic for identifying alterity, as it were, by its symptoms. But it seems to me that anthropologists are inclined to treat negation as the cause of alterity, or at least to identify the two, as if what makes, say, Cuban diviners 'different' is that they are different from 'us'. The slip is that of projection, and the prevalence of this kind of a lapse in anthropological thinking is remarkable. Indeed, spelled out, the slip sounds pretty legitimate. If I described my research project as that of explaining why some Cubans believe in their oracles, you would be forgiven for agreeing that this is a perfectly legitimate line of inquiry. Nevertheless, in doing so, you would be joining me in a tremendous muddle of projection—'negative projection', let us call it (see Holbraad 2009). The flawed syllogism would be as follows. Cubans habitually use oracles, and we do not. We do not use oracles because we do not believe in them.[2] So if Cubans do, it must be because they believe in them. This application of excluded middle would be fine, were it not for the fact that the assumption that the only way of having oracles is by believing in them is a baseless projection—the result of a lack of ethnographic imagination combined with a remarkable self-confidence that our own conceptual framework is rich enough to describe those of all others.

Nevertheless, this presumptuous approach is second nature to much anthropology. Consider, for example, the apparent dilemma between 'universalism' and 'relativism', which, although hackneyed, arguably continues to guide our instincts when it comes to placing anthropologists in theoretical space. The alleged dilemma, put simply, is about how best to deal with alterity, as we have defined it. A 'universalist' takes Cubans' apparent belief that oracles work and seeks to explain it with reference to processes that are deemed to hold for all humans (conceptually, psychologically, sociologically, etc.). A 'relativist' seeks to interpret this belief with reference to other local beliefs and practices with which the one about oracles coheres. The common premise of the two approaches is that what requires analysis (be it of explanation or interpretation) is a datum that is understood as the negation of something familiar, as with our commonsense distrust of oracles.

So if we can agree that the dilemma between universalism and relativism captures most positions in anthropology one way or the other, we may conclude that mainstream anthropological thinking relies on a remarkably uniform image of what counts as anthropological truth. Supposedly, whether our goal is causal explanation or adequate interpretation, we are basically in the business of representing others' concepts and practices that are not only interesting but also available to us (i.e., understood) as negations of our own. Indeed, the premise of negative projection is crucial to both approaches' claim to representation. For in order even to hope either to explain or to interpret something (in any case, to represent it), we must first understand it, and saying that Cubans 'believe in' oracles helps us to do so. With such an Archimedean point in place, the rest of the business of representation can get underway. Thus, universalists' explanations are 'true' if they accurately describe the causal processes that bring about native representations, while relativists' interpretations are 'true' (or adequate) insofar as they cohere with the natives' own interpretations. In both cases, truth is assumed to be a matter of 'reflecting' one set of representations (those of the natives) in terms of another (those of the analyst), and this in turn presupposes that the representations available to the analyst must in principle be suited to the job. The difficulty of producing anthropological truth, then, is supposed to lie in choosing the right concepts, that is, those that reflect native ones.

However, this image of anthropology ignores what seems like a strong possibility, namely, that ethnographic data may pose a challenge to analysis precisely to the extent that they elude description in the first place. In this view, the fact that 'alter' ethnographic data present themselves initially as negations of what we commonsensically take to be true is a result of the fact that our commonsense assumptions are conceptually inadequate to describe this data. We are getting the 'wrong' answers because we have been asking the wrong questions. Such a possibility would imply that what makes anthropological truth so special is precisely that it cannot be a matter of choosing representations that match the phenomena that they describe—that is, of getting things 'right'—since such representations simply do not exist. Rather, anthropological analysis must begin before the step of testing one set of representations against another can even be made. In other words, anthropological analysis, in this view, must turn on more than the ordinary concept of truth—that of 'telling it like it really is'. We need a different concept of truth. I argue that such a concept can be culled from an anthropological analysis of Cuban Ifá divination.

Divining Truth

Giving a full ethnographic image of Ifá divination in Havana would be beyond the scope of this chapter.[3] For present purposes, we need focus only on the main ethnographic point that relates to my argument on truth. This point is one that Ifá diviners (called *babalawos*) emphasize again and again when faced with doubting anthropologists or, indeed, doubting clients during divinatory séances. Their oracle, they say, is infallible: "Ifá no se equivoca" (Ifá doesn't make mistakes) and "en Ifá no hay mentiras" (in Ifá there are no lies). *Babalawos* themselves may certainly lie or make mistakes—since they are "imperfect humans," as one practitioner put it—but not the oracle of Ifá. During fieldwork, the most telling conversation on this matter was with a young *babalawo*, who was complaining about "exploitative" *babalawos*, as he called them. One of his main complaints was that some *babalawos* seek to impress their clients by attaching the oracle's verdicts to specific dates or to people's names (e.g., "your daughter will fall ill next Tuesday" or "the witch is your neighbor, Rossío," etc.). He told me, "I don't give people dates. Ifá speaks past, present, and future, and gives advice, but [clients] should know for themselves their own situation and act on it as they see fit ... Some [*babalawos*] do give them, but that's just showing off, and clients complain when things don't turn out that way. How can they [i.e., the *babalawos*] know these things? Ifá doesn't work like that."

So how are we to understand the claim that "Ifá doesn't work like that"? Why can Ifá give advice but not dates and names? When I asked my informant to elaborate, he reverted to a point to which *babalawos* often appeal in such conversations, namely, that "Ifá is interpretation," implying that interpretation by itself could not yield specific names and dates. Admittedly, the implication is moot since, like the famous Zande benge oracle, among many others, Ifá is sometimes used to give unambiguous yes or no answers to specific questions posed to it by the diviner. I would suggest rather that the import of *babalawos'* normative insistence on terms such as *consejo* (advice) and *interpretación* (interpretation) has more to do with the question of falsifiability than with ambiguity. Indeed, this is the gist of my informant's complaint against exploitative *babalawos*: by adding dates and names, they present the oracle's verdicts as statements of fact that may be verified or falsified according to how things actually turn out. By contrast, advice seems to him a good example of something that can be acted upon, perhaps, but not falsified. Similarly, the idea that 'Ifá speaks past, present and future', which *babalawos* often emphasize during the séance, is another normative mitigation of falsifiability. When, in a divination conducted for me, I queried—in falsifying mood—the oracle's contention that I am prone to impotence, one of the *babalawos* reminded me with macho gusto that, after all, I have no children. "And don't forget," he added with emphasis, "Ifá habla pasado, presenty, y futuro [Ifá speaks past, present, and future]".

Normativity is important here, for like the statement "your daughter will fall ill on Tuesday," an oracular verdict such as "you are prone to impotence" could easily be mistaken for ordinary, falsifiable statements of fact. My informant's dispute with exploitative *babalawos* who give names and dates can be cast precisely as a dispute over whether oracular pronouncements ought to be taken as falsifiable truth claims or not. In fact, as their occasional doubts indicate, clients—let alone anthropologists—are liable to confuse divinatory verdicts in this way, and this logical pitfall is readily exploited by *babalawos* who wish to impress. No wonder that *babalawos* should find it necessary to stress normatively that oracular pronouncements are not affirmations that might, least of all in principle, be falsified.

So it would seem that *babalawos* are inviting their clients (and us anthropologists with them) to imagine an alternative concept of truth—one that ought not to be defined by opposition to falsehood. However strange it may sound to suggest a notion of 'true' that is not the opposite of 'false', such a conceptual possibility must nevertheless be enticing for our purposes. It would seem that the notion of truth that *babalawos* are keen to avoid is the same as the one that we are trying to overcome meta-anthropologically here—namely, the idea that truth is a matter of producing statements that get things right by accurately reflecting phenomena.

Defining Truth

At this point, it is useful to introduce the concept of 'definition' because, I argue, there is a sense in which this word may yield the concept of truth we need to make sense of divination—and anthropology, too. For present purposes, we may ignore the best part of philosophical debate about what constitutes a definition, just to point out that Anglo-Saxon philosophers of language in particular tend to assume that a definition cannot but be a species of ordinary truth claim. For example, here is a horse, and the problem is to decide whether and how, say, an *Oxford English Dictionary* phrase, such as "quadruped with a flowing mane and tail," may serve to define it. Truth conditions in the sense we are seeking to overcome—let us call them 'truth-functional'—are central to this enterprise. We have a sense of what a horse is, so defining it is a matter of getting this sense right. This requirement must at some level involve using terms that hold true of horses, such as 'quadruped'. And note that this sense of definition coincides exactly with the classical anthropological strategy of negative projection. Through it, anthropologists assume that they have a sense of diviners' attitude to oracles, so defining that attitude ('representing it') is a matter of identifying concepts that, like 'belief', supposedly hold true of it—truth-functionally so.

It is remarkable that philosophers, who do nothing if not muster powers of clear thinking and creativity in order to enrich our conceptual repertoire, should presume that definitions must 'conserve' meaning in this way. Maybe defining a horse is a matter of articulating a sense one already has, but who could even begin to have a sense of a Platonic Form, a monad, the transcendental ego, and so on before philosophers ventured to define them? Indeed, those philosophers who have followed Nietzsche in thinking of philosophy as an 'untimely' enterprise have sought to theorize this possibility of conceptual invention (e.g., Deleuze 1994; Heidegger 1968; cf. Nietzsche 1997), and so have anthropologists who see the creation of new meanings not just as a philosophical prerogative but as an irreducible aspect of social living (e.g., Ardener 1989; Latour 1999; Strathern 2005; Viveiros de Castro 2002; Wagner 1981; cf. Holbraad and Pedersen in press; see also the chapter by Goldman in this book). Here we may venture a distinction between the truth-functional definitions with which analytical philosophy is mainly concerned and what I propose to call 'inventive definitions', by appeal to Roy Wagner (1981). The distinction pertains to the question of truth. As we have seen, conventional definitions are truth-functional. Now, as an example of what I take to be an inventive definition, consider a definition of inventive definition—as pudding to the proof, as it were. Let us define inventive definition as a speech act that inaugurates a new meaning by combining two or more previously unrelated meanings—something that I did just now. I took the meanings 'speech act', 'inauguration', 'novelty', and 'meaning' and combined them in order to inaugurate a new meaning, which I call 'inventive definition'. The crucial point to note here is that such a definition cannot be an ordinary truth-functional claim. 'Speech act', 'inauguration', etc., cannot be construed as properties that predicate 'inventive definition' like 'quadruped' predicates 'horse', for this would imply that the concept 'inventive definition' is not new after all: it must already exist in order to serve as the testing ground for the predicative truth claims that purport to define it. Posited as a condition for its own definition, the *definiendum* (the word to be defined) takes logical precedence over its *definiens* (the word or words that are used to define it), and hence the latter cannot be said to inaugurate it. Thus, since inventive definitions are defined as inaugurations— as inventions of (new) meanings—it follows that, unlike truth-functional definitions, inventive definitions are not predicative truth claims.

My suggestion, then, is that oracles pronounce inventive definitions in just this sense. Take the common verdict "you are bewitched" as an example. Treating this as an inventive definition implies that being bewitched is not a predicate that 'holds true' of me. Rather, it is a meaning that is being related to me so as to redefine me. The oracle transforms me from a person who stands in no particular relation to witchcraft into a person who is being bewitched. To ask whether such a shift is true or false is fundamentally to misunderstand the ontological character of the transformation by confusing it with the epistemological question of how the shift may be ascertained. The fact that practitioners of Ifá might be as likely to fall into this trap as analysts explains why *babalawos* put such normative emphasis on the requirement that the oracles' pronouncements be interpreted as non-falsifiable. Their point is that treating the truths that oracles pronounce as representational is a category mistake. Oracles turn on an alternative concept of truth, namely, that of inventive definition.

This way of thinking about divination may seem awkward. A concept can be defined afresh, but can the notion of invention really be stretched to include people as well? For, more than just a meaning (e.g., 'inventive definition'), I am a flesh-and-blood person, and it is unclear how, as such, I can be 'brought together' with ideas ('meanings') such as 'being bewitched', just as it is unclear how I, flesh and blood, can be a 'new meaning'—or new at all. In fact, is not this talk about the ability of oracles to transform people philosophically suspicious? It would seem that what is being propounded here is a version of social constructivism ('oracular constrictivism', if you will), based on the preposterously idealist notion that entities of the world can be brought in and out of existence by mere human fancy—divinatory or otherwise.

Such appeals to common sense are cheap in their professed transparency. As Bruno Latour (1999) has pointed out, from a properly anthropological perspective the dilemma between realism and idealism is false. Constructivism is indeed preposterous inasmuch as it comes as a remedy for a bias of its own premise, namely, that 'our ideas' and 'the world' cannot but constitute distinct ontological camps. Only on this premise does it become even possible—let alone necessary—to say that what 'appears' to be real and mind-independent is actually 'only' a human construct.

What this means is that to understand Ifá divination and initiation it is necessary to deny that the distinction between concepts (or meanings) and things (or people) is axiomatic (see also Holbraad 2007a; Henare, Holbraad, and Wastell 2007). Instead of reducing to the absurd our claim that oracular pronouncements have ontological effects, appeals to common sense alert us to the fact that the sense of divination, with its seemingly bizarre entailment that assertions may be unfalsifiable at the level of logical principle, is quite uncommon. And it is uncommon in just the way that Latour has envisaged. What differentiates predicative (conventional) from non-predicative (inventive) definition, and what makes the latter rather than the former appropriate to the analysis of divination, is precisely that predication presupposes the 'common' distinction between word and world, while invention does not. As we have seen, the truth-functional character of conventional definitions is premised on the logical priority of their *definienda*. And although this logical priority does not imply that the *definienda* in question exist (e.g., defining unicorns as 'horses with horns' does not mean that they exist), it does imply the existence of a domain of entities—the 'world'—from which conventional definitions may draw their truth values.

By contrast, inventive definitions do not presuppose the existence of a world of entities: such a world is their conventionalized outcome. When the oracle of Ifá defines me as a person who is bewitched, it is not speaking of an entity (myself) existing out there in the world, of whom certain properties may be said to hold (that I am bewitched). Such a construal would imply that the definition in question is conventional and open to falsification—a notion *babalawos* are keen to deny. But nor does the inevitable consequence, namely, that in defining me the oracle is bringing me about as a new person, imply the idealist notion that the world's constituents exist insofar as people (such as diviners or anthropological analysts) think or speak of them. Just as with the notion of conventional definition, idealism is premised on a logical distinction between word and world, concept and thing—in other words, precisely the distinction that is obliterated by the logic of invention.

It follows that in committing us to a notion of invention, divination leads us *a fortiori* to posit an ontological parity between what common sense distinguishes as 'concepts' and as 'things'. Thus, our analytical imagination is further stretched to include a monistically construed plane of concepts-cum-things that incorporates elements like me, witchcraft, impotence, inaugurations, novelties, meanings, and horses with horns, too. Each of these may be brought together with others so as to engender new elements, such as me-as-bewitched, inventive definitions, or even fairy tales with unicorns in them.

Conclusion

The recursive conclusion I wish to draw from this thought experiment with Cuban divination can be framed in terms of a counter-argument to the above analysis of divinatory truth—one that I owe to James Laidlaw.[4] Fair enough, the counter-argument goes, divination may not produce truth in the ordinary representational sense. But why should this be treated as an occasion for redefining truth in such a weird way as to say that the opposite of truth is not falsehood? Should we not instead just bite the bullet and say that divination is not about truth at all?

One response would be to point to the fact that diviners themselves unambiguously speak of their verdicts in terms of truth (*la verdad*), as we have already seen. However, this is a weak answer insofar as such an attempt to duck the question by appeal to ethnography would ignore the central problem that motivated our attempt to redefine truth in the first place, namely, that divinatory truth is 'alter' precisely in the sense that even our best translation (truth) is conceptually inadequate to it. A better reply would have returned to the meta-argument about the nature of anthropological analysis.

The premise of the approach outlined above is that the most interesting anthropological data are those that cannot be captured by the analyst's default concepts. Alterity, in this sense, implies that we must always begin analysis in the dark, mired in misunderstanding. We do, however, have two things to go by. First, we have our own default concepts. So when a diviner says that his oracle tells no lies and makes no mistakes, we mobilize our ordinary concept of truth and say that he is claiming that divinatory truth is unfalsifiable. Secondly, we know that when glossing native claims, our default concepts produce falsehoods. Divinatory pronouncements such as "you are bewitched" are at least pretty likely to be false, which means that they are certainly falsifiable (surely, I might not be bewitched).

Arguably, we have here the makings of a method that may allow us to approximate an understanding of native concepts and the strange statements that define them—a method I call 'ontography' for the reasons stated in the introductory comments of this chapter. One thing that we can do is to transform the sense of our own concepts. So what if, through conceptual analysis, we were to alter the premises of our concepts (here, that of truth), transforming them to such an extent that, when used to gloss native statements, they would yield statements of truth? Anthropological thought experiments would then proceed from the question, how can we redefine our own terms in order to make them behave—truth-functionally—like the natives' concepts appear to? How far do we have to change our assumptions about what counts as truth before we could say that oracles give truth? So the better response to Laidlaw's point would be that inventive definition is a new definition of truth, rather than something else, precisely because it emerged as an answer to that kind of question. Inventive definition constitutes an appropriate transformation of our default and initially inadequate concept of truth and, by that virtue, constitutes a new version of that concept.

Recursively, this brings us full circle. For, like divination, the analytic method I have just described is one that is designed to produce inventive definitions. In other words, in proposing such a method, I am proposing a new way of thinking of truth. And since the method is one of anthropological analysis, this new truth is a new anthropological truth—one, it seems to me, that is both new and radical in its consequences.

By way of closing, I would like to highlight two points. First, this image of anthropological truth is completely incompatible with what might be one of the most cherished assumptions we make about what we do as anthropologists—that we are in the business of discovering how other people (cultures, groups) see things, how they think, what they experience, etc. The version of truth I have outlined precludes this. All we have to go by are our misunderstandings of others' views—our initial descriptions of their statements and practices. What we then produce, if we are to avoid projection, is a series of concepts that imitate those statements and practices truth-functionally, but are nevertheless peculiarly ours. So let us not expect *babalawos* to have much to say on the notion of inventive definition. To subvert Maurice Bloch's (1998) formulation, anthropology is not about 'how we think they think'. It is about how we could learn to think, given what they say and do.

The second point, rather less dire in my view, is that the version of anthropological truth for which I am arguing puts clear blue water between anthropology and science, without thereby throwing us into the arms of soft interpretivism. As we have seen, both of those theoretical camps are playing at the old game of truthful representation. In overcoming that approach, we arguably come much closer to what one might take philosophers to be doing, namely, transforming concepts (coming up with new ones) through what the most rigorous philosophers—Anglo-Saxon analytic ones—sometimes call 'conceptual analysis' (see Holbraad 2007b). This is indeed contentious, although, again, recursively so, since defining philosophy is itself a philosophical problem.

Acknowledgments

This chapter draws on arguments that I have been developing in the methodological sections of a number of other publications, as well as on an oral presentation delivered at the 'Truth and Anthropology' conference at the University of Cambridge in 2005. I am grateful to João Pina-Cabral and Christina Toren for inviting me to participate in the present project and for allowing me to bring these thoughts together in an explicitly methodological context.

Martin Holbraad works in the Anthropology Department of University College London. He has conducted fieldwork on Afro-Cuban religion in Havana since 1998. His research focuses on the relationship between myth and action, the consecration of objects, and, more broadly, the logic of cosmological thought in the field of religion as well as in politics. His is co-editor of *Thinking Through Things: Theorising Artefacts Ethnographically* (2007) and *Technologies of the Imagination* (2009). His monograph on Cuban divination and anthropological truth is in preparation.

Notes

1. Alterity, in this technical sense, should be understood as neither a psychological nor a cultural condition, but rather as a purely analytical one. I may, as a matter of fact, be a practitioner of divination—indeed, I could be a Cuban diviner. The point is that the interest such practices hold for anthropology resides only in their divergence from assumptions one chooses to take for granted when writing for an anthropological audience. I could certainly write about divination starting from the assumption that deities exist, that they are able to deliver truth through particular palm nuts, and so on. But this kind of exegesis (exemplified, incidentally, by the vast literature on Ifá written by practitioners) would hold minimal anthropological interest. If, as I argue, the game of anthropology is to 'make sense' of things, assuming that they already do so is a profoundly non-anthropological move.
2. Again, the 'we' of the syllogism is not meant as a psychological or cultural generalization. Naturally, there are plenty of people who could be included in the term 'us' (Westerners, academics, anthropologists) and who do, as a matter of fact, use oracles or horoscopes or what have you. In question here is a purely analytical 'we', namely, the position from which the use of oracles in Cuba seems *not* to make sense. This is the position—to invoke the best and most famous example—from which Evans-Pritchard ([1937] 1976) was able to write of the Azande and wonder why they should think that witches exist.
3. For more details on the methods and significance of divination in Ifá, see Holbraad (2003, 2007, 2008, 2009).
4. Personal communication with James Laidlaw.

References

Ardener, Edwin. 1989. *The Voice of Prophecy and Other Essays*. Ed. M. Chapman. Oxford: Basil Blackwell.

Bloch, Maurice. 1998. *How We Think They Think: Anthropological Approaches to Cognition, Memory and Literacy*. Boulder, CO: Westview Press.

_____. 2005. "Where Did Anthropology Go? Or the Need for 'Human Nature.'" Pp. 1–19 in *Essays on Cultural Transmission*. Oxford: Berg.

Deleuze, Gilles. 1994. *Difference and Repetition*. Trans. P. Patton. London: Athlone Press.

Evans-Pritchard, E. E. [1937] 1976. *Witchcraft, Oracles, and Magic Among the Azande*. New ed., abridged and with an introduction by Eva Gillies. Oxford: Clarendon Press.

Evens, T. M. S. 2008. *Anthropology as Ethics: Nondualism and the Conduct of Sacrifice*. New York: Berghahn Books.

Fabian, Johannes. 1983. *Time and the Other: How Anthropology Makes its Object*. New York: Columbia University Press.

Heidegger, Martin. 1968. *What Is Called Thinking?* Trans. J. Glenn Gray. New York: Harper & Row.

Henare, Amiria, Martin Holbraad, and Sari Wastell, eds. 2007. *Thinking Through Things: Theorising Artefacts Ethnographically*. London: Routledge.

Holbraad, Martin. 2003. "Estimando a necessidade: Os oráculos de Ifá e a verdade em Havana." *Mana* 9, no. 2: 39–77.

_____. 2007a. "The Power of Powder: Multiplicity and Motion in the Divinatory Cosmology of Cuban Ifa (or Mana, Again)." Pp. 189–225 in Henare, Holbraad, and Wastell 2007.

_____. 2007b. "Roulette Anthropology: The Whole beyond Holism." *Journal of the Finnish Anthropological Society* 32, no. 2: 29–47.

_____. 2008. "Relationships in Motion: Oracular Recruitment in Cuban Ifá Cults." *Systèmes de Pensée en Afrique Noire* 18: 219–264.

_____. 2009. "Definitive Evidence, from Cuban Gods." Pp. 89–104 in *The Objects of Evidence: Anthropological Approaches to the Production of Knowledge*, ed. Matthew Engelke. Oxford: Royal Anthropological Institute of Great Britain and Ireland. (Originally published as vol. 14, special issue of *Journal of the Royal Anthropological Institute*, April 2008.)

Holbraad, Martin, and Morten Axel Pedersen. In press. "Planet M: The Intense Abstraction of Marilyn Strathern." In *Bureacratic Knowledge Practices: The William Wyse Professorship and the Work of Marilyn Strathern*, ed. S. Deiringer and A. Lebner. (Special issue of *Cambridge Anthropology* 28, no. 3.)

Kapferer, Bruce. 2007. "Anthropology and the Dialectic of the Enlightenment: A Discourse on the Definition and Ideals of a Threatened Discipline." *Australian Journal of Anthropology* 18, no. 1: 72–96.

Latour, Bruno. 1999. *Pandora's Hope: Essays on the Reality of Science Studies*. Cambridge MA.: Harvard University Press.

_____. 2002. *War of the Worlds: What About Peace?* Chicago, IL: Prickly Paradigm Press.

Nietzsche, Friedrich. 1997. *Untimely Meditations*. Trans. R. J. Hollingdale. Cambridge: Cambridge University Press.

Povinelli, Elizabeth A. 2001. "Radical Worlds: The Anthropology of Incommensurability and Conceivability." *Annual Review of Anthropology* 30: 319–334.

Strathern, Marilyn. 2005. *Kinship, Law and the Unexpected: Relatives Are Always a Surprise*. Cambridge: Cambridge University Press.

Taussig, Michael. 1993. *Mimesis and Alterity: A Particular History of the Senses*. London: Routledge.

Tsing, Anna. 2004. *Friction: An Ethnography of Global Connection*. Princeton, NJ: Princeton University Press.

Viveiros de Castro, Eduardo. 1998. "Cosmological Deixis and Amerindian Perspectivism." *Journal of the Royal Anthropological Institute* 4, no. 3: 469–488.

_____. 2002. "O nativo relativo." *Mana* 8, no. 1: 113–148.

Wagner, Roy. 1981. *The Invention of Culture*. Rev. and expanded ed. Chicago, IL: University of Chicago Press.

Chapter 5

EXCHANGING SKIN
Making a Science of the Relation between Bolivip and Barth

Tony Crook

> ... every understanding of another culture is an experiment with our own.
>
> — Roy Wagner, *The Invention of Culture*

An ethnographic description is also a description of the anthropology producing it. The correlate notion that descriptions of other cultures emerge from experiments with our own may sound like a license to abandon the ambition of anthropology as a theory of knowledge—the suggestion even appears deliberately to confuse the means with the ends of anthropological inquiry. But what *are* the consequences of holding that a theory of knowledge is also a theory about itself? After all, the conventional *Oxford English Dictionary* definition of epistemology as the "theory or science of the method or grounds of knowledge"

Notes for this chapter are located on page 107.

also posits both a particular notion of knowledge (something that takes a science to detect) and a theory about itself (as such a method), and so appears to carry a similar circularity.[1] In fastening knowledge to knowing, epistemology is a relational construct. Put bluntly, there is a compelling self-similarity here: epistemology is a theory of knowledge, and knowledge also is a theory of epistemology. The proposition carries an assumption that the endpoint of knowledge is bound up in the means of approach. Consequently, it stands to reflect any characterization given to knowledge back onto the characteristics of arriving at it. Indeed, before proceeding further we might pause to consider the path leading to this point.

It is telling that the so-called reflexive turn in anthropology, which directed attention to the means of production of its own knowledge, should have followed closely on the heels of an epoch of interest in Marxism (loosely, the decade from 1967 to 1977). The turn, characterized as deliberate experiments that sought to question previously held structural certainties, carried obvious allegorical overtones of the political ambitions of a generation that had lived through the turmoil of the late 1960s and the freeing up of the doors of perception. In Britain, at least, this turn is often attributed to the influential collection *Writing Culture* (Clifford and Marcus 1986) and the origins found therein for an epoch whose theory of knowledge was also revealed to be a theory about itself. But the mistake has been to take this as an endpoint for anthropological inquiry, rather than as an insight into a better means of conducting it. In the writing of anthropology, the discipline discovered the writers of it. That this should have come as a revelation says as much about the discipline's theories of knowledge that have gone before as it does about those that have followed. In turning to the question of epistemology, it pays to bear in mind how we have come to ask this question and, in keeping with the project here, what it means for anthropologists to be asking this question now. In this new turn, are we doing anything more than simply turning our attention again to the ends rather than the means, so as to rediscover some certainties?

In *The Invention of Culture* (1975), Wagner first outlined a revolutionary anthropological theory of knowledge that argued against taking the object of anthropological inquiry as separate from our engagement with it, and for taking anthropological relations much more seriously. It was the first salvo in a series of writings that culminated in Wagner's (2001) *An Anthropology of the Subject*: "Like the epistemologist, who considers the 'meaning of meaning,' or like the psychologist, who thinks about how people think, the anthropologist is forced to include himself and his own way of life in his subject matter, and study himself ... [T]he classic rationalist's pretense of absolute objectivity must be given up in favor of a relative objectivity based on the characteristics of one's own culture" (Wagner 1975: 2, 12). Instead of seeing anthropological knowledge as compromised by these admissions, Wagner urges anthropology to afford itself more seriousness and to have confidence in disconnecting from a natural science model of itself.

Rather than a philosophical endeavor seeking to square the circle, so to speak, my method here is to inspect the bases, constraints, and liberties of the circularity itself—that is, to take this self-similarity as a relation of a particular kind and to see whether we might, with Wagner, make a 'science of the relation' out of it. This chapter, then, explores the consequences of assuming that a strong hinge fastens knowledge to epistemology. That this assumption appears to create an oxymoron provides my starting point. In order to be able to ask a question of epistemology, we must first disconnect it from any questions about knowledge. Only then can we attempt a reconnection and assess the result.

In my monograph *Anthropological Knowledge* (Crook 2007a), I outline an argument about self-similarity between the imagery of a social subject and the form given to knowledge, theorizing that this holds for Anthropology and for Bolivip in Papua New Guinea. Of course, as will again be evident below, the persons, relations, and knowledge in my examples in this chapter are differently configured, and the analysis requires ethnographic demonstration. As in the book, I use Fredrik Barth's work here to illustrate his exemplification of widely held assumptions that fasten together the unit characteristics of individual subjects, individuated facts, and individualized domains. The bounded character that Barth attributed to Baktaman subjects is evident in the bounded character attributed to knowledge in Bolivip. Similarly, the monograph argues that the composition of knowledge in Bolivip reiterated the gender imagery reflected in men's and women's asymmetrical ideas about conception. Finally, it uses an experimental figure called 'the textual person' to analyze contemporary anthropological knowledge-making as separating and combining 'analytic' and 'social' relations. In a move analogous to Strathern's (2005) analysis of 'anthropology's relation' as hinging upon interpersonal and conceptual relations, the textual person suggests that anthropologists—in each of the social and analytic registers—have to demonstrate that they are both persons in their own right (having a sufficiently original voice) and persons with relations to others (being cognizant of the literature). This self-similarity in the form of relation-making among persons and relation-making among knowledge suggests that these reiterations of social imagery can be no coincidence. Nonetheless, the observation does require us to rethink what we take knowledge to be and to be about.

Min Problems

The Min or Mountain Ok region in western Papua New Guinea has long been one of the most enigmatic cultural areas in anthropological experience, proving very recalcitrant to conventional analysis. The region has gained a reputation as something of a 'black hole' and a 'graveyard' of anthropological careers. It recently led Whitehead (2000) to remark that an unusual proportion of research from over a dozen studies remains in unpublished thesis form, and to describe the corpus of published research findings on the Min as a scattered literature revealing the "tip of a large, silent iceberg" (ibid.: 36). A striking number of Min ethnographers, endeavoring to make the most of detailed materials and to synthesize complex data, have had their work cut out

for them—myself included. Min knowledge-practices present a serious challenge to certain Euro American habits of thought. The considerable problems
that Anthropology has encountered in analyzing the Min make it a particularly revealing forum in which to see the discipline's ideas of knowledge at
work. Specifically then, it is Min knowledge-making practices that have proven
exceptionally problematic to the knowledge-making practice of Anthropology.
I argue that this can be no coincidence.

It is telling that the Min remain best known through Barth's path-breaking
work on secrecy in the late 1960s, which led to *Ritual and Knowledge among
the Baktaman of New Guinea* (1975). This volume offers the radical interpretation of a people who have an epistemology of secrecy as their social organization. The assumption that the power of knowledge is a virtue of scarcity is a
central motif: '[T]he value of information seemed to be regarded as inversely
proportional to how many share it' (ibid.: 217). In his comparative exercise *Cosmologies in the Making*, Barth (1987: 9; emphasis added) regards his original
analysis to have been "strengthened *in my view* by the accounts provided by
other anthropologists analyzing cognate traditions." Toward the end of that discussion, certain "patterns and processes" are suggested to be common among
the Min (ibid.: 78): "In the [Min] case, the salient features of social organization
are four: (1) The segmentation of the population into small, localized and mutually rather suspicious local groups. (2) The differentiations of gender and initiation step within each such group. (3) The specialized role of initiator as the
authoritative knower and revealer of secrets. (4) The pulsation in the modality
of cosmological knowledge between long periods of secrecy and non-communi-
cation, and concentrated bursts of public manifestation and revelation."

In each case, of course, this geographical, social, and temporal separation
into isolated domains is the work and outcome of secrecy. Moreover, these iso-
lations provided Barth with laboratory-like conditions under which to track the
actual movements of cultural transmission between domains, grades, villages,
and ritual performances. The analytic lends a particular character to knowledge, such that bounded units of knowledge are possessed by discrete domains
of men. It carries a set of corollaries that enabled Barth to read levels of truth
into a sociology of hierarchical initiation grades, and to locate power simply by
tracking the distribution of secret knowledge revealed solely during infrequent
rituals held exclusively among men. However, as we will see, Barth's interpretation of secrecy and his analysis of cultural variation in the region both fall
down as soon as revelations outside the rituals and to uninitiated men and
women are taken into account.

Despite this, Barth's rubric on secrecy among the Baktaman has enjoyed
an extended paradigmatic reign in the Min area and remains unchallenged.
There seems to be a long-standing consensus among anthropologists that the
Min have kept all the answers to themselves. This is made strikingly evident,
for example, by one pessimistic assessment in the collection *Children of Afek*,
whose editors regard the area as "thoroughly studied." Brumbaugh (1990: 87)
contends: "Obstacles, including the extreme difficulty of the languages, the
intricate secrecy, and the collapse of the male initiation system in most areas,

provide an automatic bias tending to confirm that [Min] symbolism defies analysis in traditional terms."

With the 'secrecy rubric' holding sway, there remains a curious adherence to the Barthian path to the point that no analysis has seriously questioned Barth's interpretative terms or squarely tackled the problem of Min knowledge-making practices. Although much fine work has been produced, an intriguing kind of ethnographic quiet reigns over the Min field that is oddly reminiscent of Barthian secrecy—as if the ethnographers had taken on the concerns and habits perceived to be characteristic of their research subjects.

Moreover, Barth's exemplification of the secrecy paradigm has gone on to enjoy wider influence. By the time that Herdt surveyed the literature on secrecy and developed two contrasting models, he was able to illustrate each of them with examples from the Min. What Herdt (1990, 2003) calls the "ontological theory of secrecy" sets up a separate domain of knowledge—an "alternative, hidden cultural reality" (Herdt 2003: xi)—and an exclusive domain of persons who are party to it. Whitehouse's (2000) "modes of religiosity" rely on the case that Barth made for revelations being restricted to intermittent performances. Even Barth's (2002) recent state-of-the-art essay, "An Anthropology of Knowledge," rests one illustration of his case on the same uncompromising Baktaman foundations.

One root of the problem here is a peculiar Euro-American habit of eliding the solidity of a social relationship with the solidity of knowledge, and then taking one as a measure of the other. When Barth (1975) reports on a people whose "conceptualisation of social relations and their construction are poorly elaborated and transmitted" (ibid.: 259), and asserts that "[a] Baktaman will experience no social relation which can embody for him a conception of truthfulness and trust" (ibid.: 219), these statements provide crucial ethnographic descriptions equating a lack of sure relations with people and a lack of sure relations with knowledge. But when the Min demonstrate their agility with metaphor and image, it can appear to an anthropologist that they are also playing fast and loose with their friendship. A statement that appeared concrete only moments earlier suddenly appears as an absurd suggestion, and the social relationship can seem to be equally contingent as well. When someone seems to be withholding, lying, contradicting, or denying, this too can be interpreted as registering a comment on the terms of a social relation and, in the process, can have an impact on assessments of field data quality. In making an equivalence between the qualities of knowledge and the relational conduit, Anthropology reveals its own crucial metaphor of knowledge. Through the pretense of screening out the 'bodily-personal-relational' from the 'social science' by means of methods, the impression can also be given that our methods are doing the research on their own.

Part of the problem that Anthropology has created out of the Min is having all too familiar metaphors of knowledge easily at hand. After all, knowledge is what Anthropology 'does', and each such metaphor affords a set of relations placed within particular limits. For example, knowledge perceived in terms of domains similar to building blocks apprehends them set side by side (different spheres of knowledge for men and women, and senior and junior); on top of the other (linear hierarchies of initiation steps and truth levels); behind the other (hidden knowledge, with revelation involving displacement and redundancy); inside the other (bounded layering, like onions and Chinese boxes); or lined up (multiple alternatives, a never-ending 'mystery', or some ultimate point of truth). And each of these metaphors operates in Barth's analyses of the Min. In each instance, the separation between domains is taken as evidence of secrecy, the crux being that different levels of secret knowledge are revealed only during periodic stagings of male initiation rituals, and thus are known only to men.

What Barth's analysis starkly reveals is the poverty of an anthropological convention that approaches culture with the idea that there is a hidden order behind people's words and actions that is waiting to be revealed—an approach that we might even call 'anthropology's secrecy'. It is perhaps no coincidence that this perception of the anthropologist as the discoverer of cultural secrets should crash so dramatically among Barth's depiction of a people for whom a similar project was a matter of life and death. For a knowledge-practice premised on acquiring new knowledge, the idea of secrecy has a particular hold. For an anthropology based on field research metaphors of uncovering data, revealing connections, and entering initially opaque new cultural worlds in search of hidden meanings, secrecy has a particular fascination. Herdt (2003: 27) goes on to trace the effect back to Lewis Henry Morgan, with whom was "born what we might call the role of the anthropologist as cryptographer of secrecy."

One of the traps for Barth in taking secrecy in this way is to be lulled into thinking that it is a black-and-white matter, involving something in a state of either being known or being unknown—as if by very definition, something must be either a secret or no longer a secret. Another consequence is to imagine that there is something universal about secrecy, making it open to comparison with other examples and to theorizing on a grander scale. But on the other hand, some thinkers have suggested that secrecy informs moments of social transaction more widely. As Weiner and Glaskin (2006: 9) recently put it, "[A]ny technique of bringing-into being must conceal its own parameters as technique if it is to naturalise and legitimate the products of such action."

For Barth, what the Min describe as *awem*, which I gloss as 'important knowledge' (Crook 1999), is by very definition exclusively the secret preserve of initiated men. It is only ever revealed during periodic rituals through which scarce cultural resources are carefully distributed among grades of initiated men and from which women are entirely excluded. Our first real 'Min problem', then, is that, unless initiated men conventionally telling forbidden *awem* to women and uninitiated men still counts as secrecy, the Barthian paradigm fails to account for the data in Bolivip, where important knowledge is exchanged in respect of prior care and is described as an 'exchange of skin'.

What is it about the Min and the way that they got into Anthropology that has made them such an enigma? And what is it in Anthropology's assumptions about its own knowledge-making practices that has made such a problem out of the Min? I take these questions as sides of the same theoretical predicament, using insights into thought habits on either side as a vantage point to discuss the other.

Anthropology has become caught up here—worked on by the Min, on one side, and by archaic metaphors of knowledge, on the other. I want to query Barth's analyses of the practice of secrecy, of important knowledge as the exclusive domain of men, and of subsequent knowledge loss in Min knowledge practices. I argue that the processes of creativity that Barth takes to account for cosmological variations in the Min region are ultimately misdiagnosed.

Bolivip

This analytical loyalty to secrecy seems all the more odd when in Bolivip a long-standing conventional path exists whereby older men tell younger men about important things that they have not been shown. They also tell women what they say they must not know. These actions were related to considerations of sorrowful feelings and thoughtful care, the path that my field research was guided along.

When men were together in an important setting, I often heard them remark that women know nothing of the important stories and activities—and that they must not know. Similar dogmatic statements accompanied revelations of *awem*. The sentiment was often uttered in a whisper laden with both fright and threat, indicated by an arm cast in a quick and dismissive wave away from the closed eyes and the hidden face of a lowered head. Evoking seriousness, the gesture seemed to trace out the hurried loss of their taro plants and wider consequences so dire that they could not be faced. Women, they said, must not be told *awem*, and there was nothing playful about these threats. There was real danger here.

But I quickly realized that many more people had quite extensive knowledge of 'the secrets' than, strictly speaking, they were supposed to have. These included women and young men who had yet to be shown the initiations. Clearly, they had not come into this knowledge from an initiation ritual. After a while, I became used to hearing the men voice their threats in public, forbidding each other from revealing the secrets to women and to young men. Yet, in more secluded settings, I would also hear older men advise a younger man to start telling his wife some of the 'lighter' secrets. Women are also conventionally told about important stories, names, and practices (*awem*) that are also explicitly forbidden them. In spite of their own dogma, the men do tell *awem* to women who respect and care for them—and they always have. Referring back to the original episode when the first creator woman was tricked out of her cult house and important knowledge by her younger brother, men acknowledge that "women were the first to know."

It is not only that women do know and may know, but that they *should* know. One man explained that if women are to work hard for several years growing a pig and are allowing it to be used to support an initiation (in which women would not share), or if they harvest and roast taros from the gardens day after day to feed their sons, husbands, brothers, and cousins, then they should know how these efforts will benefit their kin. Away from women and more senior men, my close male kin would openly acknowledge that some women know a great deal about the important myths, the initiations, and the practices of the cult house. Women may informally share the initiation grade of their husbands, as well as their husbands' knowledge—and that of those whom they respect and care for—about the cult practices. However, they still say that "it is the business of the men."

One day, I was in a distant garden house with a middle-aged man and his cousin-sister. We were whiling away a hot afternoon in the cool of the house, but our snoozing was disturbed by the restless, dominant posturing of Biscuit, the largest dog. We began to talk about a magic spell that called on the taros "to grow long legs" like a dog. The man said that the spell, like other gardening spells, is well known to the women: "This spell for long stalks calls on the dog by his hidden *awem* name. Now, I know this name, and my cousin here knows this name, but neither of us can tell you this name in front of the other. You've heard this name many times already, but you don't know. If I tell you, my cousin-sister might tell the others, and they would take their shame and anger out on me. And if she tells you in front of me, then I'll bash her up. But we both know." The woman was nodding in agreement and had been miming what might happen to her while the man spoke. The man continued: "My cross-cousin knows all that we do in the cult house and initiations, and has been using her knowledge when planting the taros herself. But she cannot say. That old man was talking about just this last night—how this knowledge of important things can be given to those who have felt sorrow, who have looked after and respected them, provided that they hide it so that no one knows."

The term *weng* means talk, and the many types of talk—broken talk, turned talk, half talk, pandanus juice talk, breeze talk, serious talk—are always prefaced with whose talk it is. The image of a tree is used to describe how far one is from the origin of talk and therefore whether a person is in a position to verify it for him- or herself. People accused of bad talk about another person might defend themselves by saying that they are only in the crown of the tree and passing on gossip, or breeze talk, that another person had happened to tell them. Those in a position likened to the tree's trunk or roots would have more to answer for. The talk might be the same, but the weight put on it depends on where someone is in relation to its origin. Because of this, people remain openly skeptical about things that they have neither seen nor heard for themselves. Talk is perceived to be of and from some person, and that person remains implicated in his or her talk as it is carried about by other people.

In Bolivip, the word that people use for knowledge means 'skin', and coming to know something is expressed as 'making skin' with another person—for knowledge always comes from someone else. Often, when walking through the rain forest on the way to gardens or a bird hide, or taking part in a marsupial hunt, or looking for some seasonal fruit, people would point out a hole in a tree that their father once showed them where a marsupial lived, or a pool of water that birds use to bathe in, or a fruit tree that a relative had planted. Like talk, then, knowledge always comes of and from someone, and never goes about on its own as if alienated as some kind of object or detached from the people who hold it.

There are other words for knowledge. On such word is *wok*, which refers to a bodily liquid that can pass between people and between people and their plants through their words and actions. This water can be created by some cult house activities, for example, it is hidden inside the smoke that is released when marsupials are sacrificed to the ancestors. Another word is *lamlam*, which describes a shiny membrane inside the thigh muscle where men keep their important knowledge. Another meaning of *lamlam* is advice, such as instruction in some technique or moral advice about how to test whether your wife is cheating on you. The word is also used to describe the shining effects of advice and knowledge when manifested in the world: the sun glinting on a shiny axe is *lamlam*. A person returning from a well-tended taro garden who is walking tall, with shining skin, is described as *lamlamso* (with knowledge/water). Thus, the word 'knowledge' takes the form of bodily substances that are reserved until a person is ready and would not be harmed, and are circulated in exchanges of care. It took me some time to understand that in Bolivip knowledge is a bodily substance that passes between people. Some gardeners describe how they can also pass *wok* to their taro plants and their children by looking after them and playing with them. As one man put it, "*Wok* is another word for love."

Men in Bolivip say that there is only one path to learning important knowledge: one must "look after the skin" (*kal kiin moyamin*) of people with renown, clean the sleep from their eyes, listen to them, feel and show sorrow for them, fetch water and firewood, give them parts of marsupials and types of taro. Only then will they take equal care in making their advice and *awem* both clear and "straight" (*turon*). These relations of exchanging skin—passing on knowledge with respect to prior care—are also pursued with a father and mother's brother. Having looked after his skin, and having received his *awem*, one old man became fond of telling me that his skin had gone onto mine, that my skin had gone onto his, and that we were now "one skin." Through these exchanges and considerations, we had become encompassed by the same skin: what was ours to circulate, circulated within. This path is one that initiated men follow to learn the *awem* of their clan or ground, or the *awem* not shown in the initiations, or the initiations that they have not yet been shown. Women can also follow this path, either to learn *awem* from their father or husband, or to acquire important women's knowledge from their female relatives, for example, techniques to shape the features of a newborn to make evident the care into which it has been born.

Once I had been shown inside the cult house and had been initiated myself, my cousin-sister became more confident in talking directly about what she had learned from her mother's brother, my adopted father. She had initially heard my question as though I was trying to talk about whether she really cared for the old man. "Look, you've seen me. I always hear what he says and asks. I help him in the gardens and break firewood for him. What do you think? Am I a respectful person or not? Do I look after him or not? Are you the only one? He's my mother's brother."

The relative positions of junior and senior cultists are explained as positions in a tree. This image is reiterated by juniors, who describe asking questions of an old man only to find him unmoved—without any movement of face or body that might give something away—and who portray their own experience of learning *awem* as one of confusion, as a story seems to be moving around, branching off into many strands. Old men describe how juniors always seem to be talking about the same thing, always asking the same questions, whereas junior men say that old men do not think first before talking and keep the important parts hidden. One young man recalled that whenever he asked a question, his father just gave him another example: "Giving these old men questions only makes things difficult. They might be trying to help by bringing another example in, but they often turn their words around, and this just makes things branch more, and then you have to turn their words around again." Another man described the experience to me as *kutarkutar* (jumps and jumps again, like the *kutal* rat): "When a story does not go straight or the teller does not use straight talk (*weng turon*), when the teller goes off and starts 'breaking a path through the forest' (*saak leip, saak weng*—unconnected path, talk), when the pieces or examples seem to be jumping about, this is like *kutal*, the black-tailed giant rat, who is the most agile and hardest one to catch in the forest, even with dogs, and who might just jump from a tree, dart away, and disappear." He advised me that I should "gather up all these pieces of stories and examples and put them all together as one story (*kim kurukuru taretare*)." He explained, "You are still in the crown of the tree where all the fruit-water and flower-water hungry birds (*wok awon*) move around and sing at once, but maybe we can help you learn to see how all these pieces might be gathered up and come together into one sentence." The image of revelations of *awem* as positions on a tree suggests that for juniors in the crown, words from seniors at the base appear to branch into multiple possibilities, whereas for those at the base, juniors only demonstrate that they do not know by going on about the same thing.

Because 'doing knowledge' is about making skin, it acknowledges that contributions are required from both sides. As a junior man once put it:

When these old men try to tell you things, they only give you half (*mari*), like their advice about that hidden marsupial hunt a while ago when they told us that we should stay out in the forest house for three days and return to the village on the fourth day, because women used to confine themselves in the menstrual house for three days and return on the fourth—and you are left thinking how one story touches on the other. When they give two examples like this we call it *weng fakong* (broken talk). It is like when someone breaks a taro in two and gives you only one-half to eat. Either they do this, or they just give you another example, and again you are left thinking how the two things might touch. It is very hard. There are plenty of people who talk like this all the time, so I found out just to ask my father and mother's brother. Even though these two are trying to help me get their advice straight (*turon*), they sometimes do this by giving me only half and leaving me to use my own thoughts to realize for myself what the other half might be.

Interpretation and getting things straightened out into one story involve very particular relations through which people give other people access to their important knowledge, skills, and thoughts.

Every stage in the sequence of initiations and each small segment of important knowledge (advice, revelations, myths, spells, names, techniques) are all called *kukup* (example). As 'example', *kukup* is used to describe part and whole of this knowledge. It is also used to refer to a person's own example, that is, his or her acting out a particular combination of examples, which results in something akin to "personality," as Robbins puts it (2004). This acting out is watched and listened for with attentive care by those who may yet reveal some further *kukup*, and who are withholding knowledge until they perceive a readiness and need among a more junior grade.[2] Revealed by the way that these men talk and act, by their success in gardening and hunting, and by their problems with marriage, fatherhood, and life-cycle exchanges, these capacities and dispositions are perceived in the appearance of skin (*kal*).

With the images of trees and the different positions of crown, trunk, and roots, along with the concept of examples that are both part and whole, a sophisticated understanding of complexity and scale is clearly indicated here. People in Bolivip are aware that when dealing with knowledge, people simultaneously solve and create their own complexity. They have a lot to say about this: they have terms for 'clear' and 'hidden', but like 'the secrets', these do not constitute one state or another. It is not as simple as either being hidden or being clear. For every time something is disclosed and becomes clear, people immediately perceive that it has revealed alongside it something else that remains hidden. Inside everything that is made clear there remains something that is hidden.

Some women were also well aware of the men's belief that only vaginal mucus (*abuk gom*) and semen (*iman wok*) are necessary for conception, but they asserted that, in addition, womb or menstrual blood (*abuk kas*) is required. Where the male party regards two things as sufficient, the female party knows that the mixture contains contributions from another source. Old men say it is sufficient to look after one's father and to ask again and again until one has the stories straight. They disparage the accounts of juniors who tell of having to add things together for themselves: older men simply reiterate that this demonstrates that these people are being tricked by people who do not have things straight themselves. For old men, knowledge is the result of the joint work of a father and son. But the sons tell a different story.

Young men describe the crucial role of having *awem* from another source, notionally, from a mother's brother, and say that this will "strengthen" *awem* received from a father. They say that it is possible to hear a story again and decide which one is straighter, and to learn about the bits that have been left hidden. Contributions from a mother's brother are thus added to the joint work of a father and son. The asymmetry of male and female conception beliefs is also rehearsed by these different experiences and practices in making knowledge. In each instance, an exclusive addition from the mother's side is added to the joint work. It is as if the act of conception remains incomplete, allowing for further additions—as though certain capacities of the father's side and mother's side are released over time to help a person grow throughout life, being withheld until the person's appearance suggests readiness.

Conclusion

This chapter has pursued and developed a line of theorizing about the self-similarity of the forms of knowledge, about those who would know it, and, indeed, about the grounds of knowing. Beginning with Wagner's assertion that we acknowledge the productivity of the interrelational basis for anthropological inquiry and his exhortation that we put our own culture to work through what he called relative objectivity, the chapter opened by noting a self-similarity or circularity in a definition of epistemology. Even to ask about epistemology is already to have brought a particular theory of knowledge to it—an experiment with our own culture, so to speak—and having asked a question about epistemology is also to raise the question about what we take knowledge to be. The terms are mutually constituted, enabling and limiting each other and thus providing the literal grounds for figuring our questions. That this relational metaphor organizes our engagement—with epistemology and knowledge becoming the grounds by which the other is figured—is analogous to how Wagner describes "figure-ground reversal" (1986, 1987) as the trope of perception.

Alongside the self-similarity of epistemological ends and means, I have further developed the argument of my monograph, *Anthropological Knowledge* (2007), which sets an exchange between ethnographies of Anthropology and Min knowledge-making practices by comparing Barth's and my own analyses of Baktaman and Bolivip, respectively. Adopting this method as a science of the relation was to organize perceptions by making each the figure and ground for revealing the particular characteristics of the social imagery at work in producing them. These were experiments with our own culture, grounded in a premise that an ethnographic description is also a description of the anthropology producing it.

The wider theoretical ambitions of the monograph were rehearsed here in outlining how images of the forms taken by subjects and by knowledge were reiterated in the self-similarity of relation-making among people and relation-making among knowledge. What we have shown, then, is a series of analytical examples demonstrating ethnographically these relations and this effect. Wagner's definition of relative objectivity, philosophical definitions of epistemology, Barthian definitions of secrecy. and Bolivip definitions of exchanging skin have each yielded to this theoretical experiment. Crucially, what we are left with is the impossibility of reducing either knowledge or epistemology to any kind of generality or universal—except, that is, only insofar as these examples demonstrate the organizing capacity of self-similarity as a powerful metaphor.

Elsewhere (Crook 2007b), I have cautioned that renewed interest in the anthropology of knowledge runs the risk of privileging knowledge over those doing the knowing. We would not dream of universalizing the domain of relation-making that we call kinship, so why then the propensity to do so with the domain of relation-making that we call knowledge? No doubt, this is partly due to the cultural baggage we bring to knowledge—for example, those character-istics delineated in the opening discussion of the questions raised by asking about epistemology—and perhaps has something to do with an Enlightenment inheritance that, by definition, puts knowledge beyond the kind of inspection and doubt that I have been advancing here. These characteristics given to knowledge both amplify and curtail the kinds of question that epistemology might raise. Philosophical definitions of knowledge as 'justified, true belief' have prevented anthropology from asking what knowledge might be—and be for—in other cultures that never shared our particular inheritance, premised as it is upon certain very stubborn hinges. Although, as my discussion of Barth's work shows, it has long been possible for anthropology to deploy our own cultural ideas of knowledge and obtain some experimental results, such experi-ments cannot, as Wagner saw back in 1975, take us out of, or beyond, our own culture. Indeed, my discussion suggests that stubbornly holding to our own conceptualizations of epistemology might even begin to sound like a license to abandon the ambition of anthropology as a theory of knowledge.

I have been arguing the case for viewing epistemology as a relational con-struct. But given the self-similarity of this relation, it was only by the oxymo-ronic move to first unhinge epistemology from knowledge and to then redeploy it as a science of the relation that we were able to rethink both knowledge and epistemology. We may even find some useful analytical resources in the ethno-graphic practices we study that afford more telling theories of knowledge than experimenting with our own culture has been able to come up with.

Acknowledgments

This chapter draws together thoughts and ethnography from some previous writings and extends the argument of my monograph *Anthropological Knowledge, Secrecy and Bolivip, Papua New Guinea: Exchanging Skin* (2007), which was published in the British Academy Monograph Series. I would like to acknowledge the publishers of these previous works here.

Tony Crook is Senior Lecturer in Social Anthropology at the University of St Andrews. Having trained in Aberdeen, Manchester, and Cambridge, he held a British Academy Postdoctoral Fellowship at Edinburgh and was involved in the Cambridge-Brunel "Property, Transactions and Creations" project before joining St Andrews in 2003. A second Papua New Guinea–based research project concerns the cultural reception and cosmological impacts of the Ok Tedi mine in which Min knowledge-making now bemuses resource developers.

Notes

1. The University of St Andrews likes to think it holds a special claim over the term 'episte-mology'. The *Oxford English Dictionary* attributes the introduction of this word into the English language in 1856 to James Frederick Ferrier (1808–1864) during his tenure as a professor at St Andrews.
2. In the terms of the cult, 'elder brothers' reveal *kukup* to 'younger brothers'.

References

Barth, Fredrik. 1975. *Ritual and Knowledge among the Baktaman of New Guinea*. Oslo: Universitetsforlaget.

_____. 1987. *Cosmologies in the Making: A Generative Approach to Cultural Variation in Inner New Guinea*. Cambridge Studies in Social Anthropology, 64. Cambridge: Cambridge University Press.

_____. 2002. "An Anthropology of Knowledge," *Current Anthropology* 43, no. 1: 1–18.

Brumbaugh, Robert. 1990. "*Afek Sang*: The Old Woman's Legacy to the Mountain-Ok." Pp. 54–88, 247, 250–251 in *Children of Afek: Tradition and Change among the Mountain-Ok of Central New Guinea*, ed. B. Craig and D. Hyndman. Oceania Monographs no. 40. Sydney: University of Sydney Press.

Clifford, James, and George Marcus, eds. 1986. *Writing Culture: The Poetics and Politics of Ethnography*. Berkeley: University of California Press.

Crook, Tony. 1999. "Growing Knowledge in Bolivip, Papua New Guinea." *Oceania* 65, no. 4: 225–242.

_____. 2007a. *Anthropological Knowledge, Secrecy and Bolivip, Papua New Guinea: Exchanging Skin*. British Academy Monograph Series. Oxford: Oxford University Press.

_____. 2007b. "Figures Seen Twice: Riles, the Modern Knower and Forms of Knowledge." Pp. 245–265 in *Ways of Knowing: New Approaches in the Anthropology of Knowledge and Learning*, ed. Mark Harris. Oxford: Berghahn Books.

Herdt, Gilbert. 1990. "Secret Societies and Secret Collectives." *Oceania* 60: 360–381.

_____. 2003. *Secrecy and Cultural Reality: Utopian Ideologies of the New Guinea Men's House*. Ann Arbor: University of Michigan Press.

Robbins, Joel. 2004. *Becoming Sinners: Christianity and Moral Torment in a Papua New Guinea Society*. Berkeley: University of California Press.

Strathern, Marilyn. 2005. *Kinship, Law and the Unexpected: Relatives Are Always a Surprise*. Cambridge: Cambridge University Press.

Wagner, Roy. 1975. *The Invention of Culture*. Englewood Cliffs, NJ: Prentice Hall.

_____. 1986. *Symbols That Stand for Themselves*. Chicago, IL: University of Chicago Press.

_____. 1987. "Figure-Ground Reversal among the Barok." Pp. 56–63 in *Assemblage of Spirits: Idea and Image in New Ireland*, ed. Louise Lincoln. New York: George Braziller.

_____. 2001. *An Anthropology of the Subject: Holographic Worldview in New Guinea and Its Meaning and Significance for the World of Anthropology*. Berkeley: University of California Press.

Weiner, James, and Katie Glaskin. 2006. "Introduction: The (Re-)Invention of Indigenous Laws and Customs." *Asia Pacific Journal of Anthropology* 7, no. 1: 1–13.

Whitehead, Harriet. 2000. *Food Rules: Hunting, Sharing, and Tabooing Game in Papua New Guinea*. Ann Arbor: University of Michigan Press.

Whitehouse, Harvey. 2000. *Arguments and Icons: Divergent Modes of Religiosity*. Oxford: Oxford University Press.

Chapter 6

AN AFRO-BRAZILIAN THEORY
OF THE CREATIVE PROCESS
An Essay in Anthropological Symmetrization

Marcio Goldman

As a mixture of mistaken knowledge or ideology, illusory reality, and ethnographic peculiarity, fetishism is always situated at the confluence of three fields: epistemology, ontology, and anthropology. The word itself consists, as is well known, in an elaboration of the term 'fetish', coined in the sixteenth and seventeenth centuries by Portuguese and Dutch sailors and merchants who traveled the west coast of Africa. It was a term used to designate material objects that 'the Africans' made and then, having strangely imbued them with supposedly mystical or religious properties, went on to worship. The first theoretical use of the term was by Charles de Brosses in 1760, when he characterized it as the "first religion of humanity." From the nineteenth century onward, the term follows a curious path. It was used as a central concept by some of the

Notes for this chapter begin on page 125.

principal founders of the modern social sciences—Comte, Marx, and Freud, to name just a few. But it was also almost unanimously considered by ethnographers and anthropologists to be nothing more than an incorrect gloss of several varied and heterogeneous ideas and objects.

It seems that a series of three articles that William Pietz (1985, 1987, 1988) dedicated to the subject—published in the journal *Res* under the title "The Problem of the Fetish"—rekindled a certain interest in the ethnographic and historical aspects of the theme, if not in its dimension as a general concept. Pietz painstakingly traces the history of this "unique problem-idea." In order to do so, he considers it necessary to refute several different kinds of arguments, which, according to him, are simultaneously or alternately employed in order to exclude the possibility of using the term 'fetish'. He remains unconvinced by "universalistic" arguments (which reduce fetishism to a particular instance of universal forms of symbolism or logical error); "historical" arguments (which turn the concept into an ethnocentric projection of Western discourse); and "particularist" arguments (which condemn the concept as bad ethnography, the result of superficial and prejudiced texts written by travelers and merchants).

If fetishism was initially conceived as a kind of false physics in which the principle of causality was incorrectly applied by attributing to inanimate beings a power that they do not possess, this conception ended up being substituted or supplemented by one of fetishism as a sort of false sociology, which, according to Pietz, located social agency where it "certainly" was not. And although in both cases these sciences apparently guarantee what is real and therefore also assure the possibility of denouncing illusion, in the latter there is a sort of duplication of the critical process, as it proposes itself as a 'true' sociology, which claims not only to denounce a 'false' one, but to explain it, too. Here we should expand upon Gell's (1998: 101) observations concerning magic. Just as fetishism is not an alternative or false theory of physics but rather one that functions in the absence of a theory of physics and that is grounded in a certain type of experience, neither is it a false theory of sociology but rather a knowledge that functions in the absence of (and not because of a lack of) a sociology, that is, in the absence of the very idea of society. In the same way that the notion of causality is not the exclusive property of physics, neither is the notion of sociality that of sociology.[1]

However, this is not the central point of Pietz's text. Certainly, his objectives are not those that anthropologists in general pursue. Despite this, he touches on a question that has hung over anthropology for some time now: are we capable of saying something interesting about other ways of thinking and other forms of sociality in terms of what is different about them in relation to our own? Or are we limited to descriptions of that which resembles us and which we define as 'common' to both us and others?[2] Apparently adopting this latter position, Pietz's historical critique soon becomes mired in what Latour (1996: 29n11) considers an excessive tolerance for Freudian and especially Marxist uses of the notion of fetishism.[3] It is as if some sort of 'epistemological break' could be established between the false musings of de Brosses or the Enlightenment thinkers and the truly scientific theories attained by Marx and Freud.

Ultimately, the consequences of Pietz's method should intrigue anthropologists. However erudite his texts might be, it is difficult for us not to ask if, in the case of fetishism, the African peoples involved in this story really had no "model or truth previous or external to their own 'archive,'" or at least if they were really not party to the "series of its particular usages" (Pietz 1985: 7). More precisely, it is difficult not to ask what they would have to say on the subject and to venture that what they indubitably would have to say should at the minimum be included in the record.

Fetishism Today

It was in reaction to this absence in Pietz's text, which was actually intentional and explicit, that anthropologist David Graeber (2005: 410–411) recently complained: "In what follows, I will first consider Pietz's story of the origin of the fetish, then try to supplement his account (drawn almost exclusively from Western sources) with some that might give insight into what the African characters in the story might have thought was going on." Graeber's protest, however, ends up sounding slightly timid when we observe that, throughout his text, his notions about what Africans might have concluded was going on are limited to some ritual practices and generic cosmological speculations, alongside a theory on social order that the author peculiarly assimilates to European contractualism (ibid.: 414–415). In other words, the discourse about fetishes—or rather, those aspects of these discourses that do not resemble our ways of thinking or defining reality—continue to be silenced in favor of what Euro-Americans, whether merchants or anthropologists, consider fundamental.

Furthermore, in an immense effort to save the Marxist conception of fetishism, Graeber (2005: 425) concludes that fetishes constitute "objects which seem to take on human qualities which are, ultimately, really derived from the actors themselves." The mistake of the natives arises only, the author informs us, from the "extraordinary complexity" of the processes of creation, which inhibits the perception of a social totality, leading to the understandable illusion that one is not responsible for what one merely co-authors (ibid.: 428). Graeber remarks, generously, that from this Marxist point of view, African fetishes are particularly under-fetishized (or hardly fetishist), since their socially fabricated nature could not but be apparent to actors who are as interested in social relations as the Africans are. In fact, it is the Europeans, obsessed not with social relations but with objects of value, who project their own fetishism onto the Africans (ibid.: 432). From the African point of view, continues Graeber, "a fetish is a god under the process of construction" (ibid.: 427), and at least this pre-capitalist fetishism can be salvaged as a form of "social creativity." "The danger," concludes the author (ibid.: 431), "comes when fetishism gives way to theology, the absolute assurance that the gods are real"—excluding the commodity, of course.

However generous his position, Graeber (2005) leaves us a little confused. In the first instance, this is because his attempt to rescue the Africans is conducted in spite of themselves (ibid.: 430):

Of course it would also be going too far to say that the fetishistic view is simply true: Lunkanka cannot really tie anyone's intestines into knots; Ravololona cannot really prevent hail from falling on anyone's crops. As I have remarked elsewhere ... ultimately we are probably just dealing here with the paradox of power, power being something which exists only if other people think it does; a paradox that I have also argued lies also at the core of magic, which always seems to be surrounded by an aura of fraud, showmanship, and chicanery. But one could argue it is not just the paradox of power. It is also the paradox of creativity.

What is difficult to understand is why the author feels it necessary to limit native knowledge in a text that is intended to apprehend the African perspective of the problem of the fetish. What is also hard to understand is how the conversion of fetishism into power, or even "social creativity," could be illuminating rather than pacificatory. To maintain that "a fetish is a god under the process of construction" may be very charitable, but it is highly unlikely that this pronouncement as such would be acceptable to those directly interested in the subject (I will return to this point). And although, as Sansi-Roca (2007: 27) points out, it may be difficult to determine at what point *fetisso* became a creole word or if it remained only an expression in pidgin, which is Pietz's position (1985: 5), I would risk suggesting that the term was used by the Africans fundamentally to try to explain to the Europeans something that they could not imagine them being able to understand.[4]

Secondly, Graeber's attempt to save Marx starts with what is most problematic and least original in Marxism, namely, the scientism that he shares with most thinkers of his century. For it is only from this position that one can imagine achieving such a privileged view of the totality of social systems to which only a few have access, condemning all the fetishists, with their limited individual points of view, to glimpses of only a part of this whole. As François Châtelet (1975: 31–32) observed, what is most interesting in Marx is certainly not this type of positivist scientism, but a perspectivism that opens up several other possibilities. *Das Kapital*, Châtelet maintains, constitutes above all an ethnographic and historical description of the capitalist system as seen from the point of view of the proletariat and not the bourgeoisie. That this point of view has been considered even more totalizing, and consequently even more true or scientific, only contributes to Marxism's theoretical and political disgrace, and should be used neither as an analytic strategy, nor as a political posture intended to save it.

Finally, in order to rescue the Africans (and Marxism), Graeber seems to believe it necessary to condemn the Europeans (or at least the capitalists). They are really the only ones who have deceived themselves with respect to the nature of collective life, imagining what is in truth merely the objectification of social relations to be the origin of these same relations. In a sense, the only true fetishism is that of the commodity, and the only true fetishist is one who denounces the fetishism of others.

The evidently vicious character of this type of affirmation did not escape Bruno Latour (1996) in his short but fundamental book dedicated to fetishism.

Furthermore, in a manner very different from that of Graeber, Latour does not pretend to save the Africans or their fetishism. On the contrary, African fetishism is exactly what will rescue the Europeans from their anti-fetishism, that is, the strange notion which claims that 'modernity' has freed them from the phantom that haunts all pre-modern social formations—the phantom of belief (ibid.: 9–10, 15, 29n11, 33–35, 55).

Latour's (1996) argument is complex and sophisticated, and I will consider only one of its points here, whereby the author clarifies that his interest in the theme concerns his own society exclusively: "It was only for me, clearly, that I was interested, or rather, for these unfortunate whites who want to deprive themselves of their anthropology, locking themselves into their modern destiny as anti-fetishists" (ibid.: 96). Latour intends to demonstrate that, along with everyone else, the European is also "slightly surpassed by that which he constructs" (ibid.: 43); that between Pasteur and the fetishists, the difference is only one of degree, not of nature, since neither one nor the other is entirely realist or entirely constructivist; that it is possible to affirm that both Pasteur's lactic acid and the fetishist's fetishes were simultaneously discovered and produced. The only problem, from an anthropological point of view, is that this endeavor demands that Latour explicitly excludes what the fetishists have to say about what they do, concentrating exclusively on their "practices" (ibid.: 85–89).

This point is crucial, as it is here that Latour locates what he considers to be the fundamental difficulty of anthropology. It also probably explains the fact that from 1991 his work progressively moved away from 'symmetrical anthropology' toward a 'sociology of associations'. Thus, a few years later, Latour (2005: 41) would write that in order for sociology to "finally become as good as anthropology," it would be necessary "to allow the members of contemporary society to have as much leeway in defining themselves as that offered by ethnographers." This final apparent homage, however, paves the way for open criticism, for it seems that sociology is not merely "as good as" anthropology, but indeed better: "For better or for worse, sociology, contrary to its sister anthropology, can never be content with a plurality of metaphysics; it also needs to tackle the ontological question of the unity of this common world" (ibid.: 259). A prisoner to "culturalism" and "exoticism," anthropology is not capable of crossing "another Rubicon, the one leading from metaphysics to ontology" (ibid.: 117). Reducing the metaphysics it discovers to representations, it appeals to cultural relativism, which ultimately results in the assumption of the unity of a single world that is explicable only by science. The point is not then to try to discover the "coherence of a system of thought" (ibid.: 90). As Latour puts it, "I find more precision in my lactic acid ferment if I illuminate it with the light of the *candomblé* divinities. In the common world of comparative anthropology, the illuminations cross each other. Differences do not exist to be respected, ignored, or subsumed but to serve as a decoy for the senses, as food for thought" (ibid.: 102–103).

In studying scientists, Latour has adopted as method a privileged, if not exclusive, attention to their practice. Insofar as we give science the right to define 'reality', it is easy to understand why Latour has paid more attention to the scientists' practices than to their discourse. However, this is not the case when we listen to a fetishist or an adept of *candomblé*. Their discourses, unlike those of scientists, are normally considered to be false or are seen as enunciating a truth that is not ours. In this sense, they have the potential to destabilize our modes of thought and to define realities that, I believe, it is up to anthropologists to study. This means that the symmetry between the analysis of scientific practices and African or *candomblé* ones can be obtained only by introducing a compensating asymmetry that is destined to correct the initial asymmetry of the situation. More—or less—than a symmetrical anthropology, the matter at hand is to establish anthropological symmetrizations.

As we saw with Pietz—and up to a certain point with Graeber—the difficulties experienced by at least some anthropologists when faced with Latour seem to derive from their solidarity with the point of view of the observer, which is how many years ago Lévi-Strauss ([1954] 1958: 397) defined sociology in opposition to anthropology.[5] In fact, in their conceptualizations concerning the fetish and fetishism, all three authors (i.e., Pietz, Graeber, and Latour), each with his own motive and for different reasons, avoid a careful analysis of native theories on the subject. This is a result of the hypothesis, implicit or explicit, that only 'the unity of a common world' can guarantee the possibility of, or be the foundation for, an interest in other societies and other modes of thought.

Contrary to this, I intend to adopt a different or even opposite hypothesis to that of 'worlds in common', namely, that the value of any dialogue with other forms of thinking and living resides exactly in what there is that is *different*. The next sections of this text will therefore be dedicated to outlining the analysis of a fetishist problematic based on what those who have been referred to as such have to say on the matter. This analysis not only looks to understand better the phenomenon in question, but also may even make its illuminating effect about us more interesting, establishing connections that are richer than those to which we limit ourselves when we appeal to the necessity of a common world. In short, it follows the proposal put forward by Marilyn Strathern (1996: 521): "In anthropologizing some of these issues, however, I do not make appeals to other cultural realities simply because I wish to dismiss the power of the Euro-American concepts ... The point is, rather, to extend them with social imagination. That includes seeing how they are put to work in their indigenous context, as well as how they might in an exogenous one."

Candomblé Today

As we have just seen, Latour found "more precision" in his "lactic acid ferment" when he illuminated it "with the light of the *candomblé* divinities." It is true that in his book he deals with an example from a short ethnography about *candomblé* (in addition to a novel by an Indian author). But, more precisely, what caught his attention in *candomblé*—one of the many Brazilian religions that display elements of African origins and also embody, to different degrees, elements of Native American cosmologies, Catholicism, and European

Spiritualism—was that its deities (*orixás, voduns,* or *inquices,* depending on the 'nation' of the *terreiro,* that is, 'temple' or 'cult house') are 'made' in the process of initiation, at the same time as the persons that they will possess are made. This complex ritual of initiation is known as 'making the saint' or 'making the head' (see Goldman 1984, 1985).

The matter in question—divinities produced by humans—seems tailor-made for Latour's theses. The problem is that passing too quickly over the subtleties of any conceptual world runs the risk of missing something essential. So if you were to ask an adept of *candomblé* if he is the one who makes the divinities, the reply would certainly be negative.[6] However, if you were to ask if this or that divinity was made by someone, the answer would be positive. This is because the divinities, like people, already exist before being made—although, of course, not in exactly the same way. The crucial point, to simplify hugely, is the distinction between the 'general *orixás*' (Iansan, Ogum, Omolu), which exist as a finite number, and the intensive multiplicity of individual or personal *orixás* (the Iansan of this person, the Ogum of that person, 'my Omolu') (see Goldman 2005: 105). Only these latter could be described as having been made, the former having existed forever, since mythical times. From birth, each one of us 'belongs to' a general *orixá.* But only some of us will be called to initiation, and only in this moment will we receive 'our' personal *orixá.* This difference is generally marked by the exclusive use of the Portuguese term *santo* (saint) to designate the outcome of the process. One would say that one 'made the saint', not that one 'made the *orixá*'—even if these words, in different contexts, can be used as synonyms (see Sansi-Roca 2005: 152; Serra 1978: 59–60; 1995: 266–270).

As Serra (1978: 60) demonstrated, the saint and the *filha-de-santo* (saint-daughter) are born from a union of the *orixá* and the initiate. What is meant by 'to make the saint' or 'to make the head' is not so much to make gods; rather, in this case human beings and *orixás* make up a saint and a person. I say 'in this case' because it is not only humans who 'belong to' different *orixás,* but everything that exists and can exist in the universe: social groups, animals, plants, flowers, food, stones, places, days, years, colors, flavors, smells. All beings belong to determined *orixás,* and at the same time some must or can be consecrated, prepared, or made for them.

Scholars of *candomblé* have always been confused by this sort of ontology. Thus, in the last decade of the nineteenth century, in the first study on the theme (with the revealing title "The Fetishist Animism of the Bahian Negros"), Raimundo Nina Rodrigues (1900) encountered difficulties in deciding whether *candomblé* should be considered fetishism or 'diffuse animism'—that is, whether it has to do with the attribution of life to inanimate beings or simply the selection of certain objects as the material but momentary residence of a spiritual being. Furthermore, in the eyes of the author (an expert in medical autopsy and psychiatry), the religion of *orixás* also appeared to be a sort of confused polytheism, since the divinities seemed simultaneously to exist in themselves, to be merely represented by objects or images, and to be 'fixed' in inanimate objects. Thus, in asking, with an ulterior motive, "an African if Ogum was not a simple iron object," the reply was "yes, a simple piece of that tram track over there *is or can be Ogum, but only after the saint-father has prepared it*" (Nina Rodrigues 1900: 59; emphasis added).

The point here, of course, is not to apply this or that theory, or this or that critique, of fetishism to *candomblé*, but rather to trace a comparison between these theories and critiques and those existing in *candomblé* itself. Thus, more than a century after Nina Rodrigues's work, and more than a half-century after this theme was abandoned (for being ethnocentric or exoticizing), a new interest in the material objects of *candomblé* has provoked a return to the topics formerly grouped under the confused and certainly accusatory rubric of fetishism. A series of recent studies seems to have reintroduced, implicitly or explicitly, and to a greater or lesser degree, what we could call the problem of the fetish (or of fetishism) in *candomblé* (see, among others, Anjos 1995, 2006; Halloy 2005; Opipari 2004; Sansi-Roca 2003, 2005, 2007).

"The making of the saint," wrote Nina Rodrigues (1900: 75), "consists of two distinct operations that complete each other: the preparation of the fetish and the initiation or the consecration of its owner." The *orixá* is 'fixed' or 'planted' simultaneously in the head of the saint-daughter and in an assortment of objects arranged on a kind of dish. These objects vary greatly, but the *ferramenta* (symbolic tool) of the *orixá*, some coins, and at least one stone are encountered in almost all cases. The name *assentamento* (seat) is given to this assortment. It is viewed as a 'double' of the saint-daughter, who will have to care for it (periodically cleaning it and offering it sacrifices) for the rest of her life. At the saint-daughter's death, the *assentamento* will be dispatched, along with her spirit.

It was exactly the *assentamento* that removed any doubt in the first studies of *candomblé* that this religion was a form of fetishism, the *assentamento*s being the fetishes. And it is curious that of all the items that compose an *assentamento*, the stones (*otás, otãs,* or *itás*) always received the most attention, as if it was somehow more scandalous to attribute life to these inanimate objects. It is also intriguing to observe that, in one way or another, the more recent studies of the theme also concentrate on the stones, which constitute only one of the elements that make up an *assentamento*. Even if these stones are one of the best examples of this process, during which something becomes what it already is, maybe there is (if you will allow me the expression) a certain fixation with them that explains why we seem to continue with the same difficulty that plagued Nina Rodrigues more than 100 years ago.

At the same time, and contrary to older interpretations that supposed the entirely fortuitous nature of the selection of the stone that was to be included in someone's *assentamento*,[7] Sansi-Roca (2005) has astutely observed that even though there is a casual air around the discovery of the stone, this discovery is simultaneously a type of encounter—"a *hasard objectif,* to use the surrealist expression" (ibid.: 143)—that is determined in part by the desire of the stone itself. It is the stone that, in some way, 'asks' the future saint-daughter to find it; however, the stone can do this only because it shares something with the person whose *assentamento* it will be part of—namely, both belong to the same *orixá.* Different *orixás* demand different stones: dark and ferrous for Ogum, porous for Omolu, double-faced for Xangô, and so on: "There is recognition of the agency embodied in the stones before their consecration, although this agency is only recognizable at the right moment and by the right person—it comes out as a gift of the object to this person" (ibid.).

In his monograph about *candomblé* in Recife (northeast Brazil), Arnaud Halloy (2005) emphasizes the native distinction between a *cheche* (common) stone and an *otá* properly speaking, that is, a stone "that is an *orixá*" (ibid.: 515). In relation to this, "there is no doubt: *'the otá is an orixá'*" (ibid.: 514).[8] However, at the same time "the participants of the cult" say that "the *otá* represents the *orixá*" and that the *otá* is "the dwelling place of the *orixá*" (ibid.: 515). It is the divinatory game of cowries that determines "the ontological status" of the stones (ibid.: 531), a status that, nevertheless, is only actualized in the *assentamento* ceremony—"the investiture that establishes the passage of the ordinary object to that of a cultural one" (ibid.: 518). In other words, the stone, which becomes an *orixá* only after the *assentamento*, is the *orixá* from the beginning. Thus, all the stones of the world are divided into three apparently distinct ontological possibilities: common stones that will never be anything other than what they are, special stones that could become *orixás*, and stones that are *orixás*. This is a merely relative distinction, since all stones, even common ones, belong to specific *orixás*, and since the gap between being able to become an *orixá* and actually being an *orixá* is one that can be ritually overcome (see also Anjos 1995: 141, 145).

In this sense, we are all like stones. We too can be either common or destined for initiation, and if we are the latter, we too can become partially divine. As Valdina Pinto (1997: 54) suggested, using as an example the religion of a Bantu-speaking people, it could well be that a certain 'vitalism', rather than an 'animism', is at the heart of *candomblé*. This generalized vitalism could perhaps be likened to the 'Dakota model' (Gell 1998: 247–248), which Lévi-Strauss (1962: 144–145)[9] identified with the creative evolution of Bergson and which Gell (1998) applied to works of art.[10] In *candomblé*, modulations of a single force called *axé* (similar to other anthropologically familiar notions such as *mana* and *orenda*) make up everything in the universe according to a process of differentiation and individuation. The unity of this force guarantees that everything participates in everything else, but its modulations are such that there exist levels of participation.[11] In a more contemporary vocabulary, we could say that if we are all like stones, it is because humans, stones, and everything else are "distributed persons" (Gell 1998: chap. 7), made from reciprocal "partial connections" (Strathern [1991] 2005). Contrary to the options presented by Donna Haraway (1991: 181), a saint-daughter does not have to choose between being a goddess or a cyborg: she is both at the same time.

In her monograph on *candomblé* in São Paulo (southeast Brazil), Carmen Opipari proposes that we use the Deleuzian concepts of 'virtual' and 'actual' in order to describe this "ontology of variable geometry" (Latour 1991: 116; 1996: 78). Opipari (2004: 276) concludes: "In summary, the ritual of the 'making' could be considered a process in which the *orixá*, existing as a virtuality, actualizes. This actualization does not presuppose an individualization in the

Western sense of the individual, that is, the unification of the being, but a singularization and a personalization. In the place of an identification by an actor-adept to an *orixá*-character, we see this being substituted by an indissoluble bloc, adept-saint, which, through a mutual movement of 'becoming', appears in a performance in which the gesture is recognized by the group."[12] The only problem, it seems to me, is that the author does not emphasize the fact that, in Deleuzian thought, the pair 'virtual-actual' is opposed to the pair 'possible-real'. This is characteristic of a certain type of Kantianism, which in anthropology was developed by Lévi-Strauss. Even when not actualized, the virtual mode of existence is not that of mere possibility but instead, in its own way, that of reality. I will return to this point since, as I have already observed in passing, what appears to occur with all the beings that feature in *candomblé* is that in one way or another they already are that which they could or must become. Furthermore, it must already be clear to the reader that there is no dialectic involved in this process: the virtual is not a 'negative' whose gradual work transforms things according to their own internal contradictions. On the contrary, it is a pure positivity that has not yet been actualized.

An Afro-Brazilian Theory of the Creative Process

Before some concluding remarks, I would like to make all of this a bit more concrete. At the same time, I would like to add something to this discussion that over recent years has been moving toward a deeper understanding of the complexity involved in the ways in which *candomblé* is perceived and lived. In order to do this, I need some help from my friends from the Terreiro Matamba Tombenci Neto in Ilhéus, a medium-sized town in the south of Bahia, in northeast Brazil, where for a long time I have been conducting my fieldwork.[13]

In 1999 I bought an African bracelet as a present for Gilmar, one of my friends from the *terreiro*. I have completely forgotten the exact origin of the bracelet, but I do remember that it did not come from any of the African peoples where *candomblé* originated. I chose it because, apart from being extremely beautiful, it was made from beads that were white and red, the emblematic colors of Xangô, Gilmar's *orixá*. Some time afterwards, Gilmar told me that he was "preparing the bracelet," that is, ritually treating it with herbs, so that it could become a means of protection.

I then remembered something that I had bought when I had already started researching *candomblé*, but before starting my work in Tombenci. In 1982, when visiting one of the markets in the city of Salvador (the capital of Bahia, considered the largest center of Afro-Brazilian culture), I decided to buy a little statue of Exu. Exu is a very special divinity, the messenger of the other *orixás*—the "Mercury of *candomblé*," as Bastide ([1958] 2000) describes him. With some difficulty, since there did not seem to be many statues of Exu among the rest, I managed to find one about 15 cm long, made of iron, and, as is commonly the case, extremely phallic. I took the statue home, where it ended up in the living room of my apartment.

I decided therefore to ask Gilmar also to 'prepare' my Exu, so that he would protect me. I sent my statue to Ilhéus, and when I returned to the field, I met Gilmar, who advised me that the work was almost finished and that now we needed to 'baptize' the Exu. "By the way," he asked, "how are you going to keep him in your apartment?" Faced with my perplexed look, he explained that once prepared or baptized, the Exu would require periodic offerings to be made: palm oil, alcoholic beverage, honey, and especially the blood of an animal from time to time. How was I going to offer these things living in an apartment? It would be much better, Gilmar concluded, to keep him in the House of Exu at the *terreiro*, where every once in a while Gilmar could "feed him." As well as being the main sacrificer, Gilmar is in charge of the House of Exu at Tombenci. I realized that the Exu was becoming something very different from what he had been up until then.

As Exu is the messenger of the *orixás*, each *orixá*—and consequently each saint-daughter—has her own Exu, which must remain somewhere separate from her *orixá*. This is why every *candomblé terreiro* has a House of Exu, where all the Exus (of those in initiation or already initiated) are 'seated' or planted. We proceeded then to the ritual, during which the Exu received the requisite offerings, including the blood of a chicken that had been decapitated above the statue. Alongside this, the Exu received a name, which I cannot reveal, for should anyone discover it, they could use it against me. The name is known only by Gilmar, the saint-mother of the *terreiro*, and myself, and I can invoke it only in situations in which help is essential. Of course, if this were to occur, I would have to repay the succor with new offerings and sacrifices.

I therefore lost an almost ornamental Exu, but gained my own protector Exu. From a simple iron icon, it was transformed into a personal divinity—a fetish, as it would have been called until the nineteenth century. But was this exactly what had happened? Or, better, is this the best way to describe what had happened? The desire to buy the Exu, the difficulty I experienced and the persistence required of me in Salvador, the idea 15 years later to ask that it be 'prepared'—would not all of this suggest that, since the beginning, there was something more than iron in that statue? Could it be that there was a life therein that, in some way, had to be entwined with mine? "Even iron can put forth, even iron," as D. H. Lawrence wrote.

In this way, the preparation of the Exu liberated something that was already contained within it. The native theory of initiation maintains that no one is initiated into *candomblé* 'because they want to be', but because their initiation is demanded by their *orixá*. The *orixá* usually sends signs, which range from small unusual events and sounds to violent personal crises. On consulting the cowries, it is discovered that the person must be initiated. One of the most common forms by which the *orixá* demonstrates his desire for someone to be initiated has become known in the Afro-Brazilian literature as *santo bruto* (brute saint, which followers call *bolar no santo*). In theory, this could happen at any moment, but as a rule it occurs during a public ritual, and generally when the adept hears the music of her divinity. On doing so, she suffers such a violent possession that she rolls about in all directions on the floor of the *terreiro*, until finally she comes to a halt, lying on the floor on her back, completely rigid, and in an apparently catatonic state. She is revived with the appropriate ritual procedures and is then advised that she must start preparing for her initiation. In extreme cases, she immediately undergoes the making of the saint, and it is only when she awakens that she discovers that she has just been initiated.

One of the functions of the making of the saint is exactly the domestication of these violent and savage trances that precede initiation. As Nina Rodrigues (1900) noticed, however, "such cases are not rare ... in which the saint reveals itself even before initiation. It is what is called a *brute* saint, as yet unmade" (ibid.: 118).[14] Since this observation, practically all the scholars of Afro-Brazilian religions have taken up the idea that the trances preceding initiation are 'brute' (violent) because the saint is still not made (that is, constructed). The model of a savage or formless nature that must be conquered, domesticated, and organized by a productive or creative culture seems to underlie all of the descriptions and analyses of the phenomenon. I think, however, that both the adjective 'brute' and the verb 'to make' could mean something else. Three other ethnographic episodes and a more or less native theory will serve to point us in the direction of this other meaning.

In January 2006, while watching one of the beautiful choreographies of Iansan danced by a granddaughter of Dona Ilza (the saint-mother of Tombenci), I could not help commenting on how well she danced, even though she had not yet been initiated. Dona Ilza replied that, in fact, "she is almost ready, there is hardly anything left to do." In February 2007, I accompanied Dona Ilza to a ceremony at another *terreiro* in Ilhéus. Well after the ritual had begun, a man about 30 years old, badly dressed and looking unkempt and dirty, entered the *terreiro*. As it is generally common for beggars and other street-dwellers to wander into the *candomblé* parties looking for some food, drink, and entertainment, I thought little of it. However, when the drums began to play for Oxumarê (the *orixá* that is the snake with two heads, as well as being the rainbow that provides the essential link between the earth and the sky), the man became possessed and performed one of the most beautiful dances that I have had the pleasure of watching, coiling his body until it almost touched the ground and then quickly and sinuously stretching upwards, in a movement that perfectly evoked that of a serpent. I remarked on it the following day to Dona Ilza. Certain that the dancer had not been initiated, she replied that it had indeed been very beautiful, that he had danced very well, but that it was still necessary "to *lapidar* a little" (*lapidação* in Portuguese being the word that describes the process of gem cutting or lapidary).

Matamba Tombenci Neto is a very old *terreiro*. It was founded in 1885 by the maternal grandmother of the current saint-mother. Its organization is based on her 14 children and their respective parentage, and includes the initiates and many friends. One of these friends is Jamilton Santana (known to all as Jaco), an artist who dedicates himself to the crafting of very beautiful and ecological 'rustic furniture'. He was born in Caravelas, a small town in the very south of Bahia, and moved to Ilhéus in 1996. He soon involved himself with Tombenci, using his skill to help in the building of various different objects.

The most impressive of these without doubt is the 'throne' that he made for the saint-mother of the *terreiro*. This throne was shaped with a chainsaw out of the trunk of an ancient jackfruit tree that had been cut down when the region started to undergo urbanization. For many years before this, the jackfruit tree had been used as a sacrifice site, its roots absorbing the vital force of all the animals slaughtered on the ground above. After it was cut down, Dona Ilza insisted on keeping the trunk, which was finally transformed by Jaco into the throne on which she now sits during the public parties at Tombenci. The off-cuts of wood left over from the crafting of the throne were distributed by the saint-mother to members of the *terreiro*; they contained a great deal of *axé* and consequently would help those who kept them in their houses.

Jaco Santana has a very detailed theory about the nature of his craft. He explained to me that when he starts on a project, he has only a very vague idea as to what he wants to do. As he does not use industrially produced wood or chop down trees, he starts by looking in the forest for what he needs, collecting each piece of wood that he thinks looks promising. Over time, these pieces start fitting together as the artist establishes a dialogue with his material. Jaco maintains that it is about discovering and giving back to the wood the form that its current state is hiding.

This formulation is extremely common among sculptors, be they Bahian, Inuit, or Renaissance. Always more entranced by painting than by sculpture, anthropology does not seem to have paid much attention to what is, without question, an alternative theory of creation. More than 100 years ago, however, Freud ([1904] 1972: 260–261) referred to "the greatest possible antithesis … which, in regard to the fine arts, the great Leonardo da Vinci summed up in the formulas: *per via di porre* and *per via di levare*. Painting, says Leonardo, works *per via di porre* for it applies a substance—particles of color—where there was nothing before, on the colorless canvas; sculpture, however, proceeds *per via di levare*, since it takes away from the block of stone all that hides the surface of the statue contained in it."[15]

Not even Alfred Gell, who deals with three-dimensional objects in *Art and Agency* (1998), managed to escape the pictorial model that seems to dominate the anthropology of art. However interesting or original his theory of agency might be, it does not incorporate this crucial dimension of arts that operate through subtraction rather than addition. On the other hand, the distinction that da Vinci makes does not seem to me to be associated with a purely material operation but, above all, speaks of a process of creation that is first and foremost conceptual. Thus, as Deleuze (1984: 57) writes: "[A] series of things that you could call 'clichés' already occupy the canvas before the beginning … It is a mistake to think that the painter works on a white surface … The painter has many things in his head … Now everything he has in his head or around him is already in the canvas, more or less virtually, more or less actually, before he begins his work. They are all present in the canvas as so many images, actual or virtual, so that the painter does not have to cover a blank surface, but rather would have to empty it out, clear it, clean it" (Deleuze 1984: 57). In other words, *porre* and *levare* are not types, but two possible attitudes toward the process of creation.[16]

Certainly, as Sansi-Roca (2005: 142) has observed, *candomblé*, too, is an art form—not only because it demands special talents and gifts, but also because it creates objects, persons, and gods. However, it is necessary to add that it is a very particular art form, since all of these entities already exist before being created, which means that the process of creation involved can be understood only as a revelation of virtualities that the present actualizations 'contain'—in both senses of the word. If we wanted to lend even more of a Nietzschean air to this (already Dionysian) religion, we could say that it is a question of becoming what one 'is'—without implying any notion of a material identity to be discovered, or an original identity to which to return. In an aesthetic or more directly anthropological formulation, we might say that it is a question of the creation of new beings that are 'cut out' of a complete world in which nothing is lacking—a world where, on the contrary, everything is in excess. As Serra (1978: 310–312) demonstrated, the problem of initiation in *candomblé* lies exactly in the control and channeling of incredibly powerful forces into cult objects without reducing their potency.

Conclusion

Trying to demonstrate the potential novelty in the notion of fetishism in the second of three essays dedicated to the subject, Pietz (1987: 36–37) maintains that the genealogy of the concept is not the same as that of idolatry. Further-more, the difficulty, as opposed to medieval Christian models, derives from the fact that fetishism does not conform to any of the three models of production of beings and things recognized by theology. Neither the notion of (always divine) creation nor that of (human) generation serves to explain its genesis. Likewise, the other way in which humans generate things, manufacture, is not applicable either, as the fetish is distinct from idols, that is, from the manufac-ture of representations of false divinities. Saint Augustine did recognize that human acts that are solely dependent on free will approximate acts of creation (ibid.: 27–28), but this clearly cannot be the case with fetishes, which are made by people who are denied precisely such free will.

If, on the other hand, we listen more closely than Pietz, Latour, or Graeber to those formerly accused of fetishism, we could perhaps learn from them other ways to think about this process of creation and agency in general and gain access to other ontological modalities.[17] But to what extent are we actu-ally capable of listening to what a fetishist, or any other 'native', has to say? The only reply, as Latour (2005: 48) observes, is "as far as possible"; that is, until we are "put into motion by the informants."[18] In fact, they should not be looked on as 'informants' but as actors endowed with their own reflexivity, as theoreticians with whom we should talk and from whom we can learn. The capability to uphold the voice of the native, to take it seriously and allow it to propel anthropological reflection to its limits, seems to me the only criterion of quality relevant to our discipline—a quality that evidently is infinite and endlessly imperfect.

In the elegant text that he dedicated to the fetish in the Lusophone Atlantic, Roger Sansi-Roca (2007: 32–33) seems to reach a conclusion similar to my own: "The event in which the fetish is 'found' is not perceived by the person as arbitrary, but necessary. The value found in the object is not randomly attributed by the person, but it is seen as an immanent value of the object, something inchoate that was always there waiting for this particular person, something that he/she recognizes. It is as if the thing was offering itself to the person: as if they always belonged together. In this sense, this is a process of mediated exchange, between the person and a hidden value that is giving itself to the person." This notwithstanding, there are some important differences in our respective positions. First, Sansi-Roca (ibid.: 32) seems to suppose that there is something beyond the agent's perception, something that only the social scientist is capable of finding out: "Social actors perceive the conjuncture as a repeating traditional structures, when in fact, by repeating these structures, they change." Then, in another article, Sansi-Roca (2009: 155; emphasis added) states in the same vein:[19]

> It is clear, however, that to the historical subjects it is not always easy to *perceive* the historicity of events. In the case of *candomblé*, we see that the miracles or revelations are not *perceived* as innovations, but as rediscoveries of something forgotten or unrecognized. These revelations permit the past to be understood in different terms—more deeply, perhaps more authentically. This maybe is due to the *ideology* of mediated exchanges, of the gift, which is predominant in institutions like *candomblé*, and which takes innovation as reproduction. In this case, the function of anthropologists would be to *recognize* the historicity of these revelations, *to see* how they are *effectively* objectifications of categories with no precedents: *to see* how the desire to reproduce the traditional values of *candomblé* transforms it by incorporating the history of its country and its people.

Does this therefore signify that we have ended up back at one of the original meanings of the notion of fetishism that resides in the origin of the Marxist theory of ideology? Do social agents never know what they do, leaving it up to the social scientists to reveal it? Sansi-Roca can therefore maintain that despite what those involved think, the central characteristic of the fetish is its historicity—and it is in this sense that he concludes that "practices, objects and supposedly 'syncretic' spirits are only transpositions of personal and collective histories, incorporated into the practices of *candomblé*. The syncretism is nothing more than history" (Sansi-Roca 2009: 142).[20]

Thus, even reduced to a sort of necessary minimum, the native illusion remains. And it remains the task of social scientists to clarify it. The strategy that I have tried to follow is slightly different. Like Latour (1996), I do not think that these differences "exist to be respected, ignored or subsumed" (ibid.: 102–103); but, unlike Latour, I do not believe that it is enough to define these differences as a "decoy for the feelings" or "food for thought" (ibid.). Fetishist discourse and practice, for example, should serve essentially to destabilize our thoughts (and ultimately also our feelings). This destabilization affects our dominant forms of thought, while allowing new connections to be made with the minority forces inside all of us. In this way, if we listen carefully to what the fetishists say, we could articulate their discourse, for example, by making use of the problematization that Deleuze and Guattari subject history to, instead of trying to explain it in terms of a history that only we know and that they are unconscious of.

In this way, it is clear that the discovery of the fetish, the finding of the stone, and the determining of the *orixá* can all be understood as events when considered from a historical point of view. But these events can also be seen as the pure actualization, in historical time and in an extensive, molar world, of intensive and molecular virtualities in perpetual becoming. "[H]istory," note Deleuze and Guattari (1980: 537), "only translates in succession a co-existence of becomings." Because of this, history is always taken as a change in perspective in relation to a fixed reference with regard to which only the point of view changes. "[T]here is only the history of perception," Deleuze and Guattari (1980: 428) assert, whereas "that from which history is made is first and foremost the matter of a becoming, not of a history" (ibid.). It is for this same reason that 'internalism' and 'externalism'—the two perspectives to which studies of Afro-Brazilian religions are accustomed to resorting—are equally insufficient. If from a historical, or molar, point of view everything is in some way external or internal, then, from the perspective of the bundle of virtualities that make up the molecular dimension of existence, one could talk of neither the one nor the other. Deleuze and Guattari (1980: 536) state that "everything co-exists, in perpetual interaction," and it is necessary to "take into account the co-existence of elements" (ibid.).

Similar to Sansi-Roca, after closely following the native discourse on initiation in *candomblé*, Opipari (2004) feels obliged to emphasize the distance between this discourse and hers: "Far from being considered in its essentialist or onto-logical aspect as an 'interior force' that the adept of *candomblé* would acquire and that would increase as his development in ritual practice does so, this cre-ative potential *evidently* must be seen from a *material*, socio-historical point of view, as a motor of social and symbolic fabrication of human relations" (ibid.: 368–369; emphasis added). Given the Deleuzian perspective adopted by Opipari, this all seems to indicate that she shares with François Zourabichvilli (2004a) the hypothesis that it is not possible to speak of ontology in Deleuze's thought, since his "fundamental orientation" is the "extinction of being in favor of relation (or of becoming)" (ibid.: 6). In other words, it is in fact possible to oppose ontology and history (Opipari) or ontology and becoming (Zourabichvilli). But this is pos-sible only when we define the first, à la Latour, as unity of world or of being, that is, in an extensive mode. If, on the contrary, by 'ontology' we understand pre-cisely the intensive multiplicity of all virtualities, then, as Deleuze ([1967] 1999: 217) writes, "becoming is being ... becoming and being are the same affirma-tion."[21] As I believe that one of the central dimensions of the conceptual world of *candomblé* is exactly a universe where being and becoming are not opposed to each other, it has been in this sense—albeit somewhat crudely—that I have used the term 'ontology' and its derivatives throughout this text.

Dona Ilza told me that initiation within *candomblé* is more a problem of gem cutting than one of production. She also said that the relation between saint-daughter and *orixá* is one of mutual participation, not of property— even if she does refer to her saint as "my Iansan," and to herself as "belonging to Iansan." Likewise, it should already be clear that the expression 'brute saint', used to denote the *orixá* before initiation, cannot be understood as a 'violent' saint manifesting itself in a passive person, but rather should be perceived, as the English expression has it, as a saint 'in the rough'. Before initiation, saint and person are more like 'uncut diamonds' waiting to be discovered and 'cut', rather than wild force and inert matter awaiting animation.[22] Thus, this indicates a way of thinking about the creative process that is distinct from that which centers around a model of production and property—a model that, as Strathern demonstrated (1988: 18–19; 1996: 518), constitutes the 'root metaphor' that underpins our ways of thinking and establishing relations.

Worlds are determined by theories and practices involved in the creation of beings, persons, and gods that already exist. But this is not done according to a Judeo-Christian model of creation *ex nihilo*, in which creator is necessarily superior to created. In fact, these theories and practices seem to resonate rather with concepts such as that of "desiring-production" (Deleuze and Guattari 1972), which posits production as an uninterrupted process of cuts in fluxes, rather than as modeling of content; or with the construction of the person in Melanesia, as analyzed by Strathern (1988), where one proceeds more by subtraction than by addition; or, further, with Latour's (1996) maxim, according to which we are always "slightly surpassed" by what we create.

I do not think that these (and other) connections, even if necessarily partial, are arbitrary or forced. For these theories and practices, be they philosophical, anthropological or native, are the consequence of perspectives that refute the image of a universe where things and beings are created from nothing, and where, however much you produce, emptiness and lack are inescapable. On the contrary, these theories and practices take as their starting point the principle that we are dealing with a full world, where the fact that nothing is lacking does not mean there is nothing to do—quite the contrary.

— *Translated by Antonia Walford*

Acknowledgments

I thank Christina Toren and João de Pina-Cabral for the opportunity to present this piece in Lisbon and St Andrews, and also Peter Gow, with whom I discussed various matters and who also made important contributions to Antonia Walford's careful translation of the chapter. I am equally grateful to Ovídio de Abreu, Gabriel Banaggia, Martin Holbraad, José Guilherme Magnani, Roger Sansi-Roca, Jaco Santana, Julia Sauma, Otávio Velho, Eduardo Viveiros de Castro, and Antonia Walford for the exchange of ideas on various topics and/or for advice on specific points. My special thanks go to Tânia Stolze Lima for similar reasons and many more, not least for showing me the beautiful quotation from Lawrence. Finally, to Dona Ilza, Gilvan, Gilmar, and Marinho Rodrigues I offer my thanks for the little I know about *candomblé*.

Marcio Goldman is an Associate Professor in the Post-Graduate Program in Social Anthropology (PPGAS) at the National Museum of the Federal University of Rio de Janeiro. His research is conducted under CNPq (the National Council for Scientific and Technological Development), and he is also funded by FAPERJ (the state agency of Rio de Janeiro for founding research). He is the author of *Razão e Diferença: Afetividade, Racionalidade e Relativismo no Pensamento de Lévy-Bruhl* (1994), *Alguma Antropologia* (1999), and *Como Funciona a Democracia: Uma Teoria Etnográfica da Política* (2006). He also co-edited, along with Moacir Palmeira, *Antropologia, Voto e Representação Política* (1996).

Notes

1. I am extending here to sociology a procedure adopted by Viveiros de Castro (2009), which makes use of Gell's observation about magic and physics but in the area of kinship and biology. Viveiros de Castro (ibid.: 241) states: "Gell's point can be transposed analogically to 'kinship' ... Kinship is what you get when you proceed without a biological theory of relationality." In this sense, Viveiros de Castro concludes, kinship and magic are in fact parts, aspects, or dimensions of the same conceptual worlds.
2. As Bob Scholte (1984: 963) points out, if it is true that anthropology always looks to undermine the certainty that Western reason has of its superiority compared with that of others, no less so is the fact that it always tends to forget that "we are the ones who define what the other is or is not."
3. In his third article in the series, Pietz (1988: 109n8) states: "Here and throughout this work I am approaching the history of theories of fetishism from the standpoint of what I understand to be dialectical materialism."
4. This incidentally seems to be Joseph Dupuis' position. Writing in 1824 about his experience among the Ashanti, he maintains that "fetish is evidently a corrupt relic of the Portuguese, introduced to the country, probably, by the original explorers of that nation, and adopted by the Africans to accommodate to the understanding of their visitors, such things connected with religion, law, or superstition, as could not be explained by the ordinary use of a few common-place expressions, and that could not be interpreted by ocular demonstrations" (cited in Pietz 1988: 116n23).
5. Lévi-Strauss ([1954] 1963) wrote: "However, sociology is always closely linked with the observer ... Sociology is concerned with the observer's society or a society of the same type. But the same applies to the other example—the comprehensive 'synthesis' or philosophical sociology. Here, admittedly, the sociologist extends his investigations to much wider ranges of human experience, and he can even seek to interpret human experience as a whole. The subject extends beyond the purview of the observer, but it is always *from the observer's point of view* that the sociologist tries to broaden it. In his attempt to interpret and assign meanings, he is always first of all concerned with explaining *his own society*; what he applies to the generality are his own logical classifications, his own background perspectives. If a French sociologist of the twentieth century works out a general theory of social life, it will inevitably, and quite legitimately, reveal itself as the

work of a twentieth-century French sociologist; whereas the anthropologist undertaking the same task will endeavor instinctively and deliberately (although it is by no means certain that he will ever succeed), to formulate a theory applicable not only to his own fellow countrymen and contemporaries, but to the most distant native population. While sociology seeks to advance the social science of the observer, anthropology seeks to advance that of what is observed—either by endeavoring to reproduce, in its description of strange and remote societies, the standpoint of the natives themselves, or by broadening its subject so as to cover the observer's society but at the same time trying to evolve a frame of reference based on ethnographical experience and independent both of the observer and what he is observing" (ibid.: 362–363).

6. Thus, an important Bahian saint-mother assured Donald Pierson ([1942] 1971: 320) that "the African does not adore things made by human hands. He adores nature. What is a stone [fetish]? It's a mineral, isn't it? It wasn't made by human hands."

7. An extension, in fact, of what Pietz (1985: 8) calls the "theory of first encounter," which, since the sixteenth century, has maintained that African fetishes are found by chance, contingency, or caprice—features that are defined as characteristic of the African social order or personality.

8. In the same way, Martin Holbraad (2003: 51) argues that the "consecrated idol" received by Cuban diviners should be called "'idol-divinity', since the consecrated paraphernalia … is not seen as a 'representation' of divinity, but as divinity itself."

9. "Each thing in moving, from one moment to another, here and there, stops for a time … Thus, god stopped. The sun, so brilliant and magnificent, is where he stopped. The moon, the stars, the winds, is where he was. The trees, the animals, are all his points of stopping, and the Indian thinks on these places and directs his prayers to them, so that they reach the place where god stopped, and bring help and blessing" (George A. Dorsey, cited in Lévi-Strauss 1962: 144).

10. "What I am proposing, consequently, could be called a 'Dakota' model of an artist's work; each piece … is a place where agency 'stops' and assumes visible form" (Gell 1998: 250).

11. Roger Bastide ([1958] 2000: 295) explains that there are "a whole series of degrees of participation, from simple associations to identities."

12. See Anjos (2006) for an inspired exercise connecting Afro-Brazilian cosmology and the philosophy of Deleuze and Guattari (see also Ochoa 2007).

13. Followers of *candomblé* call their temples or cult houses *terreiros*. After my fieldwork on *candomblé* in 1983, I returned to Ilhéus in 1996 to study politics (see Goldman 2006). From 2006 onward, I took up my investigation of *candomblé* again.

14. Arthur Ramos (1934: 61) also refers to the brute saint: "The making of the saint is the first function of the *babalaos*. As I have already pointed out, for the black fetishist any natural object can be adored or worshipped as an *orixá*, but it is necessary for the saint-father to prepare it. There are, it is true, spontaneous manifestations of a determined *orixá*, but these are cases, for the blacks, of the brute saint. It is necessary to prepare it."

15. It was Stengers and Chertok's ([1989] 1990: 57–59) interpretation of the use that psychoanalysis makes of this opposition in order to disqualify hypnosis techniques, which rely on suggestion (*per via di porre*), in favor of free association, which always relies on a process of extraction (*per via di levare*) that drew my attention to Freud's observation. But it was Ovídio de Abreu—to whom I am very grateful—who drew my attention to the broader conceptual dimension of the distinction.

16. As Ovídio de Abreu notes (2003), Deleuze is referring to the painter Francis Bacon, but it is obvious that the isolated 'operation' is analogous to that in the theatre of Carmelo Bene, who wrote his plays by eliminating the dominant characters from an already existing play, an operation that Deleuze called 'minoration' or 'subtraction' (Deleuze and Bene 1979).

17. This is also, as far as I understand, the position of Alfred Gell. In the few pages directly devoted to the theme of the fetish, Gell (1998: 59–62) insists on the necessity of taking native theories into account in order to understand the phenomenon. Furthermore, he maintains that the agency of the fetish also depends on the fact that it has been made,

that it is the patient of some other agency. The only problem, it seems to me, arises from a certain indecision as to whether to extend or transform the concept of social relations in order for it to include objects (and animals and spirits), or to reduce these beings to social relations existing between humans. Thus, objects appear directly either as "persons" (ibid.: 7) or as "substitute persons" (ibid.: 5) or "in the vicinity" of social relations (ibid.: 7). Likewise, Gell's theory of agency seems to oscillate between a conception of a person as an "onion" (ibid.: 139–140), that is, as not possessing a material nucleus but made entirely of relations, and one that resembles what Stengers and Chertok ([1989] 1990: 268) call an "artichoke": under the various layers of social relations, you can always find a human nucleus. For this reason, I do not think that critics of Gell can insist that, by reformulating objects as social relations, he forfeits 'materiality'. The point, to the contrary, is to extend the notion of relations to objects. As Gabriel Tarde ([1893] 1999: 58) asserts: "[A]ny thing is a society, any phenomenon a social fact."

18. On this point, see also Favret-Saada (1990: 4–5).
19. Sansi-Roca's article also shares with this chapter some points in common. This is, I think, a proof of the possibilities opened up by the investigation of theories of world, agency, and the process of creation in Afro-Brazilian religions. As Sansi-Roca himself recently remarked, maybe it is possible to speak of a "small and humble 'paradigmatic shift' in Afro-Brazilian studies" (personal communication).
20. One of the pitfalls of the Western fetishist device, constituted historically from the fifteenth and sixteenth centuries onward, seems to be its ability to draw into itself the same things from which it, supposedly, seeks to be free. Thus, Wyatt MacGaffey's (1994) interesting criticism of Pietz starts by defending the necessity to analyze fetishism in light of "indigenous theories" (ibid.: 123), and then proceeds by reaffirming the conceptual character of native categories (ibid.: 128) and the inadequacy of Western categories to account for them (ibid.). Yet he concludes that "the ritual system as a whole thus bears a relationship to Kongo society similar to that which Marx supposed that 'political economy' bears to capitalism as its 'religion'" (ibid.: 130). He also holds that "fetishism is about relations among people, rather than about the objects that mediate and disguise those relations," "obliquely" expressing "real relations of power among the participants in ritual" (ibid.). Much ado about nothing.
21. Or, as Zourabichvili (2003: 6) describes it, becoming is an affirmation of "multiplicity as original ontological coordinate" (see also Zourabichvili 2004b).
22. As in the 'hylemorphic model', criticized by Deleuze and Guattari (1980: 457), such a view supposes an implausible exteriority between organized form and inert matter.

References

Abreu, Ovídio de. 2003. "O Combate ao Julgamento no Empirismo Transcendental de Deleuze." PhD diss., Universidade Federal do Rio de Janeiro.

Anjos, José Carlos Gomes dos. 1995. "O Corpo nos Rituais de Iniciação do Batuque." Pp. 137–151 in *Corpo e Significado*, ed. Ondina Fachel Leal. Porto Alegre: Ed. UFRGS.

_____. 2006. *Território da Linha Cruzada: A Cosmopolítica Afro-Brasileira*. Porto Alegre: Editora da UFRGS.

Bastide, Roger. [1958] 2000. *Le candomblé de Bahia (rite nagô)*. Paris: Plon.

Châtelet, François. 1975. *Le Capital (Livre I)*. Paris: Hatier.

Deleuze, Gilles. [1967] 1999. *Nietzsche et la philosophie*. Paris: Press Universitaires de France.

_____. 1984. *Francis Bacon: Logique de la sensation*. Paris: Editions de la Différence.

Deleuze, Gilles, and Carmelo Bene. 1979. *Superpositions*. Paris: Minuit.

Deleuze, Gilles, and Félix Guattari. 1972. *L'Anti-Oedipe*. Paris: Minuit.

_____. 1980. *Mille Plateaux*. Paris: Minuit.

Favret-Saada, Jeanne. 1990. "Etre affecté." *Gradhiva: Revue d'Histoire et d'Archives de l'Anthropologie* 8: 3–9.

Freud, Sigmund. [1904] 1972. "Sobre a Psicoterapia." *Edição Standard Brasileira das Obras Psicológicas Completas de Sigmund Freud*, vol. 7, no. 1: 265–278.

Gell, Alfred. 1998. *Art and Agency: An Anthropological Theory*. Oxford: Clarendon Press.

Goldman, Marcio. 1984. "A Possessão e a Construção Ritual da Pessoa no Candomblé." Masters thesis, Universidade Federal do Rio de Janeiro.

_____. 1985. "A Construção Ritual da Pessoa: A Possessão no *Candomblé*." *Religião e Sociedade* 12, no. 1: 22–54.

_____. 2005. "How to Learn in an Afro-Brazilian Spirit Possession Religion: Ontology of *Candomblé*." Pp. 103–119 in *Learning Religion: Anthropological Approaches*, ed. Ramón Sarró and David Berliner. Oxford: Berghahn Books.

_____. 2006. *Como Funciona a Democracia: Uma Teoria Etnográfica da Política*. Rio de Janeiro: Editora 7Letras.

Graeber, David. 2005. "Fetishism as Social Creativity: Or, Fetishes Are Gods in the Process of Construction." *Anthropological Theory* 5, no. 4: 407–438.

Halloy, Arnaud. 2005. "Dans l'intimité des *orixás*: Corps, rituel et apprentissage religieux dans une famille-de-saint de Recife (Brésil)." PhD diss., ULB-Bruxelles/EHESS-Paris.

Haraway, Donna J. 1991. "A Cyborg Manifesto: Science, Technology, and Socialist-Feminism in the Late Twentieth Century." Pp. 149–181 in *Simians, Cyborgs and Women: The Reinvention of Nature*. New York: Routledge.

Holbraad, Martin. 2003. "Estimando a Necessidade: Os Oráculos de Ifá e a Verdade em Havana." *Mana: Estudos de Antropologia Social* 9, no. 2: 39–77.

Latour, Bruno. 1991. *Nous n'avons jamais été modernes: Essai d'anthropologie symétrique*. Paris: Editions La Découverte.

_____. 1996. *Petite réflexion sur le culte moderne des dieux faitiches*. Paris: Synthélabo.

_____. 2005. *Reassembling the Social*. Oxford: Oxford University Press.

Lévi-Strauss, Claude. [1954] 1963. "The Place of Anthropology in the Social Sciences and Problems Raised in Teaching." Pp. 346–379 in *Structural Anthropology*. New York: Basic Books.

_____. 1962. *Le totémisme aujourd'hui*. Paris: Press Universitaires de France.

MacGaffey, Wyatt. 1994. "African Objects and the Idea of Fetish." *Res: Journal of Anthropology and Aesthetics* 25: 122–131.

Nina Rodrigues, Raimundo. 1900. *L'animisme fétichiste des nègres de Bahia*. Salvador: Reis.

Ochoa, Todd Ramón. 2007. "Versions of the Dead: Kalunga, Cuban-Kongo Materiality, and Ethnography." *Cultural Anthropology* 22, no. 4: 473–500.

Opipari, Carmen. 2004. *Le candomblé: Images en mouvement, São Paulo-Brésil*. Paris: L'Harmattan.

Pierson, Donald. [1942] 1971. *O Candomblé da Bahia*. São Paulo: Companhia Editora Nacional.

Pietz, William. 1985. "The Problem of the Fetish I." *Res: Journal of Anthropology and Aesthetics* 9: 5–17.

_____. 1987. "The Problem of the Fetish II: The Origin of the Fetish." *Res: Journal of Anthropology and Aesthetics* 13: 23–45.

_____. 1988. "The Problem of the Fetish IIIa: Bosman's Guinea and the Enlightenment Theory of Fetishism." *Res: Journal of Anthropology and Aesthetics* 16: 105–123.

Pinto, Valdina. 1997. "Nação Angola." Pp. 43–67 in *II Encontro de Nações de Candomblé*. Salvador: Centro de Estudos Afro Orientais da UFBA.

Ramos, Arthur. 1934. *O Negro Brasileiro: Etnografia Religiosa e Psicanálise*. Rio de Janeiro: Civilização Brasileira.

Sansi[-Roca], Roger. 2003. "Fetishes, Images, Commodities, Art Works: Afro-Brazilian Art and Culture in Bahia." PhD diss., University of Chicago.

_____. 2005. "The Hidden Life of Stones: Historicity, Materiality and the Value of *Candomblé* Objects in Bahia." *Journal of Material Culture* 10, no. 2: 139–156.

_____. 2007. "The Fetish in the Lusophone Atlantic." Pp. 19–40 in *Cultures of the Lusophone Black Atlantic*, ed. Nancy Priscilla Naro, Roger Sansi-Roca, and David H. Treece. New York: Palgrave Macmillan.

_____. 2009. "'Fazer o Santo': Dom, Iniciação e Historicidade nas Religiões Afro-Brasileiras." *Análise Social* 44, no. 4: 139–160.

Scholte, Bob. 1984. "Reason and Culture: The Universal and the Particular Revisited." *American Anthropologist* 86, no. 4: 960–965.

Serra, Ordep. 1978. "Na Trilha das Crianças: Os Erês num Terreiro Angola." Master's thesis, Universidade de Brasília.

_____. 1995. *Águas do Rei*. Petrópolis: Vozes.

Stengers, Isabelle, and León Chertok. [1989] 1990. *O Coração e a Razão: A Hipnose de Lavoisier a Lacan*. Rio de Janeiro: Jorge Zahar.

Strathern, Marilyn. 1988. *The Gender of the Gift: Problems with Women and Problems with Society in Melanesia*. Berkeley: University of California Press.

_____. [1991] 2005. *Partial Connections*. Lanham, MD: AltaMira Press.

_____. 1996. "Cutting the Network." *Journal of the Royal Anthropological Institute* 2, no. 3: 517–535.

Tarde, Gabriel. [1893] 1999. *Monadologie et sociologie*. Paris: Les Empêcheurs de Penser em Rond.

Viveiros de Castro, Eduardo. 2009. "The Gift and the Given: Three Nano-Essays on Kinship and Magic." Pp. 237–268 in *Kinship and Beyond: Sequence, Transmission, and Essence in Ethnography and Social Theory*, ed. Sandra Bamford and James Leach. Oxford: Berghahn Books.

Zourabichvilli, François. 2003. "Séminaire de François Zourabichvilli (Collège International de Philosophie)." Mimeo.

_____. 2004a. "Deleuze et la question de la littéralité." Mimeo.

_____. 2004b. *Le vocabulaire de Deleuze*. Paris: Ellipses.

Chapter 7

INTERSUBJECTIVITY AS EPISTEMOLOGY

Christina Toren

Extract from field notes: Sawaieke, Wednesday, 25 July 2007
A few days after the picnic (*vakatakakana*)—Sunday, I think—we're eating, and
Sefa tells us with evident satisfaction that Seini got sick from eating poison fish the
day of the picnic. "Serves her right!" (*vinaka sara ga*, lit., 'actually good'). She had
eaten fish innards wrapped in a leaf and roasted *tavu* on the hot coals. Sefa had
wanted some, but she had refused to let him have any. I say it was lucky he didn't
eat any, because otherwise he would have got sick too. He says no, if she had
given him the food she had kept to herself, it would not have been poison—they
could both have eaten it with impunity. She was punished for the fact that her
desire to eat fish (*kusima*) prompted her to refuse food to one who asked for it.

Sefa is 30 years old, an intelligent man who lived for over 10 years outside
the village of Sawaieke, working in the capital Suva and in Sigatoka and other
parts of Fiji.[1] He reasons like this not because he is incapable of understanding syllogisms[2]—his response to me makes it evident that he can—or because

Notes for this chapter begin on page 142.

he is unsophisticated, but because the obligations of kinship (*veiwekani*) and the consequences of ignoring them make it self-evident that anything bad that happens to a person is the likely result of some earlier kinship failure on their part. This idea of retribution is no doubt attributable to the inculcation of Christian teachings—all the Fijians I know are devout Methodists—but it has become one with the form taken by contemporary Fijian kinship. Immediate retribution is especially likely in an instance where someone asks for food and is refused, because the giving of food is the primary act that at once expresses and constitutes kinship. In the village, for all that people nowadays often enough eat rice and flour and tinned fish and corned beef that they buy from one of the half-dozen small stores, food is still likely to be the direct product of men's labor in the gardens and women's labor in fishing. As such, it is fitting that when men work together *vakoro* (according to the village) or *vakayavusa* (according to *yavusa*), they will be conspicuously well fed for at least one day of this collective labor.

Tuesday, 17 July 2007
This morning Makareta encourages [her son] Sefa [who's still in bed behind the partition] to get up and come and have breakfast by saying loudly that she's heard that there's lots of fish for lunch for those who are working today *vakoro* [finishing one of the teachers' houses at the primary school]. This is indeed an inducement. I notice that Mikaele too goes off to work there today, although he did not do so yesterday.

Men bake (*vavi*) root crops in the earth oven, and women boil (*saqa*) fish and vegetables over the kitchen fire. Male sexual potency is manifested in the men's ability to produce root crops for their women, especially for their wives. The sexuality of the wives is given in their ability to produce at once a man's meals and to be a man's food (lit., 'his to eat', *na kena*). The quality of a marriage—its success—is thus visible for all to see in what is eaten.

Extract from field notes: Saturday, 11 August 2007
People love to joke publicly that I am cooking for Mikaele [i.e., to imply a sexual relationship between us]. On the grounds that his wife Makareta [Ma] and I are siblings (*veitacini*), and Mika and I cross-cousins, if not spouses, they ask me what I have cooked for his dinner and whether I'm going fishing and so on … Last night, nearing dinner time, I set off for a walk beside the sea. I'm passing in front of a crowd of men on the Navure side of the village, when Mika calls out from among them, asking what is there for him to eat at home, implying that by going out walking I was failing in my wifely duty. I reply, "Kua ni leqa. E vakarau tu na kemu kakana, sa buta na vudi ka tiko na memu ti. Ko na gunu ti vudi" (Don't worry. Your food's all ready. The plaintain's boiled and the tea prepared. You'll drink tea and eat plantain). This got a huge laugh from the assembled men, tea and boiled plantain not being considered in any way an adequate meal and plantain a poor substitute for taro root when it comes to symbols of male potency.

This example manifests neatly not only the relevance of food and eating to sexuality, but also the very specificity of intersubjective relations. Such joking would not be possible, were it not that there is held to be no danger at all of any actual impropriety taking place between Mika and myself. This is not because I am an outsider (*kai valagi*, a European). Rather, it is because, as a grandmother, I am, at least publicly, considered to be beyond danger—so much so that Ma too shouts with laughter, when, on another occasion, I say, addressing myself to those who are listening: "Isa o Mika. E rui ca. Au lomani koya. E rua na watina ia e sega sara ga ni kana rawa" (Alas for Mika. It is too bad. I pity him. He has two wives, but he cannot actually get anything to eat). It is the very specificity of who I am and who Mika and Ma are that makes these jokes effective. I return later on to the importance of realizing that intersubjectivity always bears on specific relations between particular persons.

Giving Form to Kinship Relations through Food

During my last field trip to Sawaieke country, I came to the conclusion that food is the key to everything Fijian. It figures powerfully, not only in kinship relations, but in the ritualized formalities of attendance on one another (*veiqaravi*), which stipulate the obligations owed by any given clan or *yavusa* (group of clans) to other clans and *yavusa*. But if the relationships constituted and expressed through the production, exchange, circulation, giving, and consumption of food are to be inevitable—that is, apparently given in the nature of things—then the forms given to kinship relations through food have to be laid down in childhood. And of course they are.

Extract from field notes: Sawaieke, Saturday, 30 June 2007
Yesterday we ate together according to clan (*vakamataqali*), that is to say, we went, along with some others, to the Navure section of the village to eat. A *yavusa* Navure woman had died in Suva the day before, and because we couldn't be there, given the problem with boats, we devoted a day to the closing ceremony of *na i burua*. If we had been in Suva, we would have done the whole thing properly for four nights. Makareta is married into Navure, so we're closely involved.

In the morning, the men prepare *vakalolo* (pudding made of cassava and taro leaves), a plate of which I bring back home with me, and Ma and I have it for lunch. Then in the afternoon we go off to Navure to help with the cooking … and in the evening we eat largely. I confine myself to fish, but there's pig too. The pig meat is chopped up and made into a stew with rice and cassava and cabbage and noodles. The children are fed first. A large piece of blue tarpaulin is spread on the ground, and they come from all over Navure and from the houses of other *yavusa* that have reason to be involved—a good 40 to 50 or so children, of all ages from around three to ten or eleven. Even the littlest children wait patiently for their serving and then carefully carry their brimming plates to a free spot on the tarpaulin and sit down there to eat. The serving given to a child appears to depend on the size of the child and on the size of the plate, which is always filled to the brim. One boy of about eleven or so is not really given enough because the bowl in which his stew is served is small, but he says nothing, just accepts what he is given, nor do I see him comparing with his eyes the size of his serving with those of others. Later I see that one of the women simply refills his bowl without his asking for a second helping. Writing this, I realize that none of the children would, in fact, ask for seconds; they know their place. Some older children in their teens are given containers by their mothers to take home to serve and eat there. Later I … watch as the ladies cut up the baked taro into pieces and pile up plates and other containers with pork stew to send *takitaki* to the Methodist minister and the lay preacher, to a senior chiefly lady, and to many another house … The number of dishes sent *itakitaki* from the *i burua* is impressive.

Sawaieke, Wednesday, 4 July 2007
I'm struck, yet again, by how compelling and how routine are the reciprocal obligations of kinship. Sefa sends a gift of a bundle of taro to the family in Levuka (Ovalou) who are kin to his mother's clan, and they send back 10 kilos of flour, along with sugar and milk. Every day someone sends us a dish *i takitaki*—shrimp or fish or baked taro or pig or scones, etc. Makareta is much amused by the behavior of little Samisoni, aged five, which she enjoys relating to me. He comes yesterday (she says) with a plate of something (pig, I think). It must have been around lunchtime, because he looks at what she's prepared—greens and cassava—and is clearly not impressed. The cupboard being open, he asks what is in that container. At first Ma pretends she doesn't know what he's talking about. "What container?" So little Samisoni has to point it out. "That one." So then she partially relents. "Those are Christina's biscuits." Samisoni says nothing. Ma says, "Do you want some to eat?" Again Samisoni doesn't answer, he just sits silently. [Conventional good behavior requires that he refuse by saying "thank you"—meaning no.] Eventually Ma gives him a plate of cabin crackers, and at once he's off—back to his own house. Telling me the story, Ma laughs, amused by little Samisoni's making sure that he goes away with *bisikete*, rather than the cooked greens she might have given him. She says that he has in mind what he wants as he makes his way over to our house, carrying the dish sent by his mother, and that she saw him spy out the container, his eyes ranging about to see what might be had.

Extract from field notes: Sawaieke, Wednesday, 11 July 2007
Little Samisoni is assiduous in his *takitaki*—his bringing us a dish of whatever they're eating in their house; it seems he asks his mother every morning if he can take something to us. Makareta says this is because he knows that we have flour and rice and suchlike, and he wants to eat scones and dumplings (*topoi*) and biscuits. The convention with *takitaki* is that one immediately presents in return a dish of whatever is there on the cloth in one's own house, so it's a smart ploy on his part. Little Samisoni's five, very talkative and inquisitive. On Sunday he's at our house with his father (also Samisoni), and immediately he spies there in the leaf basket the *dalo vavi* that we had for lunch. He definitely wants that nice little one that he can see, even though he's eaten already and they also had *dalo vavi* (taro baked in the earth oven). He takes it and looks around, but no one encourages him to keep it—*kemu!* yours to eat!—so he puts it back; then he takes it again, giggling, and again looks around and puts it back. He takes it again and hides it under his shirt, and then, seeing me looking, puts it back. By

degrees, however, he manages to get away with it and saunters off outside with the *dalo* in his hand, there to take a bite out of it.

Little Samisoni makes so bold because our house is his—that is to say, he is in the house of a man of his own clan,' more specifically, the house of a man whom he calls Tata Lailai (Little Fathe'), who himself calls Samisoni's own father his elder brother (their respective fathers having been full brothers). It is this reliance on kinship, already borne out in his five-year-old experience, that allows Samisoni to be apparently unmoved by Makareta's sometimes grudging or mocking remarks on the frequency of his visits to us or her pretense that we are eating nothing especially desirable when he is pretty sure that she has baked buns. Often enough, she shouts at him, and I remark to her that I am surprised he is not afraid of her. He knows me, she says, laughing. Her ferocity has not managed to frighten him off, unlike many another child who lacks his specific kinship attributes.

The antithetical logic of attendance on one another (*veiqaravi*, lit., 'facing each other'), in which competitive relations of exchange between cross-cousins are in tension with axiomatically hierarchical relations between siblings, expresses itself forcibly in such relationships. Makareta is Nana (Mother) to little Samisoni because she is the wife of a man who is classificatory brother to little Samisoni's father. Formally speaking, little Samisoni owes Makareta respect and obedience, but even so he knows that he can rely on her to give him anything good that is around in the way of food. He is (perhaps) too young to know consciously that she is actually obliged to give him food. That she does so, however, is bound over time to inform little Samisoni's constitution of an idea of himself as personally effective in his relations with others, insofar as he can make them give him what he wants. The compassionate, pitying, familial love of hierarchical kinship is at once constituted and expressed in those who call themselves your kin anticipating your desires and giving you what you want, without the necessity of your asking for it— especially with respect to food. From the giver's point of view, giving places him or her in the hierarchically superior position; from the receiver's point of view, however, there may be a covert idea that he or she has coerced the gift and is thus one up on the giver. This shifting meaning arises from the way that hierarchy plays against competitive exchange. From cross-cousins you can demand food or cigarettes or anything else, and this competitive relationship between equals means that they can demand anything of you. You may be obliged to give, just as they are, but you can be defiant and dismissive too. A jokey put-down is a good substitute for giving what has been asked for. As is clear, however, in the extract from my field notes with which I began this chapter, one has to be careful with refusals—especially with regard to food. Food is the very substance of kinship, and to refuse a demand for food is a refusal of kinship, one that brings retribution. It follows that if Seini had given her cross-cousin Sefa the fish innards that he had asked for, they could both have eaten with impunity. Her greed poisoned what would otherwise have been perfectly good food.

Intersubjectivity and Human Ontogeny

I have remarked elsewhere that the clash of understanding between the ethnographer and his or her informants is an anthropological commonplace and that what is less often acknowledged is how frequently we encounter a similar incommensurability between our own ideas and the ideas of those nearest to us: our spouses, children, siblings, friends, etc. Our awareness that this is so tends to emerge only when we are in dispute with one another, although it is clear enough in the differences that emerge in, say, rival accounts of what is really happening in the economy. The problem for us as anthropologists is a particularly powerful case of the problem that we have in our daily lives: if we are really to credit other people's understandings of the world, we have also to recognize not only that the environing world provides for all the meanings that humans can make,[3] but that our own understandings are no less amenable to historical analysis—that is, no less explicable by social analysis—than the next person's. It follows that the explanatory power of our ethnographies must be made to reside in rendering our informants' categories analytical.

To render categories analytical requires a double move. First, we have to ensure that the categories in question are, from our perspective, analyzable. This is the objective of the Malinowskian project—that we be able to understand and explain what people are doing and saying because we have worked to find out the socio-political, economic, and other conditions that inform what they do and say.[4] To render our informants' categories analytical, however, requires a second move—that of demonstrating their self-evidence, their purchase on the world, their lived validity. It will be apparent that my very acceptance of the analytical utility of Fijian ideas demands a theory of human being that has historicity at its core—otherwise, I have no means of according explanatory value to Fijian ideas of the peopled world and to my own.

I began with an account of a form of reasoning whose logic is given in a certain form of social relations, not in order to explain it away, but in order to emphasize the necessity of an epistemology for anthropology that puts the close analysis of relations between people at the heart of our understanding of what it is to be human and, more particularly, at the heart of our understanding of human reasoning and its ontogeny. To do so, however, we have to have a model of human being that is phenomenologically valid.[5] It has to provide both for the analysis of social relations and for how they inform the constitution of meaning over time by particular persons in such a way as to produce meanings that are always unique (because they are the product of a constituting process in a particular person), even while they are always recognizable for what they have in common with meanings made by others (because the constituting process is intersubjective and because it bears on the human condition that they take for granted). By virtue of evolution, we humans, like other living things, inhere in the world. It follows that we inevitably make use of manifold aspects of the world in making sense of it, and that ethnographic studies of ontogeny are going to be more complete to the extent that they include the study of how objects of manifold kinds enter into people's intersubjective engagement in the environing world. But there is no mystery here, I think.[6]

I want to insist on an argument that I have made elsewhere, that mind—considered as a function of the whole person in intersubjective relations with others in the environing world—is *the* fundamental historical phenomenon.[7] This is because any human being—you and me included—is at any given point in time the dynamic self-creating product of his or her history, including the history of his or her relations with others. This process of self-creation is not self-willed. It is simply how living things function as products of continuing differentiation, which is itself informed by how the structure of living things at any given time specifies what they can make of a highly differentiated environment. In the case of human beings and other social animals, the self-creating process (which ends only with death) is embedded in close and continuing relations with conspecifics. In other words, I can become myself only in relations with other humans who are also becoming who they are.[8] The ontogeny of any given aspect of this process can be studied and delineated, more or less precisely, depending on the researcher's focus of interest. My own concern has been to describe, as clearly as I can, how humans constitute themselves as unique beings who can nevertheless be seen to be the always dynamic product of the history of intersubjective relations in whose terms they live their lives.

Given the confusion that apparently surrounds the idea of intersubjectivity (often qualified as 'difficult') it seems sensible to clarify what I mean when I use the term. Continually, over time, I constitute myself as the conscious subject of my own existence, as a function of my understanding of who I am in relation to others. They do likewise. I cannot be you, so I can have no direct access to what you mean by what you say or write; rather, I understand what you say or write in terms of my current ideas about who and what you are and of the relation between us. At any given point, I speak to my present ideas of who you are and of our relationship, and you answer back to your present ideas of who I am and of our relationship. That is intersubjectivity. It provides for the fact that we can be radically wrong about one another, or wonderfully empathetic and understanding, or prejudiced, or downright stupid. Intersubjectivity can be analytically rendered in emotional, cognitive, sociological, psychodynamic, and developmental terms.[9] Here I want simply to demonstrate why intersubjectivity has to inform our model of human ontogeny.

Edited extract from field notes: Sawaieke, Wednesday, 25 July 2007
Almost every time I see [the 32-month-old] Asaeli, he is in the company of older children, watching or trying to do the things they do. His mother describes him as [having pretensions to being grown-up] *viavia qase* [and as disobedient] *gone cikecike*, but she says this to me with affectionate pride. Asaeli is already a 'nothing ventured, nothing gained' kind of child. Yesterday I watched him struggle successfully to carry back home from the road by the seafront a new broom a good deal longer than himself—only once did he begin to let it trail along the ground. His grandmother Mere, who was a good distance away, chatting to me, called out a sharp instruction to him that it was new and he mustn't let it trail. This morning I see him in the arms of [Seini, his mother's brother's wife], who

prompts him to ask a series of questions and answers about where I am going and have I had breakfast and what did I eat.

She first speaks on his behalf in the characteristic prompting style, her gaze directed towards him and her voice somewhat lowered: "Christina, yadra" (Christina, good morning). Then she waits until Asaeli whispers, "Christina, yadra." Then she speaks again, and again waits until he repeats what she's said, "Lako ki vei?" (Where are you going?). And then, "Ko sa gunu ti oti?" (Have you had breakfast? lit., Have you already drunk tea?) "Gunu ti cava?" (What did you eat with it? lit., You drank tea with what?). Each time she waits until he's repeated her question and I've given an appropriate reply before she moves on to the next question. I then engage Asaeli himself in the same exchange: "Vakacava o iko? Sa gunu ti oti?" (How about you, have you drunk tea?). He raises his eyebrows—*degu vacu*, meaning yes—but he is not looking at me. "Gunu ti cava?" (What did you eat with it?). His whisper is difficult to hear and his gaze determinedly averted. Seini says, "E, Asaeli? Ko gunu ti cava. Mo tukuna mada. E via kila o tina i Manueli" (E, Asaeli? What did you eat with your tea? Tell us. The mother of Manuel wants to know). And somewhat louder this time, Asaeli whispers, "Raisi" (Rice).

This is a simple, but I think telling, example of how a child is inducted into relations with other human beings. What I want to stress, however, is that even if as adults we take such encounters for granted, as analysts we have to recognize that in every single case, for both adults and children, we are always looking at specific relations between specific persons. These specific relations structure the encounter and, in this selfsame process, are structured by it. Consider the people who addressed one another in this little encounter. Asaeli is a valiant child and at the time was already very articulate. Under the same circumstances, he would have been prompted politely to greet any adult, but I was a special case because he was distinctly wary of me as those village toddlers who are not very familiar with me often are. By engaging him in a prolonged conversation that was all about food, his (classificatory) mother-in-law, without either of us having to think about it, was making it as clear as could be that despite appearances, I was just another adult because, like everyone else, like Asaeli himself, I was interested in food. Between adults, the very same exchange may appear to the observer, or perhaps even to the participants, to be merely formulaic. However, I would argue that this can never be the case—that such exchanges always constitute specific social relations, such that each one of us has perforce to make sense of a specific other and of who he or she is for that other.

I want to emphasize this inevitable specificity, because only when we understand that this is always going to be the case can we see that structure and process must be aspects of one another, rather than separable phenomena. And once we see this, we are compelled too to acknowledge the theoretical problem that is given by the radical separation between any one human being and another—a separation that is given as much in ideas about what we have in common as it is in outright rejection of any commonality at all. My point here is that human sociality in general cannot help but seek to overcome what is fundamentally a real existential anxiety by virtue of projecting onto the other, in any given encounter, an idea of who it might be. If, for example, I hold that you are my enemy—indeed, that you are probably not human at all—I am constituting an idea of who you are and of the relation between us, negative though it may be. Moreover, my idea of you and of the relation between us is going to be more or less highly differentiated to the extent that I am a more or less mature person with more or less well-established ideas. When I am a child, my ideas are more open to being changed in accordance with your projection of ideas onto me than they are when I am an adult, when it may be the case that whatever you do is bound to confirm my idea of you. Little Asaeli soon became less fearful of me, even though we did not live very close to one another and I did not see him every day. He was never, however, exactly hail-fellow-well-met in his relation to me, unlike another little boy of the same age who, despite living at a much greater distance from me and seeing me much less often, would, without prompting from his mother, call out enthusiastically to me, coming out from his house to the path whenever he saw me to engage me in conversation. Why? I can only think it was because this child's mother, when she herself was a little girl of six and seven, had known me well and had loved me. It can only have been she herself who made it plain to her child in her very tone of voice that I was utterly to be trusted.

Intersubjectivity and the Specificity of Relationship

Readers who know the work of Piaget will recognize that in describing these encounters, I am implicitly talking about how, over time, through assimilation and accommodation, our schemes of knowing become differentiated in being brought to bear on the peopled world. What I am trying to do here, in part, is to show how Piaget's idea of genetic epistemology becomes more compelling once we incorporate into it a recognition of intersubjectivity in all its specificity.[10]

As soon as they are able to fetch and carry, Fijian village children as young as three or four are sent on various errands to other houses. When five-year-old Samisoni brings dishes to us *takitaki* he knows that his giving of the dish will be reciprocated, and he can brave middle-aged Makareta's frequent bad temper because he knows that, provided he waits long enough, he will get what he has come for. He has an idea of what is due to him as a function of this particular relationship, even though he could not explain what or why. More important, perhaps, is that he does indeed get what he wants by virtue of a practical understanding of Fijian politeness: he does not say no to the offer of cabin crackers, for instance, but sensibly says nothing at all. He has already learned the coercive power of the gift, and even if he is somewhat apprehensive in his relations with Makareta, one might suppose that his own mother's confidence in sending him to us with a dish of food informs the development of his idea of himself as personally effective. For Fijians, historically and up to the present day, one's idea of one's personal efficacy is bound up with what one is able to consume.[11] It is not uncommon for a villager to say of a kinsperson to whom he or she is at once close and inferior in hierarchical terms: "He [or she] gives me everything I want." So hierarchy is subverted by an idea that the receiver is in fact the instigator of the gift. Makareta is of course able to discourse at length on the obligations of kinship (*veiwekani*) and of attendance on one another (*veiqaravi*) and sees her own responses to little Samisoni as residing there.

A previous study I did of ideas of kinship held by Sawaieke children between the ages of six and fourteen suggests that this would generally be true of any Fijian villager over the age of eleven to twelve or so.[12] The children's ideas suggest that it is mutual compassion that gives rise to kinship, where for adults it is kinship that stipulates mutual compassion as its fundamental obligation. So Makareta, who had seen me watching little Samisoni when he managed to get away with the little baked taro root he so desired, was later at pains to excuse or exonerate him. When he saw the little taro root, he wanted it, she explained, because it was little, like him, and would fit easily into his hand. It did not matter that he had already eaten baked taro; his desire was kindled by "na dalo lailai vinaka" (that nice little taro), and he had to have it. Here Ma put herself in little Samisoni's place and, in doing so, explained not only why he just had to have the taro, but also why none of the adults present told him to leave it alone or teased him for it as they might have done had little Samisoni's desire not been sympathetically understood. In the relation between little Samisoni and Makareta, we can see that kinship and mutual compassion are best understood as aspects of one another, fused by virtue of an ontogeny in which intersubjectivity is rooted in the ideas and practices of kinship and attendance on one another. The adult Makareta empathizes with little Samisoni; she is not merely complying with a normative view that she must reciprocate what is given. And little Samisoni knows not only that what he gives will be reciprocated, but that it is worth pushing for his own desires in the face of adult imperviousness, for he may well manage to get what he wants. Here, as is usual everywhere in the world, adult understandings structure the conditions under which children constitute over time their own ideas of the peopled world.

I trust that it is obvious enough that ethnography is enlightening precisely to the degree that the anthropologist is able to understand and analyze the nature of intersubjectivity and the specificity of its manifold forms among the people with whom she or he works, and that the capacity to do so depends on a close understanding of his or her own intersubjective relations with those same people.[13] Indeed, one can see the ethnographic endeavor as requiring a specialized, researched, and systematically recorded form of intersubjectivity. There are, however, likely to be aspects of this process that may escape observation because they are so very much taken for granted that they cannot easily be seen. Even to posit their existence requires an anthropological take on the world that recognizes not only that other people live the world in terms of their own understanding of it, just as we do, but that—despite the fact that their ideas may be very different from our own and not at all scientific—the world confirms their ideas for them, just as it confirms ours for us.

My perspective has been profoundly influenced by the work on cognition and autopoiesis of the great Chilean neurobiologist Humberto Maturana and his colleague Francisco Varela (1980, 1987). This enabled me to realize that genetic epistemology is the psychological aspect of human autopoiesis and to make historical continuity and transformation central to my model, for if my analysis is to be valid, it has to show how ideas are transformed by means of the selfsame process in which they are maintained. One way of achieving this degree of subtlety is to study ontogeny. This is because ethnographic studies of ontogeny enable the analyst to uncover what sense children are making of the conditions in the world created for them by adults and to show how ontogeny transforms ideas in the very process of constituting them. One can study the processes that give rise to people's ideas about the way the world is, and by these means explain how, in any given case, people come to hold as self-evident ideas of the world that they themselves have made.[14] I conduct my ethnographic studies of ontogeny in Fiji, but in principle, they could be done anywhere. So, for example, to understand ideas such as 'the individual in society' or 'sex is biological and gender is cultural', to uncover the process by which people come to hold these ideas as self-evident, we could do ethnographic studies of their ontogeny among, say, English, French, or North American adults and their children.[15]

A social analysis of the process of children's language acquisition should be able to reveal how, exactly, we arrive at our most fundamental ideas, for example, the idea of what language is good for. In learning to use language, we are learning about language itself—what it does and how. We are also learning how to be in relation to others, constituting an idea of ourselves as subjects as a function of intersubjectivity—a process of continuing differentiation in which we go on and on becoming ourselves. There is a popular idea in France that the French language is more precise and analytical than other languages. English speakers are not immune to a similar view of English. It is our Euro-American idea of language as an analytical tool that gives rise to those technological innovations that most powerfully persuade us that we are the ones whose ideas are objectively true, and that other people's ideas are manifestly a function of a so-called culturally relative subjectivity, to which by reason of our technological superiority, we are immune. A systematic participant observer study of middle-class French children from, say, four to twelve years old at school, at home, and elsewhere could reveal the ontogeny of the idea that language is to be valued as an analytical tool, as a means of explaining the nature of the world and the human condition. Note, too, that in the course of this same study, we might likewise discover the ontogeny of the complementary and opposing idea—also widespread in academia, especially among followers of Foucault—that discourse itself is constitutive of what persons are and can be. For all that they seem to be antithetical, these ideas are likewise aspects of one another, each manifesting an independence that is only apparent, like the two sides of the continuous surface that is a Möbius strip. An understanding of the ontogeny of this opposition would allow us to render the ideas genuinely analytical for those whose lives they may indeed inform.

Another example of the product of an intersubjectively driven ontogeny is my concern that we derive an epistemology that provides for anthropology as the whole science of what it is to be human.[16] This particular concern is

undoubtedly the product of a long history, which, by virtue of the differen-
tiating process that over time gives rise to conceptual distinctions, I have
in common with all those many thousands of other scientists who want to
arrive at explanations of the human condition that are at once logically and
evidentially compelling. This commonality resides in the way that I (like
all those other scientists) have made and continue to make meaning out of
meanings that others have made and are making. As scientists, we hold that
we discriminate between models of human being in terms of how well they
work. We apply the principle of parsimony: the elegance and simplicity of a
model resides in its ability to take in and explain coherently a multiplicity of
data, without sacrificing any of them or disavowing their manifold interconnections. The model of human being that I propose—for all that it is rooted
in the well-established biological theory of Maturana and Varela, the phenomenology of Merleau-Ponty, and Piaget's genetic epistemology—can seem to be
arcane and difficult to understand, when, in fact, it is neither. Actually, it is
so straightforward an idea that whenever a student or colleague understands
my model, they also tend to think that it is so self-evident that they knew it all
along. This raises an issue concerning how we know what we know that has
been made often enough by others before me, but which clearly continues to
want pointing out. I find it fascinating that although the specification of this
model was the outcome of a 20-year-long process of fieldwork and analysis
and working through various possible formulations, it is taken to be quite
another matter actually to demonstrate that mind is a function of the whole
person in intersubjective relations with others in the environing world—as if
the model and the ethnography that demanded its development were quite
independent of one another.

Conclusion

My general point is that relations between people mediate the processes in
and through which, over time, mind constitutes its own transforming products
and is constituted by them. The challenge, then, becomes that of fleshing out
a theory that is able to recognize that biological, psychological, and socio-
cultural data give us access not to different 'levels' of integration (and thus
of explanation) but to aspects of one and the same phenomenon. It follows
that we cannot build genuinely explanatory psychological or biological models
without reference (at least in principle) to the fact that our biology and psychology are embedded in a long history of specific intersubjectivities, whose
analysis is going to be germane to any biological and psychological model that
purports to be explanatory.

Christina Toren is Professor of Social Anthropology at the University of St Andrews. Her regional interests lie in Fiji, Melanesia, and the Pacific, and her anthropological interests in theories of human being, kinship, ritual, and exchange processes. She is the author of numerous articles and two monographs, *Making Sense of Hierarchy: Cognition as Social Process in Fiji* (1990) and *Mind, Materiality and History: Explorations in Fijian Ethnography* (1999).

Notes

1. Real names are not used in these field notes.
2. A syllogism entails formal deduction from major premise to minor premise to conclusion. For example, all parts of a fish are edible excluding the intestines. These internal organs are part of a fish and not intestines. Therefore, they can be eaten safely.
3. This observation is, I think, a new one—at least in the sense that, given that the world provides for all the meanings that humans can make, this has to be provided for in our conceptualization of mind. For a case study, see Toren (2007b).
4. In *Coral Gardens and Their Magic*, Malinowski (1935) draws out his idea of 'the context of situation', first put forward in an essay published twelve years earlier: "[T]he conception of meaning as *contained* in an utterance is false and futile. A statement, spoken in real life, is never detached from the situation in which it has been uttered" (Malinowski [1923] 1952: 307). Malinowski's ([1948] 1974: 239–40) empiricism was always tempered by an awareness that "[a]ny belief or any item of folklore is not a simple piece of information ... [it] must be examined in the light of diverse types of minds and of the diverse institutions in which it can be traced. To ignore this social dimension [of belief] ... is unscientific."
5. My phenomenology is derived primarily from the works of Merleau-Ponty ([1945] 1962, 1964, 1974) and Husserl ([1954] 1970, 1965).
6. Along with no mystery, there is also no need for any additional ideas such as 'actor-network theory' or 'extended cognition'. In the former case, the 'agency' attributed to objects is a real problem, not because objects are objects, but because it is questionable whether agency illuminates our understanding of human beings. In the latter case, one needs to extend cognition only if mind is characterized as a function of the brain, as in information-processing models of mind, or of the embodied nervous system, as in neuro-constructivist models (see note 10 below).
7. This formulation is derived from a synthesis of the works of Maturana and Varela (1980, 1987) on autopoiesis; Piaget ([1968] 1971) on genetic epistemology, especially with respect to his idea of the cognitive scheme as a 'self-regulating transformational system' (i.e., as an autopoietic process); Husserl's and Merleau-Ponty's phenomenology; and certain of Vygotsky's ([1934] 1986, [1936] 1978, 1981) insights on language acquisition. For a description of how this model works and how it may be applied to studies of ontogeny, see Toren (1999a, 1999b, 2002, 2004, 2007a, 2007b). For a recent, superb synthesis of biology, phenomenology, and mind sciences, see Evan Thompson's (2007) *Mind in Life*—a work that should become foundational for all the human sciences, including anthropology. 'Culture' remains a problem for Thompson's theory, but it is one that we can solve by taking the approach I argue for here, as elsewhere.
8. It has been suggested to me that my model of mind is more or less identical to that proposed by George Herbert Mead in his various works. This is true enough, insofar as Mead proposed a model of mind that is social through and through, his endeavor being, as Charles Morris put it in his introduction to *Mind, Self and Society*, "to show that mind and the self are without residue social emergents" (Mead 1934: xiv). Mead also adumbrates,

where he does not actually address, a number of the issues that have concerned me. For example, Mead (1934: 186) emphasizes "the temporal and logical pre-existence of the social process to the self-conscious individual that arises in it." We part company, however, with respect to the place of pragmatism in our models. I characterize mind as a function of the whole person that is constituted over time in intersubjective relations with others in the environing world. But for all this, mine is primarily an intentional model of mind, not a functional one. Here I depend on Merleau-Ponty, for whom intentionality "has two components: (i) that all consciousness is consciousness of something and (ii) that the 'unity of the world—before being posited by knowledge in a specific act of identification—is "lived" as readymade or already there' ([1945] 1962: xvii). Merleau-Ponty's idea of intentionality is important for the theoretical synthesis I [have proposed] because it asserts both that consciousness is a material phenomenon and that what we take for granted as given in the very stuff of the world ... is brought into being by ourselves as a function of our lived experience of the peopled world and of ourselves as given in it. So for example, for some years before I begin consciously to posit my own existence *as an object of knowledge*—who am I? where did I come from? what am I doing here?—I have already embodied a sense of the spatiotemporal dimensions of the world I live" (Toren 1999b: xx). Compare this with what Morris (1932: 276) has to say about Mead's functional theory: "The functional theory of mind may be said to take two main directions, depending on whether the term 'function' is meant to refer to purpose or role ... One may ... insist that mind is an instrument in the service of organic needs, that furnishing such organic aid is the function of mind, without thereby subscribing to any specific theory as to the nature of mind. Similarly, one could maintain that mentality is a characteristic of events in a certain role without holding that this functioning which constitutes mentality has as its purpose or function the furthering of organic behavior. The essential characteristic of the pragmatic interpretation is that both of these uses of the term 'function' are employed—the theory is doubly functional: mind, on the one hand, serves the purpose of furthering organic action, while, on the other hand, mind is regarded as the functioning of events that are not intrinsically mental." It is crucial to my model of ontogeny that the environing world of people and things is lived as 'readymade, already there', *before* it is explicitly (i.e., consciously) posited as an object of knowledge.

9. Note that intersubjectivity is not properly characterized as the communication of shared meanings; intersubjectivity entails an openness to others, an inevitable 'making sense' of others, but it does not entail ideas of 'role' or that a person be able to take the 'role of the other'. Contrast Mead's (1932: 86–87) social behaviorist theory of communication: "A society is a systematic order of individuals in which each has a more or less differentiated activity. The structure is really there in nature, whether we find it in the society of bees or that of human beings. And it is in varying degrees reflected in each individual. But ... it can get into the separate individual only insofar as he can take the parts of others while he is taking his own part. It is due to the structural organization of society that the individual, in successively taking the roles of others in some organized activity, finds himself selecting what is common in their interrelated acts, and so assumes ... the role of the generalised other." Mead (1934: 254) also contends that "[i]n the human group ... there is ... communication in which the person who uses this gesture and so communicates assumes the attitude of the other individual as well as calling it out in the other. He himself is in the role of the other person whom he is so exciting and influencing. It is through taking this role of the other that he is able to come back to himself and so direct his own process of communication ... The immediate effect of such role-taking lies in the control which the individual is able to exercise over his own response. The control of the action of the individual in a co-operative process can take place in the conduct of the individual himself if he can take the role of the other."

10. I have in mind here the neuro-constructivist approach to child development proposed by the neo-Piagetian psychologist Annette Karmiloff-Smith and her biological-connectionist colleagues (see, e.g., Elman et al. 1996; Karmiloff-Smith 1992, 1995, 1998). As

in Piaget's original model, development itself is the key to understanding how cognitive processes become structured in specific ways, with cognitive development being understood "in terms of self-organizing emergent structures arising from the complex interactions between both organism and environment" (Elman et al. 1996: 113). The careful experimental work that justifies the model comes to grips with the dynamism of organism and environment. However, various problems remain—primarily, that the neuro-constructivist model is founded in a representational theory of the mind/brain and, concomitantly, in an idea of the person in which sociality is one among numerous emergent developmental structures rather than inherent in every aspect of human being in the world. It follows that there is no awareness here that development is a historical process, that is to say, one that is always and in all respects inevitably embedded in historically constituted intersubjectivity.

11. Toren (1998) shows how the ultimate act of consumption, cannibalism, annihilated the other and evinced the *mana* of the eater 1998.

12. Toren (1999a) shows how the ontogenetic process of constituting kinship as intentionality makes any given Fijian able ideally to be kin with any other and, further, makes kinship serve at once as the expression of collective order, as the domain of relations in whose terms libidinal desire is structured, and as the ground of ideas of self and other.

13. Again, I have to emphasize that the character of intersubjectivity is always specific to the social relations that are engaged. See, for example, Evans (2006) for evidence not only that the nature of intersubjectivity is emphatically *not* to be taken for granted, but that it cannot be said to vary as a function of any gross formulation such as culture, class, or gender. Rather, the person/child is at any point in time continuously making sense of his or her self in relation to the ideas that various likewise unique others—peers, siblings, parents, teachers—have about who he or she is expected to be and become in the future.

14. "All economic and psychological explanations of a doctrine are true, since the thinker never thinks from any starting point but the one constituted by what he is. Reflection even on a doctrine will be complete only if he succeeds in linking up with the doctrine's history and the extraneous explanations of it, and in putting back the causes and meaning of the doctrine in an existential structure. There is, as Husserl says, a 'genesis of meaning' ... which alone, in the last resort, teaches us what the doctrine 'means'" (Merleau-Ponty [1945] 1962: xix). It follows that to understand how children constitute intersubjectively, over time, ideas such as hierarchy, god, kinship, and so on necessarily entails an analysis of the social relations that mediate the constituting process and, insofar as this is possible, their history (see, e.g., Toren 1990, 1999a, 1999b, 2002, 2004, 2007a, 2007b).

15. Since the publication in 1992 of *Beyond Modularity: A Developmental Perspective on Cognitive Science*, Annette Karmiloff-Smith (1995, 1998) has focused ever more closely on demonstrating that, rather than being innately specified, so-called cognitive modules are the outcome of developmental processes. I have made the same argument with respect to my work on the constitution over time of certain Fijian concepts, as well as in principle (Toren 1990; 1999b: intro., pt. 2). The idea is at once central to Piaget's ([1968] 1971) genetic epistemology and crucial for understanding how ideas come to be understood as self-evident, given in the stuff of the world: "[Cognitive] structures—*in being constructed*—give rise to that necessity which a priorist theories have always thought it necessary to posit at the outset. Necessity, instead of being the prior *condition* for learning, is its *outcome*" (ibid.: 62).

16. Compare Kapferer (2007: 78), who argues that anthropology is "a rigorous knowledge practice, by and large non-positivist in orientation, that claims the knowledge it produces has a degree of validity which, like any scientific practice, is never beyond contestation or immune from radical doubt or contestation."

References

Elman, Jeffrey L., Elizabeth A. Bates, Mark H. Johnson, Annette Karmiloff-Smith, Domenico Parisi, and Kim Plunkett. 1996. *Rethinking Innateness: A Connectionist Perspective on Development*. Cambridge, MA: MIT Press.

Evans, Gillian. 2006. *Educational Failure and Working Class White Children in Britain*. Basingstoke: Palgrave Macmillan.

Husserl, Edmund. [1954] 1970. *The Crisis of European Sciences and Transcendental Phenomenology: An Introduction to Phenomenological Philosophy*. Trans. and intro. David Carr. Evanston, IL, Northwestern University Press.

———. 1965. *Phenomenology and the Crisis of Philosophy*. Trans. with notes and intro. Quentin Lauer. New York: Harper Torchbooks.

Kapferer, Bruce. 2007. "Anthropology and the Dialectic of Enlightenment: A Discourse on the Definition and Ideals of a Threatened Discipline." *Australian Journal of Anthropology* 18, no. 1: 72–94.

Karmiloff-Smith, Annette. 1992. *Beyond Modularity: A Developmental Perspective on Cognitive Science*. Cambridge, MA: MIT Press.

———. 1995. "Annotation: The Extraordinary Cognitive Journey from Foetus through Infancy." *Journal of Child Psychology and Psychiatry* 36, no. 8: 1293–1313.

———. 1998. "Development Itself Is the Key to Understanding Developmental Disorders." *Trends in Cognitive Sciences* 2: 389–398.

Malinowski, Bronislaw. [1923] 1952. "The Problem of Meaning in Primitive Languages." Pp. 451–510 in *The Meaning of Meaning: A Study of the Influence of Language upon Thought and of the Science of Symbolism*, ed. C. K. Ogden and I. A. Richards. London: Routledge & Kegan Paul.

———. 1935. *Coral Gardens and Their Magic: A Study of the Methods of Tilling the Soil and of Agricultural Rites in the Trobriand Islands*. 2 vols. London: George Allen & Unwin.

———. [1948] 1974. *Magic, Science and Religion*. London: Souvenir Press.

Maturana, Humberto R., and Francisco J. Varela. 1980. *Autopoesis and Cognition: The Realization of the Living*. Dordrecht: D. Reider.

———. 1987. *The Tree of Knowledge: The Biological Roots of Human Understanding*. Rev. ed. Trans. Robert Paolucci; foreword J. Z. Young. Boston: Shambhala.

Mead, George Herbert. 1932. *The Philosophy of the Present*. Ed. Arthur E. Murphy. London: Open Court.

———. 1934. *Mind, Self and Society: From the Standpoint of a Social Behaviorist*. Ed. with intro. Charles W. Morris. Chicago, IL: University of Chicago Press.

Merleau-Ponty, Maurice. [1945] 1962. *Phenomenology of Perception*. Trans. by Colin Smith. London: Routledge & Kegan Paul.

———. 1964. *Signs*. 9th ed. Trans. and with intro. Richard C. McCleary. Evanston, IL: Northwestern University Press, 1964.

———. 1974. *Phenomenology, Language, Society: Selected Essays of Merleau-Ponty*. Ed. John O'Neill. London: Heinemann.

Morris, Charles W. 1932. *Six Theories of Mind*. Chicago, IL: University of Chicago Press.

Piaget, Jean. [1968] 1971. *Structuralism*. Trans. Chaninah Maschler. London: Routledge & Kegan Paul.

Thompson, Evan. 2007. *Mind in Life: Biology, Phenomenology and the Sciences of Mind*. Cambridge, MA: Harvard University Press.

Toren, Christina. 1990. *Making Sense of Hierarchy: Cognition as Social Process in Fiji*. L.S.E. Monographs in Social Anthropology. London: Athlone Press.

———. 1998. "Cannibalism and Compassion: Transformations in Fijian Notions of the Person." Pp. 95–115 in *Common Worlds and Single Lives: Constituting Knowledge in Pacific Societies*, ed. Verena Keck. London: Berg.

———. 1999a. "Compassion for One Another: Constituting Kinship as Intentionality in Fiji." 1996 Malinowski Lecture. *Journal of the Royal Anthropological Institute* 5: 265–280.

_____. 1999b. *Mind, Materiality and History: Explorations in Fijian Ethnography*. London: Routledge.

_____. 2002. "Space-Time Coordinates of Shame in Fiji." Pp. 215–231 in *Representing Space in Oceania*, ed. G. Bennardo and A. Duranti. Special issue of *Pacific Linguistics*.

_____. 2004. "Becoming a Christian in Fiji: An Ethnographic Study of Ontogeny." *Journal of the Royal Anthropological Institute* (N.S.) 10: 222–240. [Orig. 2003; republished because of major printing error].

_____. 2007a. "How Do We Know What Is True? The Case of *Mana* in Fiji." Pp. 307–335 in *Questions of Anthropology*, ed. Rita Astuti, Jonathan Parry, and Charles Stafford. Oxford: Berg.

_____. 2007b. "Sunday Lunch in Fiji: Continuity and Transformation in Ideas of the Household." *American Anthropologist* 109, no. 2: 285–295.

Vygotsky, L. S. [1934] 1986. *Thought and Language*. Cambridge, MA: Harvard University Press.

_____. [1936] 1978. *Mind in Society*. Cambridge, MA: Harvard University Press.

_____. 1981. "The Genesis of Higher Mental Functions." Pp. 144–188 in *The Concept of Activity in Soviet Psychology*, ed. J. V. Werstch. Armonk, NY: Sharpe.

Chapter 8

CAN ANTHROPOLOGY MAKE VALID GENERALIZATIONS?
Feelings of Belonging in the Brazilian Atlantic Forest

Susana de Matos Viegas

When we read Malinowski we get the impression that he is stating something which is of general importance. Yet how can this be? He is simply writing about Trobriand Islanders. Somehow he has so assimilated himself into the Trobriand situation that he is able to make the Trobriands a microcosm of the whole primitive world.

— Edmund Leach, "Rethinking Anthropology"

One of the defining features of anthropological knowledge is its capacity to challenge and renew through the experience of living among people with whom anthropologists form ongoing relationships. The transformation of these relationships into ethnographic descriptions with general validity is thus a fundamental starting point for anthropology's epistemological procedures and is the main subject of this chapter. Among the many definitions of the word 'general' (from the Latin word *generalis*), a particularly useful meaning for the approach proposed here is that "general" is what is "true in most instances but not without exceptions"; it can thus be seen as the "opposite of universal"[1] and as a procedure that aims to evaluate "the extension of a concept whose content or understanding is determined by abstraction."[2] Adopting this specific meaning of generalization, the principal goal of this chapter is to depict the epistemological procedures of generalization, specifically concerning ethnographic descriptions in anthropology, which are influenced by phenomenological perspectives. It begins by recognizing the centrality of experience and relation in the constitution of ethnographic knowledge in anthropology. Certainly, one of the singularities of this knowledge is its immersion in the world (cf. Engelke 2008: 3; Hastrup 2004: 456; Pina-Cabral 1992: 7; 2003). Fieldwork experience constitutes a complex web of engaged knowledge, in which the subject of experience is both the 'trained researcher' and the 'character in the local drama' (Hastrup 2004: 464; Pina-Cabral 1992). As is largely accepted, it is due to this engaged knowledge that anthropological ethnographies are in a privileged position to overcome any type of formal division between objectivity and subjectivity (Wilson 2004: 15). Moreover, as already noted by Wilhelm Dilthey, experience incorporates not only what is 'habitual, typical, and customary' (*Erfharung*), but also what is 'idiosyncratic, exceptional, and singular' (*Erlebnis*) (see Dilthey [1924] 1945; Jackson 1996: 27; Rickman [1976] 1986; Viegas and Gomes 2007: 12). Thus, when we make meaning of a face-to-face relationship, we are already making connections to a multiplicity of platforms of knowledge. The concept of intertextuality attempts to broaden this dimension, but it does so in a manner so foreign to the centrality of experience that it results in focusing exclusively on linguistic and textualist references, thereby depriving it of those connections.

Starting by conceiving ethnography as engaged and experience-like knowledge, this chapter will therefore depict how we achieve generalization in ethnographic descriptions. This will be explored through an ethnographic analysis of 'feelings of belonging' to territory as experienced by the Tupinambá of Olivença—an indigenous people who live in the Atlantic forest region of the south of Bahia (Brazil). For this study, I will use anthropological fieldwork carried out since 2003 in support of an indigenous land claim made to the Brazilian federal government, at the request of the Tupinambá, with whom I had worked several years ago (1997–1998).

In contrast to current procedures for land claims elsewhere, in Brazil the validation of anthropological knowledge in these processes is mainly an anthropological ethnographic study. This study has to represent a certain scale, because it is aimed at understanding the Tupinambá people and territory claimed as indigenous land (*terra indígena*) (cf. Viegas 2007b). The land claimed by the Tupinambá covers an area of approximately 50,000 hectares between a strip of coastline and a mountainous region connected by several rivers. Nowadays, this 50,000-hectare territory is inhabited by roughly 3,000 Tupinambá; 50 tradesmen, landowners, and tourist-resort owners; and about 10,000 peasants. The Tupinambá live scattered across the whole region, and their manner of inhabiting the territory presents significant differences at a social, economic, and even symbolic level.

In order to go from an ethnography centered in one area (the locality of Sapucaeira), where my former fieldwork was conducted, to the totality of the Tupinambá people and territory, a reflection over the scales of analysis becomes unavoidable. This is what this chapter explores, by showing how ethnography based in intersubjective analysis produces anthropological generalizations. This approach is in line with theoretical proposals and ways of doing ethnography in anthropology that consider experience and communication in its immersion in the world of relationships (e.g., Gow 2001; Pina-Cabral 2002; Toren 1999a, 1999b). In this way, it differentiates from existential anthropological perspectives that regard experience closer to cultural meanings and existential dilemmas (e.g., Jackson 2002, 2005), contributing to epistemological perspectives that need further consolidation. The main contribution of this chapter to ways of thinking about epistemological procedures in anthropology is to show that valid ethnographic generalizations can be achieved through the analysis of how people become beings in the world.

The chapter discusses how, for the Tupinambá, in the process of becoming a being-in-the-world, living in a 'residential compound' is at the heart of feelings of belonging to the territory. A residential compound is constituted by an extended family, and in this rural region of Olivença, people call these residential compounds *lugares* (lit., places). In 1998, I lived for a period of time in one of these kinship compounds in Sapucaeira. The 2003 fieldwork was, of course, very different from what is usually practiced in anthropology. Two particular distinctions should be highlighted as relevant to the aim of this chapter. The first is that the fieldwork carried out in 2003 was 'official', which meant that (1) a government decree had to be published, giving the exact time that the anthropologist would arrive and leave the region of fieldwork, and (2) until the research was handed in, the anthropologist was not to visit the area or carry out fieldwork without the knowledge and permission of FUNAI,[3] who would send a person to accompany the anthropologist during any visit he or she might choose to make. Under these conditions, increasing the time of fieldwork for a period longer than one or two months becomes unfeasible because, among other reasons, it is an expensive way of doing fieldwork and places limits on the availability of funds budgeted by FUNAI.

In Brazil, the fieldwork required by the anthropologist in indigenous land claims is intended to be carried out, in principle, by a researcher who has already done fieldwork in the region. Validation of the anthropological ethnographic argument developed by previous ethnographic descriptions and the capacity to make valid concepts are thus unavoidably put at stake. I will use the research requirements for the validation of ethnography to expose the epistemological issue that was particularly incisive in this case, and which gives this chapter its title, that is, "Can Anthropology Make Valid Generalizations?" And if so, then how?

Is Generalization Important to Anthropology?

The issue of generalization was highly contested by the literary and reflexive turn in cultural anthropology and postmodern perspectives. Let us take just one emblematic example: the argument by Lila Abu-Lughod ([1991] 2006), in which the author holds against the use of the concept of culture and considers generalization as part of the problem in the use of this idea in anthropology. Alternatively, she proposes that anthropology should do "ethnographies of the particular" (ibid.: 475). Among other reasons, she maintains that the problem with generalization is that "anthropologists commonly generalize about communities by saying that they are characterized by certain institutions, rules, or ways of doing things," for instance, saying things such as "the Bongo-Bongo are polygynous" (ibid.). We agree with this statement, of course, and she is also right to say that anthropologists should ask, instead, "how a particular set of individuals—for instance, a man and his three wives in a Bedouin community in Egypt … —live the institution that we call polygyny" (ibid.). What is apparent in this otherwise interesting point of view is that, for Abu-Lughod, there appears to be no alternative except to refuse all generalization, full stop.

A further problem arises when the author connects the issue of generalization to the critique and rejection of the concept of culture. Culture is not useful, follows Abu-Lughod's argument, because it implies a generalization of meanings among a group of individuals, which therefore could be defined as shared meanings ([1991] 2006: 475):

> When one generalizes from experiences and conversations with a number of specific people in a community, one tends to flatten out differences among them and to homogenize them. The appearance of an absence of internal differentiation makes it easier to conceive of a group of people as a discrete, bounded entity, like 'the Nuer', 'the Balinese' and the 'Awlad 'Ali Bedouin' who do this or that and believe such and such. The effort to produce general ethnographic descriptions of people's beliefs or actions tends to smooth over contradictions, conflicts of interest, and doubts and arguments.

In sum, Abu-Lughod asserts that anthropology should refuse to make generalizations in order to write ethnographies of the particular, wherein people's power of negotiation and agency in social life would be highlighted. However, there is a problem in identifying generalization with the opposite of particular, with the representation of the parts by the whole, with the substitution of feelings by the norm.[4] In this view, only the parts can be multi-vocal—only the parts live in tension, in dissonance, and even in inequality.

If we assume, however, as suggested above, that what is general can be opposed to the universal and that the experience in which ethnography is based incorporates the particular as much as the general, the ordinary as much as the exceptional, tensions as much as consensus, feelings as well as norms, then there is no need to identify generalization with uniformity, univocality, and normativity, and thus to reject it out of hand. If we assume that experience is the starting point of ethnographic analysis and that "the agents always relate to one another in a field historically marked by domination and power" (Pina-Cabral 2008: 77), it does not make sense to identify culture with more consensual or even more *groupal* entities. Recognizing this centrality of experience in the construction of ethnographic knowledge in anthropology, Hastrup (2004) proposes that we move on from a "horizontal generalization," whose objective would be to proceed to the identification of shared systems (such as those rejected by Abu-Lughod), to a "vertical generalization," "the processes by which meanings are established, challenged and altered" (ibid.: 466).

While Abu-Lughod identifies generalization with uniform, normative, and reified knowledge, arguing for ethnographies of the particular, Edmund Leach's ([1961] 1982: 1) famous argument accuses anthropology of doing "impeccably detailed historical ethnographies of particular peoples" that refuse to make generalizations. In a way, the preoccupations of Abu-Lughod in the 1990s and those of Leach in the 1960s seem absolutely antithetical. Leach is concerned that by doing such detailed historical ethnographies, anthropology stops making "comparative generalisations" (ibid.). He raises an idea that is of the utmost importance for the present discussion. He argues that by refusing to make generalizations, anthropology can very easily turn to generalized abstractions, such as the fictitious category of 'the primitive man'. This appears in functionalist ethnographies, as Leach explains in the quotation from the epigraph of this chapter, when they describe a located place like the Trobriands as "a microcosm of the whole primitive world" (ibid.).

The refusal of generalization, therefore, does not appear to be a viable option for anthropology. To recognize and identify the epistemological tools that make of ethnography general knowledge, and at the same time to understand how we effectively evaluate the extension of the phenomena that we describe, is fundamental for our ability to acknowledge the types of categories that we use and to avoid abrupt epistemological leaps. The question of the scale of analysis we are using is therefore inevitable to consider, and of course we know that ethnographic descriptions of details of daily life are not an anthropological scale of analysis. As Charles Stafford (2008: S128, S133) has put it, anthropology looks at the human experience with microscopic eyes, but as it speaks of human experience and considers its vast (at times holistic) connections, its scale of analysis is far from being small—even when compared with the scales of other social and human sciences.

Another important issue, which is sometimes forgotten in contemporary reflections about generalization and scale, is anthropology's disciplinary legacy and its epistemological consequences. As the post-structural and postmodern turns were taking place, anthropology was also reaching a point of sophisticated theoretical reflection that was fueled by comparative analysis. Examples include Strathern's (1988) theory of personhood, which interlinks Melanesia, Marxist theory, and feminism; João de Pina-Cabral's (1986, 1991a, 1991b) discussion of the primary social units in southern Europe, which covers debates on kinship theory, the Mediterranean, and social theory; and Viveiros de Castro's (1998) Amerindian perspectivism thesis, which is fueled by ethnographic Americanist debates of the last two or three decades and theoretical reflection on the nature-culture debate. I would argue that, at this level, comparison does not constitute a method of analysis but rather a generalizing epistemology of particular phenomena in anthropology.

This perspective on comparison and scale allows us to consider that what is at issue is "comparing the incommensurable." Formulated by Marcel Detienne, this expression was adopted by Goldman and Viveiros de Castro (2006) to suspend the idea of sustaining comparisons in the obsessive evaluation of similarities of scale, type, theme, or even the nature of objects being compared: "The notion of commensurability supposes that what commensurates two things is external to them. Two things are commensurate as a function of a third, supposedly nature in itself … We believe that one of the things that anthropology demonstrates is that commensurability is an internal, not an external, process" (ibid.: 186).

The ethnographic analysis by Tânia Stolze Lima (1999), which illustrates and is at the base of the theoretical proposals of Amerindian perspectivism, helps us to understand this idea of comparing the incommensurable, as well as to apprehend that certain ethnographic concepts have a general validity. Lima (1999, 2005) describes the daily life of the Juruna, along with their greatest desires and ideals (e.g., hunting pigs in the river), which are sometimes expressed in their dream life and are regularly brought into conversation. These (almost) holistic articulations contribute toward the understanding of certain general principles. These include, for example, how for the Juruna certain animals, and principally wild pigs, have a 'point of view' and thus occupy the position of subject. They have the same habits as the Juruna: they drink a lot of fermented drinks, for example; return to the abandoned locations where the dead are buried; live in communities divided by family relations and led by a chief with shamanic powers, and so on (Lima 1999: 109). The ethnographic texture of Lima's analysis allows the conceptual understanding of a point of view as being a simultaneously ontological and epistemological position (ibid.: 113): "A proposition such as 'the Juruna think that animals are humans,' besides deviating appreciably from their discursive style, is a false one, ethnographically speaking. They say that 'the animals, to themselves, are human.' I could, then, rephrase this as 'the Juruna think that the animals think they are humans.' Clearly, the verb 'to think' undergoes an enormous semantic slippage as it passes from one segment of the phrase to the other."

The identification of the point of view with a subject is also expressed in language. It is in translation to Portuguese that the Juruna epistemic subjectivism gains grammatical expression. Lima (1999: 116) describes how even she had difficulties in admitting this radical subjectivism, when it reached the point of saying "to me, it rained":

Certain phrases spoken to me in Portuguese, such as 'this is beautiful to me', 'for him the animal turned into a jaguar,' 'to us, there appeared prey while we were making the canoe', seemed to refer exclusively to the grammatical structure of a language which I did not master but which nonetheless became transparent through the Juruna's Portuguese. Even after I began to put together one or two phrases, the constructions which invited these types of translation never ceased to sound strange; without doubt, I would classify them as the most difficult Juruna practice to assimilate. *Amdna uhe w'I*—it is not easy to utter these words without becoming disconcerted, unpleasantly or otherwise. I felt I was saying 'to me, it rained' and not 'it was raining there, where I was.' This way of relating even the most independent and alien phenomena to the self leaves its mark on Juruna cosmology.

This description and understanding of the concept of point of view becomes clear in a range of epistemological procedures. It is worth noting the following three, due to their relevance on the issue of scales and generalization. First, stemming from the long-term fieldwork experience of the anthropologist with the Juruna is Lima's ability to contrast her first impressions in the field with those resulting from the maturation of her knowledge over time.

A second procedure, which signals the general and generalizing character of the concept of point of view, results from the holistic articulation between the diverse dimensions of Juruna life, for instance, between daily life and cosmological understandings of the world. We could call this 'the procedure of contextualizing through partial connection', which would thus be part of the evaluation of the expansive scale of ethnographic knowledge by showing that "everything is embedded in, and connected to, everything else" (Stafford 2008: S133). Contextualization would also be "constituted by the world of things as it is presented to human experience" (Jackson 1996: 11; see also Dilley 1999a: 31). From the point of view of the most incisive debates on the question of context in anthropology, we could also recognize other types of contextualizations, closer to Strathern's notion, of "partial contexts in the form of partial connections wherein different frames or 'scales' … are adopted to generate competing orders of knowledge that each make sense of social life" (Dilley 1999a: 32). Contextualization constitutes, at this level, diffuse referential worlds (cf. Pina-Cabral 2003), at the same time referring to the specific type of holistic or internal connection that implies our recognition of "the idea that knowledge/understanding is achieved via interaction and concrete situated practice" (Harvey 1999: 217).

Finally, the third procedure highlighted here illuminates not only the life of the Juruna but also that of many other Amerindians. We could refer to this last epistemological procedure as multiple strategies of comparison. They appeal to the overlap of levels that weave the value of anthropological generalizations. The concept of the point of view directs us to many other Tupi and other Amerindian ethnographies, thus allowing for broader levels of abstraction implied in the Amerindian perspectivism (see Viveiros de Castro 1998).

From the perspective debated and examined here, we must of course state clearly that important achievements based on generalizations are reached by means of the history of anthropology. In refusing to think seriously about the specifically generalizing character of producing ethnography in anthropology, the discipline may end up making abstractions related to more normative and reified categories, such as (after 'the primitive world') 'the globalized world', 'the capitalist world', or 'the Arab world'. Thus, a first answer to the question mark in this chapter is that generalization must undoubtedly be taken seriously in contemporary methods of producing ethnographic knowledge in anthropology.

The World in *Lugares*

I will now explore the construction of generalized ethnographic concepts from a phenomenological perspective about feelings of belonging among the Tupinambá. This will be based on the idea that living in a residential compound, as observed in a universe of 300 people (in the locality of Sapucaeira), may be extrapolated to apply to 3,000 people who inhabit a 50,000-hectare territory. The apparently obvious solution to this issue would be to use quantitative data, which was in fact a requirement for the indigenous land claim study and was thus effectively done. We organized and carried out a survey, as extensive as possible, into how the Tupinambá whom we visited were making their residential arrangements. We made use of GPS and genealogical diagrams to quantify the distribution of indigenous people into types of residence: (1) residential compounds, (2) separate houses, and (3) houses located in large farms, as shown in the following table. This information clearly shows that (1) a far greater number of Tupinambá live in residential compounds (965) than in separate houses (418), and (2) a far greater number of houses exist in residential compounds or *lugares* (227) than in separate areas (93).

This quantitative approach, which is nothing but the 'elementary statistics' so often present in anthropological studies (cf. Pina-Cabral 2008: 71), allows

TABLE 1 The Number of Houses and People in Extended Family Residential Compounds and in Separate Houses by Locality, 2003–2004

Localities	Residential compounds	Separate houses	People in residential compounds	People in separate houses
Sapucaeira Cima, S. de Baixo, Gravatá	61	25	260	103
Acuípe de Cima, A.do Meio	29	18	123	82
Curupitanga, Pixix, S. Negra, C. Sº Pedro	39	10	146	55
A. Baixo, A. Olivença (Atlantic coast)	34	11	166	61
Santana, Santanha and Sierras	64	29	270	117
Total	**227**	**93**	**965**	**418**

Source: Genealogical survey (2003–2004 fieldwork).

FIGURE 1 Diagram Chart Representing the Information in Table 1.
Created by Vivóeusébio Graphic Design Studio.

us to translate an ethnographic argument into numbers. The GPS survey created a map showing the location of all the residential areas visited. However,
the data fail to provide effective generalizations based on ethnographic-like
thinking (i.e., based on experience and relatedness). The precise reasons why
quantitative data help ethnography gain an empirical reference but fail to
confer elements that could assist in the making of abstractions should then be
further considered.

In order to develop generalized ethnographic concepts from a phenomenological perspective, the point of departure is the idea that "as humans, we cannot
help making meaning of the world—but we never do this in isolation. Rather,
we make meaning intersubjectively" (Toren 2002: 107). From my observation of
everyday life in Sapucaeira, the dynamics of affects and belonging are constituted in the *lugares*. Take the daily life of children who live in the same residential compound: they move freely between houses as they play together, bathe
together, prepare manioc roots, fight to get an adult's attention, and experience
the affective dynamics between relatives, especially between women who may
become their mothers. As soon as they learn to walk, they move about between
houses to play. This freedom of movement, however, does not come about as a
result of shared parental roles, as often happens in other contexts where these

kinds of residential compounds are crucial for the making of sociality. The child grows up in the world of kinship residential compound relations, but at every instance of its life it belongs to only one mother and one house.

In the first months of life and until it can walk, a baby is carried in its mother's arms and then perched on its mother's hip. It is very rare that someone thinks of holding another person's baby and does so only if the mother is present. Thus, growing up from the baby's point of view would be letting go of its mother's arms and then joining other children to play: first, siblings, who live in the same house, and then cousins, who live in other houses in the same residential compound. It is rare to see small children visiting other *lugares*; this usually takes place only on special occasions. Their lives are confined to the space in the *lugares*—the ravine, houses, trails, forest, and gardens. Children begin to move about more and go farther afield when they are between the ages of nine and eleven (cf. Viegas 2003).

When they marry, the movement between these residential compounds is of the utmost importance. Regardless of how a husband and wife began their courtship, whenever the start of a relationship is described, it is frequently said that the boy 'fetched' a woman. The expression has various meanings that I will not go into now, but it also describes very objectively the idea of going forth to fetch a wife outside the kinship residential compound where one lives and bringing her back (cf. Viegas 2008a). Daily life in a house built by and for the couple will eventually produce the conjugal relationship.

From the first years of marriage, since mothers-in-law live in the same residential compound, they tend to assist their daughters-in-law after childbirth. This starts off a process of mutual support but also one of affective dynamics, at various levels. Among the Tupinambá of Sapucaeira, I observed that the integration of wives into the life of the residential compound is comparatively easy compared to what has been observed in other virilocal Amerindian contexts. This happens, at least in part, because they often come to the compound early in their lives (sometimes when they are just 12 years old) and may become peers of their sisters-in-law, who live in the same compound. As the years go by, girls of the same age may have interests in common. This is sometimes connected to the solidarities that arise out of gender dynamics. There are also events in life that may pit sisters-in-law against each other. This happens, for instance, if the couple separate and their offspring become the children of the sister-in-law (cf. Viegas 2007a: 143–180). As a result, young married women maintain links with their parents in the residential compound where they were born. Even when their parents live in other localities in the Olivença region (some of them far away), the young girls try not to lose touch with their relatives and visit them regularly. If a couple separate, the wife may have to leave her children and return to her parents' house, which also explains hegemonic gender values that identify women with a tendency to change place (cf. Viegas 2008a).

The consequences of the changes that occurred in the lives of the Tupinambá since 2002–2003, when they formalized their indigenous identity and land claim to the federal state of Brazil, were immediate and involved a range of aspects. For instance, the Tupinambá who inhabited different parts of the territory and who, in many cases, had never met each other face to face were now engaged in political meetings and exchanging life experiences. They also elected one sole political leader to represent them at the federal state level and with NGOs. The government health services for indigenous people began to provide the Tupinambá with medical assistance. Public ceremonies, during which the Tupinambá dressed in 'indigenous clothes', were performed in order to change the public image of them as being rootless, scattered, and assimilated among the rural population. And, of course, conflicts between landowners and indigenous people in the region erupted immediately—mainly, because if the land is returned to the Tupinambá, these landowners will have to sell their investments to the federal state and leave the region.

The change in the life of the Tupinambá was felt at once in the kinship residential compounds that I had got to know well during my stay in 1997–1998. In March 2002, my hosts sent me a letter describing this change: "Dear friend Susana: First, I want to tell you that after you left *many new things have happened in this community*" (emphasis added). They then mention new types of 'indigenous' activities: "We have a woman *cacique* [main leader], other leader, a health team and indigenous schools ... our indigenous community has projects for an individual *roça* (land clearing), a collective *roça*, medicine, handicraft, and ceramics. Jupará and Care of São Paulo [two NGOs] are providing support. Alice and Mauro [a young couple who were also part of the residential compound where I lived] are well and are working in handicrafts and make necklaces and rings from *dende* coconuts and *buri*."

Mauro, the man referred to in this letter, was only in his forties when he became unable to earn a living as a rural laborer due to health problems. This is why they mentioned to me that in 2002 he was able to work again. Doing indigenous 'handicraft'—an activity I never saw in the Sapucaeira region in 1998—was more suitable to his physical condition than rural activities and could be carried out in the residential compound where he lived. Even if the handicrafts that the Tupinambá are producing are not very successful in the Brazilian market, they would never have entered the market in the first place if they did not have the 'indigenous' trademark.

When I returned to the Olivença region in 2003, the relevance of the *lugares* as places of belonging became even more apparent to the understanding of processes of change that had occurred since 1998. Changes were shaped most intensively in the experience of living in *lugares:* new networks between *lugares* became possible, new ways of belonging to the territory and landscape were achieved—namely, by having a *cacique*, or main leader, and through webs between residential compounds that were now spread throughout the landscape. Statistical or numerical data did not help in the effective understanding of these changes. The epistemological procedures mentioned in the previous section—long-term fieldwork experience, contextualizing through partial connection, and multiple strategies of comparison—were more helpful to the understanding of lived experience and historicity among the Tupinambá, even in these changing times.

Generalization

A first point to make is that the ethnographic descriptions in the previous section are in themselves filled with knowledge about other ethnographies on the subject. In terms of kinship dynamics among the Tupinambá, for instance, they are strongly inscribed in comparisons of ethnographies on Amerindian contexts (see, e.g., Gow 1991, 1997, 2000), especially the Tupi in Amazonia (cf. Fausto 2001; Viveiros de Castro 1992), as well as ethnographies on raising children in lower-class urban areas of Brazil (Fonseca 2004), on matrilateral Afro-Bahian family dynamics (Marcelin 1999; Pina-Cabral 2007), and on the extended patriarchal family in northeastern rural areas in Brazil (Woortman 1995).

To understand how the Tupinambá developed a sense of belonging to their territory, a second layer of abstraction is necessary to account for the experience of inhabiting a territory during a constant processes of land expropriation between the Tupinambá and different social actors. The story of each kinship residential compound and the memories of where people lived and how they moved between localities are crucial to the Tupinambá, because they also explain how memory of the territory is connected to the historical experience of living in this territory. In fact, areas of cultivation that have been abandoned and fruit trees that were part of residential areas where people used to live are the memory markers of the lived territory for the Tupinambá (Viegas 2006; 2007a: 85–88, 207–224, 288–295; 2008b).

Another layer of abstraction arises from comparison in anthropology. Sociality produced in the *lugares* begins to gain a generalizing value in relation to, for instance, Americanist and Melanesian debates on sociality, with the latter emphasizing relation as the core of sociality, and the former focusing on the idea of investment in small solidarities, as described in various contexts for Amazonia (Rivière 1984; Strathern 1988; Viveiros de Castro 1992). A further comparative approach, which helps to explain the centrality of life in *lugares*, arises from the concept of producing sociality through 'immediacy'. This idea has been developed by Nurit Bird-Davis (1994: 590, 593) in relation to the Nakaya, who live in a bamboo forest region in South India that was partially destroyed in the early twentieth century for the cultivation of rubber and coffee. The notion of immediacy focuses on relatives with whom personal, intense contact is maintained in daily face-to-face relations, instead of those of more distant generations, for instance. In this explanation, Bird-David draws our attention to the type of relations that compare to the value given to direct personal experience among the Tupinambá of Olivença in the *lugares*—that is to say, to the importance of the ties of immediacy in the daily production of social life.

More abstract ideas may then arise from these debates. It allows us, for example, to refute theories on acculturation and assimilation that have in the past accounted for the disappearance of the Tupi people inhabiting the Atlantic coast of Brazil. These theories state that the Tupi were quickly assimilated into the regional way of life because their social organization was based on 'dispersed family models' whereby solidarity was restricted to local groups scattered in the territory (Darcy Ribeiro in Turner 1993: 44). An ethnography of the Tupinambá's lived experience in *lugares* provides us, however, with a different picture of that history of solidarity. In fact, if the Tupinambá have survived in the region of Olivença and maintained relations of belonging to that territory, it has been at least partially because, in the course of their lived experience in the area, sociality has not depended on aggregative processes of solidarity, based on large social units, but rather has encompassed investment in immediacy, mainly through the constitution of meaningful relationships in the residential compound.

Conclusion

The argument developed in this chapter allows us to recognize the importance of generalization and comparison in the organization of levels of knowledge in anthropology. If anthropology produces a body of knowledge that distinguishes itself from other forms of knowing the world, it is inevitable that the validity of concepts in anthropology arises, first of all, from experience and relation, which then constitute and are constituted by different layers of contextualization and comparison. It becomes important, thus, to find a combination of "comparative strategies" that "illuminate, at the same time, the phenomenon that we observe and the epistemological profile of our questions" (Gregor and Tuzin 2001: 15). In a similar sense, it is necessary to recognize the plurality of qualitative comparative methodologies (Gingrich and Fox 2002b: 2, 9, 12, 19; Strathern 2002: xvii).

This is why the equivalence between the 'worlds' that we compare should not be considered commensurable. Comparison is more of an epistemic kind, a relation *de jure*. Finally, in this chapter the multiple commitments between theoretical tradition, in which comparison has a prominent position, and the broad field of ethnographic knowledge, as a central part of the anthropological project, have been reaffirmed. This allows us to evaluate the importance of successive generalizations, which are always constituted in and through ethnographic descriptions (cf. Pina-Cabral 1991a; Sanjek 1996; Toren 2002; Viveiros de Castro 1999: 154).[5]

As a final conclusion, we can thus argue that generalization, as an operation that aims to fix the extension of a concept, is carried out in anthropology by means of experience, contextualization, and multiple strategies of comparison. In a way, the epistemological tools that allow us to reach valid generalizations correspond simply to the axis of anthropological training. Through the case discussed in this chapter, I have argued that valid generalizations, which do not necessarily mean uniformity, will always need to be sustained in processes that combine intersubjectivity with the analysis of data and the abstractions that arise from comparative thinking. From this point of view, we can say that anthropology is now better equipped to make valid generalizations than it was decades ago. We should not waste this moment.

Susana de Matos Viegas is a Senior Research Fellow in Social and Cultural Anthropology at the Institute of Social Sciences, University of Lisbon. Her main research interests are the study of place and kinship, ethnicity and identity among Amerindians, and the Tupi, in Lowland South America. She has carried out fieldwork among the Tupinambá who live in the south of Bahia (Brazil). Among her publications is an ethnographical and theoretical analysis of the Tupinambá, *Terra Calada* (2007).

Notes

1. *Shorter Oxford English Dictionary on Historical Principles*, vol. 1, 2nd ed. (Oxford: Clarendon Press, 1939): 783.
2. *Enciclopédia Verbo Luso Brasileira da Cultura* (Lisbon: Editorial Verbo, 1963): 317.
3. FUNAI (Fundação Nacional do Índio, or the National Indian Foundation) is the department of the Brazilian Ministry of Justice that deals with indigenous affairs.
4. This problem has been largely identified as a type of sociocentrism from which cultural constructionism could not detach itself (cf. Pina-Cabral 2008: 78–81).
5. In the ethnography of the Tupinambá de Olivença, I systematically develop this rehabilitation of an open and comparative vision of regionalism through plural strategies of comparison, which say as much about the socio-structural aspects of cultural experiences (cf. Viegas 2007a).

References

Abu-Lughod, Lila. [1991] 2006. "Writing against Culture." Pp. 466–479 in *Anthropology in Theory: Issues in Epistemology*, ed. Henrietta Moore and Todd Sanders. Oxford: Blackwell Publishing.

Bird-David, Nurit. 1994. "Sociality and Immediacy: Or, Past and Present Conversations on Bands." *Man* 29: 583–603.

Dilley, Roy. 1999a. "Introduction: The Problem of Context." Pp. 1–46 in Dilley 1999b.

_____, ed. 1999b. *The Problem of Context*. New York: Berghahn Books.

Dilthey, Wilhelm. [1928] 1945. "La vivencia." Pp. 419–423 in *Psicologia y Teoria del Conocimiento*. Mexico: Fondo de Cultura Económica.

Engelke, Matthew. 2008. "The Objects of Evidence." *Journal of the Royal Anthropological Institute* (N.S.): S1–S21.

Fausto, Carlos. 2001. *Inimigos Fiéis: História, guerra e xamanismo na Amazônia*. São Paulo: University of São Paulo.

Fonseca, Claudia. 2004. "The Circulation of Children in a Brazilian Working-Class Neighborhood: A Local Practice in a Globalized World." Pp. 165–181 in *Cross-Cultural Approaches to Adoption*, ed. Fiona Bowie. London: Routledge.

Gingrich, Andre, and Richard Fox, eds. 2002a. *Anthropology, by Comparison*. London: Routledge.

_____. 2002b. "Introduction." Pp. 1–24 in Gingrich and Fox 2002a.

Goldman, Marcio, and Eduardo Viveiros de Castro. 2006. "Abaeté, Rede de Antropologia Siméstrica: Entrevista com Márcio Goldman e Eduardo Viveiros de Castro." *Cadernos de Campo* 14/15: 177–190.

Gow, Peter. 1991. *Of Mixed Blood: Kinship and History in Peruvian Amazonia*. Oxford: Clarendon Press.

_____. 1997. "Parentesco como consciência humana: O caso dos Piro." *Mana* 3, no. 2: 39–65.
_____. 2000. "Helpless: The Affective Preconditions of Piro Social Life." Pp. 46–63 in *Love and Anger: The Aesthetics of Conviviality in Native Amazonia*, ed. Joanna Overing and Alan Passes. London: Routledge.
_____. 2001. *An Amazonian Myth and Its History*. Oxford: Oxford University Press.
Gregor, Thomas A., and Donald Tuzin, eds. 2001. *Gender in Amazonia and Melanesia: An Exploration of the Comparative Method*. Berkeley: University of California Press.
Harvey, Penelope. 1999. "Culture and Context: The Effects of Visibility." Pp. 213–236 in Dilley 1999b.
Hastrup, Kirsten. 2004. "Getting It Right: Knowledge and Evidence in Anthropology." *Anthropological Theory* 4: 455–472.
Jackson, Michael. 1996. "Introduction: Phenomenology, Radical Empiricism and Anthropological Critique." Pp. 1–50 in *Things as They Are: New Directions in Phenomenological Anthropology*, ed. Michael Jackson. Bloomington: Indiana University Press.
_____. 2002. "The Exterminating Angel: Reflections on Violence and Intersubjective Reason." *European Journal of Anthropology* 39: 137–148.
_____. 2005. *Existential Anthropology: Events, Exigencies and Effects*. New York: Berghahn Books.
Leach, Edmund. [1961] 1982. "Rethinking Anthropology." Pp. 1–27 in *Rethinking Anthropology*. New York: Athlone Press.
Lima, Tânia Stolze. 1999. "The Two and Its Many: Reflections on Perspectivism in a Tupi Cosmology." *Ethnos* 64, no. 1: 107–131.
_____. 2005. *Um peixe olhou para mim: O povo Yudjá e a perspectiva*. São Paulo: University of São Paulo.
Marcelin, Louis Herns. 1999. "A linguagem da casa entre os negros no recôncavo baiano." *Mana* 5, no. 2: 31–60.
Pina-Cabral, João de. 1986. *Sons of Adam, Daughters of Eve: The Peasant Worldview of the Alto Minho*. Oxford: Clarendon Press.
_____. 1991a. "A unidade social primária na Europa mediterrânica e atlântica." Pp. 135–159 in Pina-Cabral 1991c.
_____. 1991b. "As categorias de comparação regional: Uma crítica à noção de Mediterrâneo." Pp. 69–89 in Pina-Cabral 1991c.
_____. 1991c. *Os contextos da antropologia*. Lisbon: Difel.
_____. 1992. "Against Translation: The Role of the Researcher in the Production of Ethnographic Knowledge." Pp. 1–23 in *Europe Observed*, ed. João de Pina-Cabral and John Campbell. Basingstoke: Macmillan Press.
_____. 2003. "Semelhança e Verossimilhança: Horizontes da narrativa etnográfica." *Mana* 9, no. 1: 109–122.
_____. 2007. "Mães, pais e nomes no Baixo Sul (Bahia, Brasil)." Pp. 63–88 in *Nomes: gênero, etnicidade e família*, ed. João de Pina-Cabral and Susana de Matos Viegas. Coimbra: Almedina.
_____. 2008. "Sem palavras: Etnografia, hegemonia e quantificação." *Mana* 14, no. 1: 61–86.
Rickman, H. P. [1976] 1986. "Introduction." Pp. 1–31 in *Dilthey: Selected Writings*, ed. H. P. Rickman. Cambridge: Cambridge University Press.
Rivière, Peter. 1984. *Individual and Society in Guiana: A Comparative Study of Amerindian Social Organisation*. Cambridge. Cambridge University Press.
Sanjek, Roger. 1996. "Ethnography." Pp. 193–198 in *Encyclopedia of Social and Cultural Anthropology*, ed. Alan Banard and Jonathan Spencer. London, Routledge.
Stafford, Charles. 2008. "Linguistic and Cultural Variables in the Psychology of Numeracy." *Journal of the Royal Anthropological Institute* (N.S.): S128–S141.
Strathern, Marilyn. 1988. *The Gender of the Gift: Problems with Women and Problems with Society in Melanesia*. Berkeley: University of California Press.
_____. 2002. "Foreword: Not Giving the Game Away." Pp. xiii–xx in Gingrich and Fox 2002a.

Toren, Christina. 1999a. "Introduction: Mind, Materiality and History." Pp. 1–21 Toren 1999c.
_____. 1999b. "Making History: The Significance of Childhood Cognition for a Comparative Anthropology of Mind." Pp. 102–115 in Toren 1999c.
_____. 1999c. *Mind, Materiality and History: Explorations in Fijian Ethnography*. London: Routledge.
_____. 2002. "Anthropology as the Whole Science of What It Is to Be Human." Pp. 105–124 in Gingrich and Fox 2002a.
Turner, Terence S. 1993. "De cosmologia a história: Resistência, adaptação e consciência social entre os Kayapó." Pp. 43–67 in *Amazônia: Etnologia e história indígena*, ed. Eduardo Viveiros de Castro and Manuela Carneiro da Cunha. São Paulo: University of São Paulo.
Viegas, Susana de Matos. 2003. "Eating with Your Favourite Mother: Time and Sociality in a South Amerindian Community (South of Bahia/Brazil)." *Journal of the Royal Anthropological Institute* 9, no. 1: 21–37.
_____. 2006. "Nojo, Prazer e Persistência: Beber fermentado entre os Tupinambá de Olivença (Bahia)." *Revista de História* 154: 151–188. (Special issue, "Dossier: História dos Índios," ed. John Monteiro.)
_____. 2007a. *Terra Calada: Os Tupinambá na Mata Atlântica do sul da Bahia.* Rio de Janeiro: 7Letras.
_____. 2007b. "Ethnography as Mediation: Public Categories and the Anthropological Study of a Land 'Traditionally Occupied by Indians' (Brazil)." *Ethnografeast III: Ethnography and the Public Sphere—Wenner Gren Foundation International Symposium*, Categories, Questions, Agendas (21.06), Lisbon, ISCTE, 20–23 June.
_____. 2008a. "The Materiality of the Past: Non-archival Memory among the Tupinambá of Olivença." Paper presented to the panel "Amazonian People's Visual and Material Worlds," SALSA Fifth Sesquiannual Meeting, Oxford and Paris, 17–21 June.
_____. 2008b. "Mulheres transitivas: Hegemonias de género em processos de mudança no feminino (Tupinambá de Olivença Brasil)." Pp. 623–640 in *Itinerários: A investigação nos 25 anos do ICS*, ed. Manuel Villaverde Cabral, Karin Wall, Sofia Aboim, and Filipe Carreira da Silva. Lisbon: Imprensa das Ciências Sociais.
Viegas, Susana de Matos, and Catarina Gomes. 2007. *A Identidade na Velhice.* Porto: Ambar.
Viveiros de Castro, Eduardo. 1992. *From the Enemy's Point of View: Humanity and Divinity in an Amazonian Society.* Chicago, IL: University of Chicago Press.
_____. 1998. "Cosmological Deixis and Amerindian Perspectivism." *Journal of the Anthropological Royal Institute* (N.S.) 4: 469–483.
_____. 1999. "Etnologia Brasileira." Pp. 109–219 in *O que ler na ciência social brasileira (1970–1995)*, ed. Sergio Miceli. São Paulo: Editora Sumaré.
Wilson, Richard A. 2004. "The Trouble with Truth: Anthropology's Epistemological Hypochondria." *Anthropology Today* 20, no. 5: 14–17.
Woortman, Ellen F. 1995. *Herdeiros, parentes e compadres: Colonos do Sul e sitiantes do Nordeste.* São Paulo: Hucitec; Brasília: Edunb.

Chapter 9

THE ALL-OR-NOTHING SYNDROME
AND THE HUMAN CONDITION

João de Pina-Cabral

For the past 50 years, most socio-cultural anthropologists have avoided addressing frontally the issue of our common humanity, which was central to the
launching of the discipline. More recently, the very notion that the concept
'human condition' might be a useful heuristic device has come to be questioned by many of us. On the whole, even those who did not go as far as that
failed to turn their explicit attention to the issue.

Over the decades, the accumulation of ethnographies taught anthropologists
about the profound diversity of culturally specific definitions of humanity. More
recently, a feeling of gloom concerning the 'scientific' value of anthropological
knowledge became prevalent. After a half-century of continued self-reflexive
critique, anthropologists were caught in their own trap. They became loath to
claim any special kind of authority concerning the parameters of humanity that
they adopt in the course of their studies, as opposed to the specific versions of
humanity espoused by the people whom they study.

Notes for this chapter are located on page 175.

One of the more sophisticated contemporary thinkers in our discipline, Eduardo Viveiros de Castro, puts it in the following terms: "[T]he aim of contemporary anthropology cannot continue to be that of finding the substitute [*succedaneum*] for the pineal gland that makes humans 'different' from the rest of 'nature'. As much as it might interest nature, such a difference cannot make much difference. Anthropologists will be far better occupied studying the differences that humans are effectively capable of producing; the difference between them and the remaining live beings is only one among many, and not necessarily the clearest, the most stable or the most important of them" (Viveiros de Castro 2007: 109). Of course, one has to agree that the Cartesian search for the 'pineal gland', the ultimate causal link with nature, is vacuous. And one must agree further still that the difference between humans and other living beings might be construed as being small, if seen from the perspective of God or of nature. But seen from the perspective of humans, I doubt whether it can simply be pushed aside as irrelevant. "The differences that humans are effectively capable of producing," as Viveiros de Castro (ibid.) so aptly puts it, can be studied only if we have identified the notion of 'human' and the fact that it is humans identifying themselves as such that is at stake.

In the wake of Marilyn Strathern's theorization (see, especially, Strathern 1992a), this type of approach came to be identified as a call for ontology (that which exists) and a rejection of the possibility of epistemology (that which can be known). Briefly put, it would supposedly be unethical for 'Euro-American' anthropologists to claim precedence for the knowledge that they produce over the knowledge produced by the 'Other' whom they study.

This state of affairs, to my mind, is deeply unsatisfactory as it sits on a series of self-contradictory postures. It fails to account for the specificity (and essential cosmopolitanism) of the knowledge produced by scholars and scientists. It does not explain how it is at all possible to produce ethnographic knowledge. It makes ethical claims that breach the cultural divide without accounting for what justifies them. Finally, it is essentially paternalistic in the presupposition that all contemporary heirs to the anthropology of the past have to be Euro-American or, in any case, have to position themselves in an essentially 'Western' subject position (cf. Pina-Cabral 2006). The problem, however, is not simply to do with our failure to theorize the way in which we generalize about human behavior. It goes much further. These postures—much like the similarly dystopian fantasy that human specificity has been eroded by the arrival of thinking machines—are dependent on a discursivist notion of human interaction that, as will be argued later, is wholly illegitimate.[1]

In this chapter, I argue that behind the acceptance of these limitations lies a form of self-defeat that I have named the 'all-or-nothing syndrome'—that is, the condition of those who, because they cannot have the whole truth, despair of having any truth at all. This relies on a logical procedure that is fallacious, the after-effects of which lead to a pervasive leaning toward skepticist solutions—in Donald Davidson's (2001: 45) phrase, "the fallacy of reasoning from the fact that there is nothing we might not be wrong about to the conclusion that we might be wrong about everything."

Truth

Over the past two decades, the all-or-nothing syndrome has become hegemonic in our discipline. The post-war generation had been brought up in the hope that, through science, they would come to know truth, absolute truth, with which they would be able to control the world. They did control the world increasingly, that much is certain. But absolute control and absolute truth evaded them, and, what is worse, they could no longer trust the world beyond science. From the point of view of a heightened physicalist type of materialism, the impossibility of reducing all truth to physical objects came as a major setback. They had endowed truth with such grandeur and such powers that, in the end, nothing could satisfy them enough.

This is how Paul Veyne (1988: 27) expresses it in his brilliant essay on the belief in myths in ancient Greece:

> [M]odalities of belief are related to the ways in which truth is possessed. Throughout the ages a plurality of programs of truth has existed, and it is these programs, involving different distributions of knowledge, that explain the subjective degrees of intensity of beliefs, the bad faith, and the contradictions that exist in the same individual. We agree with Michel Foucault on this point. The history of ideas truly begins with the historicization of the philosophical idea of truth. There is no such thing as a sense of the real. Furthermore, there is no reason—quite the contrary—for representing what is past or foreign as analogous to what is current or near.

Approaches of this kind, which maintain that truth is simply not a property, that it does not point to any real characteristic of our thoughts or beliefs (cf. Lynch 1998: 111–118), are labeled 'deflationist' by philosophers. A singular result of holding such views is that, being disappointed with the material world, people who maintain them turn for refuge to the world of meaning. A tendency then arises to focus on discursive behavior—on language games, but not in a Wittgensteinian sense.[2] In anthropology, this turn of attention opened up a number of fascinating perspectives, but, in the end, it came to pose practical problems, as it threw into question the very purpose of the anthropological enterprise. Are we, after all, just pleasantly engaged in constructing yet another self-enclosed program of truth?

I propose that we now address the issue of truth frontally by starting with W. V. Quine's notion of 'the indeterminacy of translation'. Analytical philosophers such as Quine argue that the various aspects of mental phenomena are essentially interdependent in such a way that a person cannot possibly have anything like "a single, isolated, thought" (Davidson 2004: 7–12); that is, "each belief require[s] a world of further beliefs to give it content and identity" (Davidson 2001: 98).[3] This they refer to as 'the holism of the mental'. If the meaning that we attribute to a concept is indissociable from all other meaning—that is, if it is holistic—then no two persons and no two communities of speakers can ever attribute the precise same meaning to a concept. Of course, philosophers of language do not stop here. They go on to show how interpretation is actually possible, not in spite of but due to this basic indeterminacy.

The reason why this notion is useful to my argument at this point is that if anthropologists were to take their skepticism seriously—and not as a literary conceit, as I believe they do—then the indeterminacy of translation would mean that there could not be any communication both between cultures and between individual human beings. In short, why do anthropologists accept the notion of grounding their skepticism at the level of cultures yet fail to understand that if there is reason to be skeptical at that level, there is also reason to be skeptical at the individual level? And if that is the case, why do they write at all?

The time has come for us to make our way back again to a more serious engagement with our own scientific task. For that, we have to abandon our idealist romance with virtuality and return to our marriage with empirical research and critical analysis. My claim is that there is no possible description of what actually occurs in the ethnographic encounter that does not presume some form of realism. In stating this, I am not making any sort of positivistic declaration of access to unmitigated truth or to a disembodied condition. All I ask for is the recognition that if we do not ascribe at least to a minimal kind of realism, of a type akin to what philosophers such as Michael Lynch (1998) have advocated, we will never be able to understand what we do when we go to the field; learn a people's language or adapt a language we already know to their local speech; learn to use local etiquette; learn to live with their food, their daily and monthly routines, their climatic conditions, their basic domestic tasks, their regular use of plants and other consumables, and so on.

One might argue that the minimalist realism that I am advocating is a truism. When faced with the magnitude and complexity of human intercultural difference, this requirement for a basically shared world is so primitive, so hidden beneath the layers of subsequent meaning, that it can simply be forgotten and left aside. That is how Marilyn Strathern (1999: 171), for example, apparently sees it. Yet this argument is not convincing, for anthropologists, of all people, should be aware that it is on the bedrock of such minutiae that the possibility of ethnography stands. A fieldwork situation wherein the ethnographer's world and the native's world are mutually unknown in an extreme fashion is not conceivable. The social context being studied is always already largely familiar to the ethnographer. On top of that, growing globalization over the past five centuries has meant that the ethnographic encounter has been increasingly mediated by an immeasurably complex chain of interactions.

Sharing a world is an essential condition, not only for thinking and speaking, but also for interpreting, and thus it is an unavoidable condition of the ethnographic exercise. Davidson (2001: 213) explains that "our view of the world is, in its plainest features, largely correct. The reason is that the stimuli that cause our most basic verbal responses also determine what those responses mean, and the contents of the beliefs that accompany them. The nature of interpretation guarantees both that a large number of our simplest perceptual beliefs are true, and that the nature of these beliefs is known to others."

Ironically, what the word 'world' should be taken to mean is something that, in a way, I think anthropologists and historians should have been better equipped to explore than analytical philosophers. Behind the play of words that goes from the singular 'world' to the plural 'worlds', we can identify another version of the all-or-nothing syndrome. Of all people, anthropologists-as-ethnographers, as much as anthropologists-as-theorists, should be prepared to know that a condition of there being 'worlds' (in the plural) is that there should be 'world' (in the singular), for we would never have been able to reach any knowledge concerning the world's plurality if we had been stuck in a solipsistic universe, which would necessarily be singular. The deflationist interpretation of the indeterminacy of translation—which chooses to be skeptical about the possibility of intercultural knowledge but takes as unproblematic the possibility of intersubjective knowledge and of temporally discontinuous interpersonal knowledge—is not logically sustainable and can have crept into anthropology only as a kind of unstated dogma due to the institutional need to preserve the concept of 'culture', a form of conformism.

I find recent criticisms of the Malinowskian concept of holism essentially misguided.[4] The adaptation of the term for ethnographic methodology that Malinowski proposed brings to the fore the fact that meaning, thoughts, beliefs, concepts, and institutions are both internal aspects of the mind and part of an intersubjectively shared world. As Christina Toren (2002: 122) emphasizes: "Mind is a function of the whole person constituted over time in intersubjective relations with others in the environing world." In the course of social life, our propositional attitudes become objectified as part of the socially appropriated environment that surrounds us, both in words and practices, and in objects. Thus, it is not only that in order for two minds to communicate they require a world external to them, but also that this world is always marked by the processes of communication that pre-date the new act of communication.

An important corollary of this is that, as the holism of the mental applies to all forms of thought, one is also engaged to be a holist as far as one's academic or scientific endeavors are concerned. Thus, all anthropological concepts are related in a variety of complex ways to all others that have preceded them. But there is more. Any understanding on your part about what I write is dependent on your sharing with me not only the concepts, as learned in books or lectures, but also a common world—that is, a context, a condition before the world.[5]

The call for the historicization of the 'philosophical idea of truth' made by scholars such as Michel Foucault and Paul Veyne is no doubt correct; there is no thought outside of history, if by history we mean an always already socially constructed environment of human interconnectedness. I disagree only because they consider that to be a historicist concerning knowledge one has to deny meaning to the concept of truth. But the fact that one can encounter (even at the same time, in the same person) what they call different 'programs of truth' does not imply that there is no truth at all. Their historicism runs counter to truth only because they confuse the existence of difference with the absence of relevant similarity: they will have all or nothing.

Veyne (1988: 128) reckons that "[t]he idea of truth appears only when one takes the other person into account. It is not primary; it reveals a secret weakness ... Truth is the thin layer of gregarious self-satisfaction that separates us from the will to power." Where he goes wrong is not in his historicism, but in his entrenched individualism. That will not stand. There is no such thing as thought that does not take "the other person into account." Gregariousness is no "thin layer"; rather, it is the bedrock that makes interpretation possible and without which there would be no thought. "The possibility of thought comes with company," insists Davidson (2001: 88). And, sure enough, there is no sociality without power.

In order to be able to interpret others, however, it is not enough to share a world. One must also attribute to other people's acts some basic logical consistency, that is, some form of rationality. A condition for the interpretation of others is to accept that they, too, interpret us in much the same way. There can be thought only where there is sociality, and for that to be the case, many of my beliefs about the world must be true. Thus, we all share the means to start constructing bridges for interpretation. This being the case, all socio-cultural difference and all interpersonal difference in thought will always be a matter of relative difference and relative similarity. The fact that our world is socially constructed should never be held to mean that it is not a common world. To study socio-cultural difference is to study *relevant* socio-cultural difference *and* similarity. That means that, much as it may evolve in the course of history, there will always be a human condition.

Anthropology can happen only because there is a human condition, that is, a relation not only between humans and the world, but also among humans—an ethical relation, inasmuch as it applies to *all* humans. Morality as formulated in codified fashion is a socio-culturally specific phenomenon. Yet ethical relatedness is something that goes way beyond socio-cultural difference and that sits on our common human condition. As Mary Midgley (1983) and Philippa Foot (2001) have argued, we would even find it difficult to imagine anything one might count as culture that would not assume some version of the Golden Rule—that is, treat others as you want to be treated by them. Why have anthropologists failed to explore such an obvious precondition for the very feasibility of ethnography? We have failed to concern ourselves with the investigation of the basic problem of how knowledge of the 'other' is acquired. Our anthropological 'other' continues to be sociocentrically defined in terms of corporate collectivities, even among recent critics of sociocentrism, oddly enough.

I use the expression 'human condition' in reference to the work of Hannah Arendt (1958: 9), where she states: "Men are conditioned beings because everything they come in contact with turns immediately into a condition of their existence." I rather prefer this term to that of 'human nature'[6] for the reasons that Arendt gives for her own choice: "It is highly unlikely that we, who can know, determine, and define the natural essences of all things surrounding us, which we are not, should ever be able to do the same for ourselves—this would be like jumping over our own shadows" (ibid.: 24).

But why would it be "like jumping over our own shadows"? I am inclined to interpret Arendt's 'shadow' as being that which one might otherwise call 'rationality'. This would, therefore, be another way of stating what Davidson (2004: 123) means when he speaks of the "irreducibility of the mental to the physical." Why have so many anthropologists failed to grasp this? We seem to have broken the bridge, effaced our steps, and wiped out the trail that led from our common human condition to our complex ethnographic grappling with human difference. Yet these are mutually interdependent.

Epistemology and Free Will

As we attempt to understand better the conditions of possibility posed by anthropological (and, by implication, ethnological) knowledge, ours is an issue of epistemology. One often thinks of epistemology, however, in purely intellectualist terms, as if one could discuss thought without also discussing the relationship of humans to the world. This, however, is both impossible and undesirable. In response to sense perception, social beings construct beliefs about the world, and the selfsame stimulation also implies that they have an investment in the world. Humans are geared conjointly to both thought and action. Human thought, of course, is free from immediate physical determination—our will is, to a large extent, free; that, however, should not lead us to propose that the mental and the physical are distinct phenomena (Davidson 2005: 277).

That free will appears to be paradoxical is due as much to the way in which rationality inserts a new form of causality into the world as it is to the implicit presuppositions about the human actor—the disposition to consider the person not as socially constructed but as a bounded individual. Viveiros de Castro (1996: 121–122) calls our attention to the perpetual oscillation in Western thought, as he puts it, between "a naturalist monism (of which 'sociobiology' is one of today's avatars) and the ontological dualism of nature/culture (of which 'culturalism' is the contemporary expression)." His diagnostic is absolutely correct. However, driven as it is by an all-or-nothing dynamic, his discursivist medicine does not soothe our malaise.

A more sensible and constructive solution would be a compromise of the kind suggested by Davidson's (2004) 'anomalous monism', that is, "the position that says there are no strictly lawlike correlations between phenomena classified as mental and phenomena classified as physical, though mental entities are identical, taken one at a time, with physical entities. In other words, there is a single ontology, but more than one way of describing and explaining the items in the ontology" (ibid.: 121).

I emphasize that in anthropology, this is no 'retro-prophecy', to use Viveiros de Castro's own ironical expression. Rather, it is only a more guarded solution to our present epistemological quandary. In his influential disquisitions concerning Spinoza and the neurobiology of affects, António Damásio (2003) supports an approach essentially similar to mine. We must avoid the all-or-nothing disposition to think that when we highlight the importance of personhood, we are necessarily relaunching the modernist polarity individual/society; or that, as we identify the anomaly in our monism, we must be building upon the nature/culture polarity; or, finally, that to sustain the scientific character of anthropology means to engage in a modernist utopia of progress based on the primitive/civilized opposition.

Four Negatives

To this I want to add some insights that I have derived from reading Hannah Arendt's (1958: 233) debate on action. There, she explores a problem that is, in many ways, similar to the paradox of free will: humans act for reasons, yet their reasons can never fully explain their actions.

> While the strength of the process of production is entirely absorbed in and exhausted by the end product, the strength of the action process is never exhausted in a single deed but, on the contrary, can grow while its consequences multiply; what endures in the realm of human affairs are these processes, and their endurance is as unlimited, as independent of the perishability of material and the mortality of men as the endurance of humanity itself. The reason why we are never able to foretell with certainty the outcome and end of any action is simply that action has no end. The process of a single deed can quite literally endure throughout time until mankind itself has come to an end.

Again, the source of our confusion lies not only in pretending to separate action from the world, but also in the nature of the presumed unit of reckoning: the boundaries of personhood and of conscience can hardly be seen as the limits of action. Action is undertaken by persons and other social entities in a pre-existing world and is constitutive of them and of that world. To that extent, in Arendt's image, it reverberates throughout time until mankind itself comes to an end. From this, Arendt derives the two main characteristics of action: it is both irreversible and unpredictable. Indeed, as it is constitutive of the actor/s and of the world, action can never be undone, unlike most processes of physical manipulation of the world that normally can be reversed or unmade. Furthermore, as it depends on free will, action cannot be predictable. This leads us again to the initial question, to which we responded with the Davidsonian notion of anomalous monism.

The ethnographer is not free from the epistemologist's quandary of having to explain how he knows what he knows. In fact, in ethnography, two epistemological injunctions meet: the first is that of the ethnographer's mode of knowing/acting; the second is that of the knowing/acting as that which she is studying. Ethnography and anthropology are activities aimed at communicating knowledge. So the issue of the reception of what is 'done'—the epistemology of the receiver—is not to be discarded. Of course, how I write anthropology/ethnography is deeply related to the ethnography/anthropology I have learned. We will soon find ourselves in a hall of mirrors—a perverse hall of mirrors, for it is one that sidetracks the essential issue, focusing on secondary phenomena and thus giving the appearance of irresolubility.

In fact, the essential issue is not these dialectics of knowledge reception (discourse on discourse), but rather the relation of 'triangulation', where meaning and action are at play. It is not all a matter of thought; it is a matter of thought *in the world*. Thus, the three sides of the triangle are all equally in need of being taken into account: (1) the thinker, (2) his or her others, and (3) the world that surrounds them and gives sense to what they do. The indeterminacy of meaning—which sustains that I will never be able to pin down precisely any meaning whatsoever (any other person's meanings, but also my own)—appears to enter into contradiction with the fact that we all share a common humanity, a human condition, which makes it possible for any two humans to reach a very considerable amount of understanding between them. These two injunctions, however, are hardly contradictory. They do not counter each other because they apply to different aspects of the same phenomenon. Their relation is necessarily one of constant approximation and constant differentiation. This is a sphere in which the paradox of Achilles and the arrow actually works. It will never have a final absolute solution, for this is 'the realm of human action and speech', and therefore Hannah Arendt's injunctions are inescapable: action is always irreversible and unpredictable. It is the gap caused by the anomaly in our monism. The creative dialectic between the communality of the human condition and the ultimate 'indeterminacy' of communication explains why human action is not subject to a means-ends analysis. It is ultimately 'underdeterminate'.

Bearing in mind this difference between indeterminacy and underdetermination, let us explore further this issue of meaning, for I believe that it clears the way to interesting insights concerning the possibilities and the limits of ethnographic reporting and anthropological theorizing. Essentially, following Quine, the argument is that "what we can say and understand about the propositional attitudes of others should be what we can capture by matching up our own sentences to those attitudes" (Davidson 2001: 77). This is essentially a negative thesis, that is, one that establishes limits, countering more optimistic views concerning the possibilities of interpretation. Davidson (2005: 317) asserts that this approach "is an attack on the idea that meanings can be captured in exactly one way" (2005: 317). As Davidson puts it: "[S]entences can be used in endless different ways to keep track of the attitudes of others, and of the meanings of their sentences ... there is no more to the identification of meanings than is involved in capturing those complex empirical relations" (ibid.). Thus, as it is never absolute, interpretation is always basically indeterminate and dependent on a relationship between the one who interprets, the one who is interpreted, and the world that surrounds them and without which there would be no referential context for interpretation.

The point of the matter is not that what is described is in any way less real. The notion of having direct access to other people's categories is, after all, an absurdity, once we give up a representational theory of meaning. Nor is indeterminacy a factor of there being two or more persons involved. Davidson (2005: 316) reminds us that "[i]ndeterminacy occurs whenever a vocabulary is rich enough to describe a phenomenon in more than one way," and that, "[g]iven the richness of all natural languages, it would be surprising if it were not always possible to describe the facts of any discipline in many ways" (ibid.: 317). I take "richness" here to mean the fact that in language and in what anthropologists call culture is inscribed a vast plurality of different and divergent perspectival objectifications. Language and culture accumulate the traces of an innumerable series of diverse perspectives, identifications, options, practices, and gestures.

One preliminary point is that one must follow Davidson's lead in setting aside the concept of 'translation', substituting instead 'interpretation'. The notion that ethnography involves translation is often used in a misleading fashion (even though part of what the ethnographer does is, indeed, to translate) because of the centrality it places on the purely ideational aspects of social engagement (languages, cultures, discourses). On the contrary, ethnography involves the setting of what one hears into contexts of what one observes; without that triangulation, it would not be ethnography but literary analysis.[7] The equating of ethnography with translation presumes that there is some sort of equivalence between the ethnographer and his or her subjects, as if what the ethnographer does is to translate between two languages of the same kind—the native's language and 'our' language (that mysteriously underspecified first person plural of imperial anthropological theory).

Both of these are grave errors, for, contrary to when I carry out textual analysis, what I do when I write an ethnographic monograph is not, and is not intended to be, of the same nature as what the people I describe do when they do what I describe. Ethnography presumes anthropology in the same way that anthropology presumes ethnography. In no way can the ethnographic encounter be satisfactorily described as a "discourse about the discourse of a native" (Viveiros de Castro 2002: 113). Such a description goes clearly against the accumulated evidence of our methodological legacy. As is so often the case, Malinowski's frankness has a quality of depth and innocence that reveals what later came to be hidden. In the preface to the first edition of *The Sexual Life of Savages*, Malinowski ([1929] 1931: xlviii) declares that in this study, "when I make a simple statement without illustrating it from personal observation or adducing facts, this means that I am mainly relying on what I was told by my native informants. This is, of course, the least reliable part of my material."

Concerning the relationships between ethnography and anthropology, we must attend to Davidson's (2005) argument that "there are endless things that may happen next, many of which would confirm theories at odds with our present theories. This is *underdetermination. Indeterminacy* is not like this; no amount of evidence, finite or infinite, would decide whether to measure areas in acres or hectares" (ibid.: 318; emphasis added). It is easy to see that both underdetermination and indeterminacy play a role in both anthropology and ethnography, but they do so differently. In anthropological theorizing, we aim to provide means to *compare* the practices of humans in social environments, whereas in ethnographic description and interpretation, we aim to *describe* these same practices.

From this perspective, then, we could see ethnography as being doubly indeterminate. This is so, firstly, because the act of someone interpreting what others think and do always presumes a level of indeterminacy in the interpretation (*a fortiori* if the two parties come from different socio-cultural backgrounds). Secondly, when I engage in ethnography, I am, so to speak, shifting modes of knowledge, that is, from practical knowledge that is applied in real-life circumstances to a theoretically informed style of knowledge that is meant to be transmitted, not in the practical forms of real-life engagements, but in a mediated mode (written, read, or in audiovisual record) that is interpreted by reference to a comparative framework controlled by the critical methods of scientific reporting and citation. Ethnography presumes a shift in the mode of interpretation: from general lived practice to theoretical practice, a distinctly idiosyncratic type of lived practice. Ethnography presumes anthropology. The ethnographer interprets not for herself but for others whose further interpretations occur in a context that is radically different from that within which the ethnographer gathered her information. Whether or not we choose to believe in the automatic privilege of illumination that such 'distancing' confers on us—as Bourdieu and others have done—is quite another matter.

To proceed with the argument, however, we could see anthropology as being characterized by a 'double' underdetermination. Firstly, like all scientific accounts, it can capture only part of the causes that determine social becoming and thus will never be able fully to predict them. Secondly, it depends on ethnography for the gathering of its materials, and the latter is limited by the indeterminacy of interpretation. Thus, anthropology, like all other social and human disciplines, will never be able "fully [to] explain or predict any event under a physical description" (Davidson 2005: 309).

Again, to follow Davidson (2005: 306) in his essay on Spinoza, "mental and physical concepts belong to independent explanatory systems." And yet, due to the very requirements of interpretation, the anthropologist will never be able to account for human social behavior without making some reference to the world of things, the physical world within which it all takes place. In short, ultimately, there is no such thing as 'virtual' sociality. The anthropologist must 'triangulate' between (1) her understanding, (2) the thoughts and deeds of others, and (3) the physical world within which all social life occurs. Here, we come back to Needham's (1985) fascinating parable concerning the actual impossibility of inventing an ethnography and sustaining its verisimilitude—the story of Dr. Johnson's friend, Psalmanazar, who concocted an apparently realistic account of an invented society in the far-off island of Florida, today's Taiwan (cf. Pina-Cabral 2003).

All this becomes especially relevant when one addresses the complex issue of affects—the way in which external events affect one's own internal dispositions toward one's self. In particular, any anthropological approach to affects (cf. Damásio 2003) must take into account the indeterminacy of interpretation, since any one of us possesses more than one language to describe our own affects, let alone those of others, and the underdetermination of explanation, since it will never be possible to identify all the factors that would be involved in the complex triangulation between what a person feels, how that is determined by his relations to others, and how all that is dependent on complex modes of physical causation (both environmental and organic).

By now, it will have been noted that these four categories—irreversibility, unpredictability, indeterminacy, and underdetermination—are all in some way negations. That might lead us to throw down our arms and give up on a task that is so dependent on what it is not. But here, precisely, is where we return to

Quine's luminous insight: indeterminacy does not prevent translation; on the contrary, it is a condition for it. Once meaning stops being for us something that actually exists in a person's head (a kind of picture present in the individual mind) and becomes a form of action—an activity of relating—indeterminacy is no longer to be seen as a negative, limiting feature, but as a positive asset. Furthermore, we must be aware that behind our capacity to translate (or better yet, in Davidson's terms, to interpret) the speech and action of others, there is an ethical posture that Davidson called a 'charity'—a disposition to believe that other people can make sense. Our capacity to understand others is based on our ethical constitution as human beings.

Faced with the incapacity to formulate basic human interchange in terms of crisp Aristotelian concepts and a theory of representations, anthropologists opted for a kind of instinctivist notion of human empathy in a Geertzian mold.[8] This, however, was a weak-kneed, conservative response. It should have been clear from the start that concepts based or dependent upon natural language cannot be susceptible to the Aristotelian 'laws of bivalence' (the famous laws of the 'excluded middle' and of 'non-contradiction') and should not be seen as a limitation. The industrial success of 'fuzzy logic' should help us realize that. What is suggested by the four features of action and interpretation identified above is that, as with fuzzy logic, we must focus on human sensitivity to error. Our dependence on error may allow for the possibility of getting things at least partially right. These are not variables that apply solely to ethnography/anthropology; rather, they apply to all action and to all interpretation.

Conclusion

This being the case, my conclusion is guardedly realist. Much like Davidson and Arendt, I believe that those who choose to dabble in virtuality and hall of mirrors aesthetics are giving up too soon. They are failing to see something very essential, not about anthropology as such, but about the human condition. Apparently, some of our more distinguished colleagues have toyed with the idea that the discursive reduction would bypass the epistemological problem, but the fact is that so long as we remain bound to the sort of things social scientists do (i.e., empirical research and systematization, critical analysis and theoretically informed reporting, claims to specialist status), the epistemological question is not going to go away.

In fact, by now, as the years run their course, the all-or-nothing syndrome is becoming increasingly depressing. After all that soul searching, after the deeply humbling experience of discovering that the knowledge we produced was just like any other knowledge, we found out that we had no courage to ask for a divorce. We continued to receive our salaries, to train students, to draw out research funds, to stick to methodological procedures, to observe critical standards, and even to claim a privileged voice concerning politically weighted social issues.

Such a situation cannot last much longer. Sooner or later, we will have to ask ourselves whether we really have done away with science, in what we stubbornly continue to call the social sciences, and with concern for the human condition, in what we stubbornly continue to call anthropology. And the evidence is that we have not, which suggests that, after all, our deflationist fancies are not much more than a conservative literary conceit.

João de Pina-Cabral is Research Coordinator at the Institute of Social Sciences of the University of Lisbon, where he was Scientific Director from 1997–2003. He was Founding President of the Portuguese Association of Anthropology (1989–1991), President of the European Association of Social Anthropologists (2003–2005), and Malinowski Memorial Lecturer in 1992. He has carried out fieldwork and published extensively on the Alto Minho (Portugal), Macau (China), and Bahia (Brazil). He has been a Visiting Professor in the UK, US, Brazil, Spain, France, and Mozambique.

Notes

1. Note that I use the word 'discursivist' here in a very general sense to cover all types of theoretical dispositions that focus essentially on the communicational aspects of human sociality and favor intellectualist analyses over a grounding of human interaction in a shared world. Thus, I include in the category not only the explicit culturalist approaches inspired by Geertz and David Schneider but also those inspired by Foucault or Deleuze.
2. Compare with the debate in *Anthropology Today*, which followed from our original discussion of these issues in the panel "Anthropological Evidence and Its Culture" at the 2003 American Anthropological Association meeting in Chicago. See Richard A. Wilson (2004), Knut C. Myhre (2006), and Brian Morris (2007).
3. Note that here I am using the term 'belief' in the sense of 'propositional attitude'—not in the sense of 'believe *in*', which Needham (1972) rightly criticized in *Belief, Language and Experience*, but rather in the sense of 'believe *that*' (cf. Ruel [1982] 2002).
4. While one cannot fail to agree with Marilyn Strathern's criticism of sociocentrism (see Strathern 1992b: 97), throwing holism as a methodology down the drain with it is a serious error of judgment, to my mind.
5. And that shared world, of course, includes a body—as Christina Toren (2002: 106) puts it, "the kind of body of which [the mind] is an aspect is crucial to its workings."
6. Compare with Toren (2002: 110–113).
7. And even literary analysis requires triangulation with the world.
8. Compare with the canonical formulation of this notion in the introduction to Vincent Crapanzano's *Tuhami* (1980: xi).

References

Arendt, Hannah. 1958. *The Human Condition*. Chicago, IL: University of Chicago Press.

Crapanzano, Vincent. 1980. *Tuhami: Portrait of a Moroccan*. Chicago, IL: University of Chicago Press.

Damásio, António. 2003. *Em busca de Espinosa: Prazer e dor na ciência dos sentimentos*. São Paulo: Companhia das Letras.

Davidson, Donald. 2001. *Subjective, Intersubjective, Objective*. Oxford: Clarendon Press.

_____. 2004. *Problems of Rationality*. Oxford: Oxford University Press.

_____. 2005. *Truth, Language and History*. Oxford: Oxford University Press.

Foot, Philippa. 2001. *Natural Goodness*. Oxford: Clarendon Press.

Lynch, Michael P. 1998. *Truth in Context: An Essay on Pluralism and Objectivity*. Cambridge, MA: MIT Press.

Malinowski, Bronislaw. [1929] 1931. *The Sexual Life of Savages in Northwestern Melanesia*. London: Routledge and Kegan Paul.

Midgley, Mary. 1983. "Duties Concerning Islands: Of Rights and Obligations." *Encounter* 60, no. 2: 36–43.

Morris, Brian. 2007. "Wittgenstein Revisited." *Anthropology Today* 23, no. 1: 28.

Myhre, Knut Christian. 2006. "The Truth of Anthropology: Epistemology, Meaning and Residual Positivism." *Anthropology Today* 22, no. 6: 16–19.

Needham, Rodney. 1972. *Belief, Language and Experience*. Oxford: Blackwell.

_____. 1985. "Psalmanazar, Confidence-Man." Pp. 75–116 in *Exemplars*. Berkeley: University of California Press.

Pina-Cabral, João de. 2003. "Semelhança e Verosimilhança: Horizontes da Narrativa Etnográfica." *Mana* 9, no. 1: 109–122.

_____. 2006. "Anthropology Challenged: Notes for a Debate." *Journal of the Royal Anthropological Institute* 12, no. 3: 663–673.

Ruel, Malcolm. [1982] 2002. "Christians as Believers." Pp. 99–113 in *A Reader in the Anthropology of Religion*, ed. Michael Lambek. Oxford: Blackwell.

Strathern, Marilyn. 1992a. *After Nature: English Kinship in the Late Twentieth Century*. Cambridge: Cambridge University Press.

_____. 1992b. "Parts and Wholes: Refiguring Relationships in a Post-plural World." Pp. 75–104 in *Conceptualizing Society*, ed. Adam Kuper. London: Routledge.

_____. 1999. *Property, Substance and Effect: Essays on Persons and Things*. London: Athlone.

Toren, Christina. 2002. "Anthropology as the Whole Science of What It Is to Be Human." Pp. 105–124 in *Anthropology Beyond Culture*, ed. Richard Fox and Barbara King. Oxford: Berg.

Veyne, Paul. 1988. *Did the Greeks Believe in Their Myths? An Essay on the Constitutive Imagination*. Trans. Paula Wissing. Chicago, IL: University of Chicago Press.

Viveiros de Castro, Eduardo. 1996. "Os pronomes cosmológicos e o perspectivismo ameríndio." *Mana* 2, no. 2: 115–144.

_____. 2002. "O Nativo Relativo." *Mana* 8, no. 1: 113–148.

_____. 2007. "Filiação Intensiva e Aliança Demoníaca." *Novos Estudos Cebrap* 77: 91–126.

Wilson, Richard A. 2004. "The Trouble with Truth: Anthropology's Epistemological Hypochondria." *Anthropology Today* 20, no. 5: 14–17.

Chapter 10

EVIDENCE IN SOCIO-CULTURAL ANTHROPOLOGY
Limits and Options for Epistemological Orientations

Andre Gingrich

Any assessment of the epistemological basis for socio-cultural anthropology and ethnography requires a consideration of the nature of evidence in these fields (Engelke 2008). What assumptions prevail with regard to evidence, and what can we say about corresponding practices? In the first section of this chapter, I approach these questions by summarizing briefly the differences of relevant legacies in some neighboring disciplines. As we will see, I believe that socio-cultural anthropology's dialogical, fieldwork-based orientation places it in a unique position to overcome a subjectivist-objectivist dichotomy that prevails in some of these related fields. In the chapter's second section, I examine several specific epistemological legacies of socio-cultural anthropology that have been actively engaged in this dialogical enterprise during recent decades.

References for this chapter begin on page 189.

This leads me to identify some of the challenges of what has been called a 'second modernity', which we are said to be about to enter. In the third and final section, I inquire about the epistemological and evidence-related contents of the challenges imposed upon us by this second modernity and explore the available options for reinvigorating our epistemological skills.

Leaving 'Amongitis' Behind

Most authors who deal with the subject will agree that epistemology is concerned with human knowledge—with its conditions, its possibilities, and its limits. In the present context I thus focus on the conditions, the possibilities, and the limits of ethnographic and anthropological knowledge. Unavoidably, this involves answers to questions such as "knowledge about what, and about whom?" Here is where the notion of evidence enters our discussion, either implicitly or explicitly. Epistemological implications can and should be considered from various other angles as well, but addressing them through a perspective on evidence helps to emphasize the empirical foundations of socio-cultural anthropology. In one way or another, the discipline has always been embedded in ethnographic fieldwork and rooted in ethnography. For this very reason, it is clear what kind of evidence is most important to ethnography and, by implication, to socio-cultural anthropology: the 'particular' case. We teach with it and about it. We use and interpret it for our publications. Our field notes, field diaries, interview recordings, visual documentation, and so on, relate to the unique cases that most of us study. These field-based materials are informed and prearranged by the researcher's curiosity and research interests. They are elaborated on the basis of intersubjective fieldwork interactions, and, ideally, they also are stored and maintained in ways that keep them accessible for intersubjective assessments by other members of the research community. Because our field-based evidence relates to particular cases, I call it 'micro-evidence'.

Since our usual micro-evidence relates to the particular, we often hesitate when colleagues from other disciplines—historians or archeologists, linguists or economists, biologists or medical scholars—ask us what kind of evidence socio-cultural anthropology might have to offer regarding this or that kind of problem that they are investigating. I see two main sets of underlying reasons for our caution.

The first set of reasons has to do with our reluctance to communicate the kind of 'macro-evidence' that is often expected from us by colleagues in other fields. We usually prefer to offer particular examples, which may or may not confirm those colleagues' questions. Edmund Leach (1962) once jokingly remarked that most socio-cultural anthropologists suffer from a contagious disease that he called 'Amongitis'—that is, our tendency to answer macro-questions from others by replying that "among the Nuer" (or "among the Kachin" or "among the so-and-so"), things are organized in this or that way. 'Amongitis', of course, is a nickname for implicit particularism and, at the same time, for implicit Popperianism. The implicit logic behind this attitude would argue that either there are, perhaps, no universals at all—which is implicit particularism—or if there are any plausible theories about universals, then one negative example is enough to falsify them—which corresponds to Popper's methodology of critical rationalism. (I shall continue to use the term 'Popperianism' as a shorthand reference to this specific version of neo-positivism, which is particularly popular among natural science theorists in the tradition of Sir Karl Popper and among anthropologists inspired by the work of Ernest Gellner.)

Because of socio-cultural anthropologists' well-known reluctance to answer questions about macro-evidence in any other way than by referring to particular examples, we have gained the increasingly problematic reputation of delivering no evidence at all. A scholarly discipline runs into the danger of undermining its own standing if it remains careless about such a reputation—that is, if it communicates nothing but particular cases. The danger increases in an era when humanity is facing global problems and challenges, and while anthropology continues to claim expertise about human diversity and the human condition at large. I have argued elsewhere (Gingrich and Fox 2002) that, to a certain extent, new forms of anthropological comparison might be one way to improve our skills in processing micro-evidence toward the formulation of conceptualizations and theories along an intermediate scale or range. These 'medium-range' methodological operations, it was pointed out, are based primarily upon qualitative and comparative assessments. This is why they have very little in common with the sociological tradition of medium-range theories in the legacy of Robert Merton and others, but share the social science tradition of 'grounded theory' approaches.

These medium-range conceptualizations and empirically saturated hypotheses are thus related to groups of cases that we might label 'meso-evidence'. As in the case of micro-evidence, the identification, choice, and arrangement of meso-evidence is also informed by the researcher's—or the research team's— interests, questions, or hypotheses. Meso-evidence introduces additional levels of abstraction into the particular examples of micro-evidence, thereby transforming it toward a level of interpreted abstraction that allows comparability. These processes of excluding and including medium ranges of circumstances and classes (or sets) of examples thus define the empirical basis for the elaboration of medium-range concepts and theories.

Later in this chapter, I follow João de Pina-Cabral (this volume) by arguing that the time also seems right for addressing in new ways, and in a number of carefully selected fields, the question of socio-cultural universals, or what could be called macro-evidence. Again, macro-evidence is created along with the questions we pose (see also Hastrup 2004). Processing new forms of meso- and macro-evidence, on the basis of our existing expertise in micro-evidence, not only would enhance our potential for communicating with other academic fields, but also could improve our reputation. More importantly, addressing meso- and macro-evidence in careful and self-reflexive ways would also substantiate our own discipline's theorizing, which has not exactly been thriving in recent years.

In addition to 'Amongitis', or what I have called our implicit particularism and implicit Popperianism, our continuing reluctance to communicate about meso- and macro-evidence across disciplinary boundaries also has to do with a second set of factors. Implicit particularism and implicit Popperianism are safe because they are rooted in our own empirical practices: we prefer to speak only about what we know for sure. At the same time, however, we are also well aware that even the particular case examples that we know so well depend, to a larger or smaller extent, on what others have told us during our fieldwork. Our micro-evidence itself is contingent upon other subjectivities. Because we are so conscious of the weight of subjective factors in our micro-evidence, we display a healthy and critical skepticism toward meso- and macro-evidence, which often is presented as if it consisted of nothing but objective facts. To my mind, this skepticism represents a potential strength, despite the fact that it is currently perceived as our weakness. Socio-cultural anthropology has a very long record of assessing subjective and objective factors in relation to each other. It is because scholars in some other disciplines do not have the same kind of critical self-awareness practiced by anthropologists that communication across disciplinary boundaries tends to be difficult. In short, our 'bad reputation' with regard to evidence has to do not only with our insistence on the safety of micro-evidence (and ensuing attitudes of implicit particularism and Popperianism), but also with our skepticism toward the alleged objectivism of micro- and macro-evidence, and with our critical awareness that objectivism tends to distort reality.

I will use the terms 'objectivism' and 'subjectivism' here along the lines elaborated in the early works of Pierre Bourdieu (1972) and Bruno Latour (1988), that is, in the sense of implicit and inherent epistemological ideologies that inform research practices. These ideologies tend to accept evidence only under the condition either that evidence is objectified (in the case of objectivism) or, alternatively, that it is an authentically subjective expression (in the case of subjectivism). The two categories imply problems of their own, of course, which I will not discuss here. For the time being, I use these terms for a very brief illustration of major differences in epistemological legacies between socio-cultural anthropology and neighboring fields. I will employ the two examples of biological anthropology and linguistic anthropology to highlight this point.

Physical or biological anthropology exemplifies perhaps the most explicit objectivist record concerning evidence. In this sub-discipline, more-or-less hard data relate to hypotheses and to accessible and replicable conditions of generating those data. There can be little doubt that biological anthropology largely follows an objectivist legacy. Still, science studies (and many socio-cultural anthropologists working in that field) have confirmed and clarified what Thomas Kuhn and Paul Feyerabend had theorized previously—that even the most refined objectivist epistemologies cannot flatly ignore the subjective element. Ever since the theorizations of Albert Einstein and Werner Heisenberg, more refined epistemologies from the world of the natural sciences have included key topics such as the 'unknown', the 'necessary impreciseness', and, in general, the 'researcher's perspective' (Knorr-Cetina 1981, 1995; Mol [2002] 2005).

Linguistic anthropology and its intersections with discourse analysis, media studies, and studies of performative arts, on the other hand, unavoidably have to rely largely on a subjectivist record of dealing with evidence. Indeed, an individual act of performance through body or speech may never be duplicated under comparable conditions. Likewise, its interpretation may very well depend upon one researcher's very specific perspective—to such an extent that very little 'evidence' may remain accessible for others. But that small remaining part is important. It includes documentation and scholarly debate about the contents and the conditions of documentation. In fact, few researchers in linguistic anthropology—or performative art, for that matter—would be prepared to give up that remaining part. A minimum record has to exist that can be assessed by others through intersubjective means and by reference to an empirical foundation. The subjectivist legacy certainly prevails in this field, but a minimum of objectivist reference is retained (Duranti 2001, 2004).

We thus may identify in biological anthropology a dominant discourse of objectivism, with irreducible, minor, and implicit elements of subjectivism, which is quite typical for a general life science orientation. By contrast, we may refer to a dominant discourse of subjectivism, with irreducible, minor, and implicit elements of objectivism in linguistic anthropology, which is typical of a more general humanities orientation.

If we insist—as I think we should—that socio-cultural anthropology, at least in its European version, is part of the social sciences, it thereby becomes clear that an apparent weakness of our field actually represents potential strengths and advantages. In fact, the social science legacies of socio-cultural anthropology differ in important ways from what I have just outlined. Indeed, the cases of biological anthropology and of linguistic anthropology may serve as examples for larger trends in the life sciences and humanities, respectively. In this sense, they exemplify dichotomies of relations between objectivism and subjectivism. In socio-cultural anthropology, however, the main epistemological legacy represents less a dichotomous arrangement than a dialogical relationship between subjectivism and objectivism.

That dialogical legacy in our field makes us skeptical when others appear too enthusiastic about either the objectivist or the subjectivist legacies in their own record. I believe that this specific dimension of socio-cultural anthropology's dialogical legacy thus offers us the chance to engage others and to move beyond the '-isms'. But in order to do this, we have to give up the false security of limiting ourselves to micro-evidence.

Toward a New Realism

In this second section, I begin to think through some of the implications of what I have identified in a Bakhtinian sense as a dialogical relationship between objectivism and subjectivism in our own epistemological legacy. As an academic field, socio-cultural anthropology emerged in the second half of the nineteenth century in a context that followed the model of the natural sciences. Evolutionism and, to an extent, the diffusionist interlude were elaborated along objectivist forms of logic. It has been argued that socio-cultural anthropology's so-called meta-narratives of the twentieth century continued that logic by further establishing objectivism through new theoretical models that were processing field data into theories (Clifford and Marcus 1986). But this is true only to a certain extent. Actually, as soon as ethnographic fieldwork was established as the discipline's key methodological procedure, an earlier monopoly of objectivism became decisively challenged. Since then, two epistemological elements have remained vital for our enterprise: (1) the ethnographer, from the outset, is being exposed to a socio-cultural context that differs decisively from his or her own—one that constantly questions and challenges the fieldworker's own epistemological horizon; and (2) this challenge is pursued and promoted primarily through local worldviews that usually include other epistemological horizons.

By definition, then, the ethnographer has to enter into a constant self-reflexive dialogue with subjective alterities, even if the ethnographer's own epistemological horizon remains the most solid version of objectivism. In socio-cultural anthropology's formative phases of evolutionism and diffusionism, elements of fieldwork did occur, as in the case of Lewis Henry Morgan or the Torres Straits expedition. However, fieldwork's epistemological status remained marginal during that developmental era, and an exclusively objectivist monopoly prevailed. As soon as ethnographic fieldwork was introduced, a dominant objectivist legacy entered into a continuously dialogical relationship with subjectivist elements (Young 2004).

This dialogical relationship has shaped socio-cultural anthropology's so-called grand narratives of modernity, or what we may now call its 'first modernity'. The merits of this dialogical legacy should not be underestimated: native views and self-reflexivity in the field have constantly imposed themselves as limiting factors on any excessive objectivist extreme. Simultaneously, fieldwork's empirical roots and the logic of everyday life in the field have functioned as factors that serve to limit any excessive subjectivist extreme. By and large, objectivism and subjectivism have kept each other in check through this dialogical relationship. This is valid for the period of socio-cultural anthropology's so-called meta-narratives of our first modernity, when an objectivist legacy dominated that dialogical relationship. I would argue that it has continued to be true during the past two decades of our postmodernist phase, when, by contrast, a subjectivist legacy dominated that dialogical relationship. The result has been that extremism on either side has never survived much more than one generation of scholarship in our field. This becomes quite evident if we consider, for instance, Marvin Harris's cultural materialism as an excessively objectivist endeavor, or, for that matter, if we remember Clifford Geertz's claim that ethnography is nothing but 'faction' as an excessively subjectivist agenda. The short life spans of extremes such as these again underline the vitality of the dialogical relationship inside anthropology's practice (Barth et al. 2005).

Although the epistemological vitality of objectivist-subjectivist dialogues inside our field are hard to deny in practice, their theorizing is still underdeveloped. We lack major epistemological debates and instead often compensate by importing epistemological theorizing from other fields. At present, this leaves us with an apparent paradox. We have seen that, thanks to its own legacies, anthropology is far better positioned than other disciplines to move beyond the '-isms' of objectivism and subjectivism, and that this represents a great opportunity. At the same time, we appear to import too much from elsewhere without theorizing the epistemological implications of this borrowing, at the risk of transforming ourselves from an active into a passive agent in interdisciplinary interactions. We thus are entering a phase not only of great risks but also of great opportunities for socio-cultural anthropology.

To my mind, this intra-academic phase of risks and opportunity represents but one dimension of larger public and global transformations. In line with many others, such as sociologists Shmuel N. Eisenstadt (2002) and Ulrich Beck (2007) and anthropologists Ulf Hannerz (1996) and Arjun Appadurai (1996, 2006), I see these transformations as the emergence of a second modernity, one that includes multiple and alternative trajectories in this globalizing world. If we accept this assessment, then socio-cultural anthropology's reorientation requires a serious reassessment of its epistemological foundations. My own position in this discussion about broadening and reinvigorating socio-cultural anthropology's epistemological basis is to propose a 'new realism' and, as part and parcel of that new realism, new practices of processing meso- and macro-evidence. These forms of evidence help to substantiate our frequent claims about the 'wider significance' of particular cases. They also support the ways in which we conceptualize and theorize that wider significance in and for the world we inhabit.

A new realism, therefore, does not imply a return to the old forms of objectivism, to Popperian or other forms of neo-positivism. Instead, new realism introduces a maximum of qualitative research and of self-awareness about the power of social and ideological constructions and representations into the research process itself, as much as into the interpretation of results. At the same time, new realism addresses the problems of the world we inhabit, a world that is globalizing and has, in fact, been globalizing for quite a while. In this globalizing world of multiple trajectories and complex transnational connections, the human condition is again central to our enterprise. If more and more people are connected by processes that begin and end beyond local contexts, then our epistemologies, as much as our empirical practices, must of necessity move beyond the particular and address the medium-range cases of wider—and sometimes even of global or 'universal'—dimensions of the human condition. A new realism therefore moves beyond the documentation of fragments and combines anthropology's original question about human diversities and commonalities with those about human life and human subjectivities in the present and in the future.

Two Modes of Reinvigorating Anthropology's Epistemology

In this last section, I would like to suggest two non-exclusive and mutually supportive modes of reinvigorating our epistemological basis for the purpose of facing the challenges of a second modernity along the lines of a new realism. These two modes seek merely to expand, strengthen, and continue elements that already are part of what I have called our dialogical epistemological legacy.

One of these two modes is situated inside European and Western cultural traditions. The other is not.

The first of these two modes is inspired by the legacy of European and wider Western social theory and philosophy. Any epistemology for socio-cultural anthropology must have some relation to the broader context of social theory and philosophy. Indeed, it would be difficult to envision an epistemology for socio-cultural anthropology that had no connection at all to the larger academic enterprises of which we are part. In one way, then, strengthening our broader epistemological foundations inside transnational and global academic worlds is a timely development that will bring us closer to dialogical opportunities with others. But the global academic world itself sometimes experiences short-lived trends and cycles of fashion, particularly so in the humanities and social sciences. A small discipline such as socio-cultural anthropology has to be especially careful not to become too dependent on them. To some extent, these fashions in the humanities and social sciences are a response to the fact that philosophy has lost much of its previous status as a meta-science for other academic fields. Some intellectuals experience this as a great loss and are searching for substitute ontologies. I count myself among those who, by contrast, are convinced that the demise of philosophy's former status need not be seen as a deplorable crisis that has to be overcome by waves of fashionable substitute ontologies. Instead, I sense the opportunity for a period of newly liberated cross-fertilization among a plurality of disciplines. In these new contexts, Western philosophy is just one among several interesting disciplines with good potential for inspiring epistemological debates in socio-cultural anthropology. The reverse is also true: anthropology might indeed inspire philosophy.

In these new contexts, a short examination of major inspirations from European and Western philosophy and social theory indicates three significant trajectories that stand out. First is the inspiration from language philosophy, in general, and from Ludwig Wittgenstein's philosophy, in particular. A number of socio-cultural anthropologists are continuing earlier endeavors, such as those of Rodney Needham (1975), by absorbing Wittgensteinian orientations. Among them are Veena Das (1998, 2007), in some of her recent work about the constitution of local subjectivities, and Thomas Csordas (2004), in his work on embodiment and physical experience. I have developed an attitude of friendly skepticism toward these endeavors. I can see why, for subjectivity-centered approaches, Wittgenstein's later work may indeed provide some fundamental epistemological orientation. Still, this work continued to be almost exclusively focused on language and language-based forms of representations, which I find difficult to accept as an exclusive trajectory for the new realism that I think is our central challenge.

Second, several scholars in the social sciences have become engaged with various combinations of pragmatism. By definition, pragmatism orients toward the real world by pursuing central questions about social effects and the results of social intentions. In this sense, pragmatist epistemologies seem to be much more straightforward and successful in addressing key anthropological concerns regarding the empirical dimensions of ethnographic fieldwork. Moreover, some versions of pragmatism have absorbed significant dimensions of phenomeno-logical epistemologies, and pragmatism has a somewhat less relativistic take on language than does Wittgenstein. One may remain doubtful about some of the ethical foundations of pragmatism, which tend to be somewhat incoher-ent and eclectic. Still, pragmatism's evident intersections with anthropology's fieldwork concerns—and also with an orientation toward a new realism—are clearly attractive to many in our field. Various socio-cultural anthropologists have in fact embraced one or another version of pragmatism, among them João de Pina-Cabral, several former postmodernists, and some Scandinavian scholars, including Kirsten Hastrup (2004, 2005). I find a degree of sympathetic skepticism toward pragmatism to be appropriate.

The third philosophical trajectory, phenomenology, has been gaining increas-ing attention among quite a few socio-cultural anthropologists. To some extent, this seems to be connected to our cyclical search for fashionable substitute ontologies, as mentioned above. Something similar, in fact, can be said about growing interests in Wittgensteinian and pragmatist epistemologies. But what is less explicit there is more conspicuous among those who embrace Heide-gger's phenomenological work—without any question mark—as the ultimate truth in epistemological reasoning. Steven Feld and Keith Basso's (1996) edited volume *Senses of Place* is a case in point. In it, a number of very coherent local ethnographic studies of a particularist kind are combined with a universalist Heideggerian epistemology and ontology. As I have already argued in "Con-ceptualising Identities" (Gingrich 2004), a basic reliance on Heidegger tends to lead toward a new particularism legitimized by a universalist ontology that asks few other questions than those about difference. This emphasis on differ-ence, together with Heidegger's problematic record in the Nazi period, leads me to a position that is neither friendly nor sympathetic toward this trajec-tory for socio-cultural anthropologists. Heidegger and phenomenology in its entirety, however, are not identical with each other—as much as Heideggerians would want us to believe that they are.

In fact, there is a whole realm of phenomenology that stands apart from Heidegger's specific way of reasoning. That other, wider realm of phenomenol-ogy has a lot to offer to socio-cultural anthropology. In addition to Hannah Arendt's work, we can look to much of the earlier and some of the more recent German phenomenological traditions, including Husserl, Schütz, and Walden-fels, but also to the crucial French phenomenological tradition, from Sartre to Merleau-Ponty to Levinas. A broad and heterogeneous group of socio-cultural anthropologists has been working for some time now with phenomenologi-cal approaches, ranging from eminent scholars in neighboring fields, such as Achille Mbembe (2001), to anthropologists Paul Rabinow (1997) and Alessan-dro Duranti (2006) and several contributors to this volume, including Christina Toren (2002). These phenomenological orientations combine well with micro-evidence, but it remains to be seen whether they will also develop their poten-tial toward a new realism. Still, it seems obvious that the phenomenological inspiration is bound to stay with us for quite a while.

I see advantages and opportunities in this development—in particular, empirical openness, temporality, and intersubjectivity. In most of its versions, phenomenology is in fact quite open to the empirical record, which fits well with socio-cultural anthropology's own roots in micro-evidence. In fact, phenomenology has been actively absorbing subjective experience and empirical inspiration, as in the work of Alfred Schütz and his concept of *Lebenswelten* (life-worlds). In turn, this openness to empirical routine in research itself, and as a field of research, has been picked up by critical theory, as in Jürgen Habermas's (1981) notion of a "colonization of lifeworlds" being a central feature in current phases of globalization.

Temporality had been crucial for Husserl's endeavors from the outset. In his sense of the term, temporality relates not only to the historical rhythms producing the conditions of the present, but also to the experiential modes of duration in subjective agency itself (Gingrich, Ochs, and Swedlund 2002). In turn, compressions of time and space and a shift toward charging the present with the goals and dangers of the future are two fundamental movements toward a second modernity (Harvey 1990). In this perspective, phenomenology's emphasis on temporality represents a very clear asset in facing the challenges of globalization, especially in contrast to the more limited kind of help that would be offered in this regard from pragmatism, let alone Wittgenstein.

Both its empirical, life-world-centered orientation and its emphasis on temporality thus strengthen and upgrade socio-cultural anthropology's established epistemological competencies in terms of a new realism. Intersubjectivity, however, the third among these three major advantages, relates most clearly to my present concern with meso- and macro-evidence. Here I would like to confine myself to phenomenology's crucial link between intersubjectivity and evidence. That link was elaborated by critical theorists during the 1950s and 1960s, when Adorno and Horkheimer pointed out during the *Positivismusstreit* of German sociology that their criticism of Popperianism and objectivism by no means implied an abandonment of research evidence as such. In spite of critical theory's explicit and well-argued point, this insight became somewhat lost during the postmodern moment, which is why we have to retrieve it, put it back into the central epistemological position to which it belongs, and organize our academic practices accordingly.

My point is that intersubjectivity is central to our academic endeavor as social scientists and as socio-cultural anthropologists. If the evidence we present on the micro-, meso-, and macro-levels is not intersubjectively accessible, together with our research interests that generated the evidence, then our research is a failure. Intersubjectivity thus lies at the core of our academic culture. Abandoning intersubjective scrutiny would transform our practices into something that would more closely resemble art than academic research. What has been said by Adorno ([1970] 1995) and others about art as an independent and equivalent source of insight and understanding remains valid, of course, and I am convinced that many spheres of transition between the arts and academic research yield productive results—from Lévi-Strauss's ([1955] 1993) literary excursions in *Tristes tropiques* to some good examples of the present. Still, art deals with aesthetic and experiential criteria of intersubjectivity, whereas academic research deals with criteria of logical coherence and intersubjectively accessible evidence. So although I acknowledge all creative potentials of art and all productive transition zones between art and academic research, I would maintain that fluid boundaries are not the same as no boundaries at all. There is some difference between art and academic research, and intersubjectively available evidence is one of its markers (Waldenfels [1990] 1998).

The intersubjective qualities of evidence therefore allow us to establish new norms and practices of democratic and pluralistic scholarship. These norms and practices ensure basic standards of quality as much as they require a maximum of freedom and diversity of research. We have been living far too long in tacit complicity with Clifford Geertz's dictum that in our field, anyone can do what he or she wants to do and then call it anthropology. This is acceptable only for those who seriously believe that in socio-cultural anthropology it is impossible to decide, after debate and reflection, if some evidence is more appropriate than others and if some insights are better suited to understanding a problem than others. If we do not support such extreme subjectivism, the rest of us will have to move on to a new culture of academic intersubjective pluralism in which, after debate and reflection, appropriate and adequate evidence will be maintained and inadequate evidence will be left aside. Intersubjectivity thus encourages scholarly debates about concepts, theories, methods, and evidence in a field in which they have been absent far too long, due to changing fashions and tastes and to the intellectual star cult.

On the basis of improved scholarly debate, it will be much easier to assess which kind of meso- and macro-evidence is inspiring, productive, and useful, and which is not. If anybody can write up his or her piece of micro-evidence and call it anthropology, while the others shrug their shoulders in response (because we all do nothing but 'faction', anyway), then meso- and macro-evidence will not stand a chance. If, however, we discuss and debate a volume such as *Shamanism, History, and the State*—an excellent study co-edited by Nicholas Thomas and Carolyn Humphrey (1994)—and if, 15 years later, we still think that it contains valid material and insights on the medium-range phenomenon of shamanism in its various particular settings (because a whole load of studies since then have basically confirmed and further elaborated what Thomas and Humphrey demonstrated), then we can and should use this material for our field's meso-evidence on shamanism.

Intersubjectivity, in my view, invigorates the possibilities and potentials for comparison and for becoming explicit about the solid macro-evidence we have. But some would argue that to be more explicit about macro-evidence is both unlikely and unrewarding. Can this be true? Did Arnold van Gennep, almost 100 years ago, really say everything that there is to say about ritual on a very general level, for instance? I believe he did not. I think most socio-cultural anthropologists would agree that no human society exists without rituals. And most would also agree that a vast amount of evidence has been produced during the past century that contains more than just a plethora of particular examples. It might be difficult to accommodate our different theoretical preferences in its interpretation, but I remain convinced that the identification of a few socio-cultural universals not only is possible on the basis of existing forms of micro- and meso-evidence, but also is necessary because of the new interest in global questions. Best practices in intersubjectivity among the scholarly communities would be an indispensable prerequisite for such an exercise in macro-evidence on ritual. The same can be said about kinship or myth or any other major concept of the anthropological repertoire. The time has come, therefore, also to consider macro-evidence.

At the beginning of this section, I mentioned two modes of elaborating our epistemological basis: a Western one and a non-Western one. After adding a caveat on the first, Euro-American mode, I will present a self-reflexive concluding remark about the second mode. I have articulated my sympathy for strengthening phenomenological elements in socio-cultural anthropology's epistemological reorientation, because, to my mind, it helps us to cope with some of the requirements of evidence in the second modernity we now face. My caveat is intrinsic to this sympathetic attitude. From Husserl to Arendt, and from Merleau-Ponty to Levinas, phenomenology has not yet been able to transcend the objective-subjective distinction in any satisfactory manner. It is true that phenomenology performs the dialogical movement between object and subject more elegantly, and more pervasively, than most other approaches. But in its elaborate and refined ways, phenomenology still remains caught up inside that basic distinction between subject and object. In this sense, phenomenology indisputably remains part of our specific, Western European and Eastern Mediterranean cultural heritage. The distinction between object and subject goes back not only to Hegel and to Descartes. Their philosophies were the secularized versions of what Maimonides and Augustine had already conceptualized many centuries earlier, through the theological distinctions between the creator and the created or creation. The monotheist legacy of creator and created still informs those secular legacies in which the object-subject distinction remains central—and phenomenology is one of them.

I am therefore convinced that in addition to more sophisticated and improved imports from European philosophy and social theory, it also will be rewarding for socio-cultural anthropologists to connect our epistemology in new ways to the non-European intellectual records that exist. This has already been realized to an extent since the introduction of ethnographic fieldwork, which absorbs 'the native's point of view' and native epistemologies by implication. Perhaps now is the time to broaden and strengthen that central element in our own epistemological legacy as well. We have engaged with particular local epistemologies wherever we have carried out ethnographic fieldwork. In more than one way, however, we have for the most part ignored the non-monotheist epistemological and philosophical traditions that are not based upon one creator—traditions in which the dichotomy between subject and object is not as central as it continues to be in most Western traditions. Perhaps now is also the right time to envision a comparative anthropology of epistemologies.

Acknowledgments

I would like to thank João de Pina-Cabral (Lisbon) and Christina Toren (St Andrews) for the inspiration they provided through editing this volume and by convening the conference that preceded it. The editorial assistance of Joan K. O'Donnell (Harvard) is gratefully acknowledged. I am also most grateful for discussions with Alessandro Duranti (Los Angeles), Kirsten Hastrup (Copenhagen), John Comaroff (Chicago), and Eva-Maria Knoll (Vienna) on various aspects and a first draft of this chapter, as well as for an anonymous reviewer's comments. Parts of this chapter's first section are based on an earlier presentation at a panel sponsored by the Wenner-Gren Foundation at the 2003 meeting of the American Anthropological Association, and parts of the second and third sections also were presented and discussed in February 2008 on the occasion of a guest lecture at the Central European University in Budapest.

Andre Gingrich directs the Austrian Academy of Sciences' Institute for Social Anthropology (ISA) and has been a panel chair at the European Research Council's Advanced Scholars Grant since 2008. He has lectured in the US, the Middle East, and several European countries. His areas of ethnographic fieldwork include Saudi Arabia, the Yemen, and Austria. Among Gingrich's recent publications are "Honig und Tribale Gesellschaft: Historischer Hintergrund, sozialer Gebrauch und traditionelle Erzeugung im südlichen Hijaz" (2007), in a collection edited by Walter Dostal; *Neo-Nationalism in Europe and Beyond* (2006), co-edited with Marcus Banks; and *One Discipline, Four Ways: British, German, French, and American Anthropology* (2004), co-authored with Fredrik Barth, Robert Parkin, and Sydel Silvermann.

References

Adorno, Theodor W. [1970] 1995. *Ästhetische Theorie*. Frankfurt am Main: Suhrkamp.
Appadurai, Arjun. 1996. *Modernity at Large: Cultural Dimensions of Globalization*. Minneapolis: University of Minnesota Press.
_____. 2006. "Fear of Small Numbers: An Essay on the Geography of Anger." Durham, NC: Duke University Press.
Barth, Fredrick, Andre Gingrich, Robert Parkin, and Sydel Silverman. 2005. *One Discipline, Four Ways: British, German, French, and American Anthropology*. Chicago, IL: University of Chicago Press.
Beck, Ulrich. 2007. *Weltrisikogesellschaft: Auf der Suche nach der verlorenen Sicherheit*. Frankfurt am Main: Suhrkamp.
Bourdieu, Pierre. 1972. *Esquisse d'une théorie de la pratique, précédé de trois études d'éthnologie kabyle*. Geneva: Droz.
Clifford, James, and George E. Marcus, eds. 1986. *Writing Culture: The Poetics and Politics of Ethnography*. Berkeley: University of California Press.
Csordas, Thomas. 2004. "Evidence of and for What?" *Anthropological Theory* 4, no. 4: 473–480.
Das, Veena. 1998. "Wittgenstein and Anthropology." *Annual Review of Anthropology* 27: 171–195.

_____. 2007. *Life and Words: Violence and the Descent into the Ordinary*. Berkeley: University of California Press.

Duranti, Alessandro. 2001. "Performance and Encoding of Agency in Historical-Natural Languages." Pp. 266–287 in SALSA Proceedings 9, ed. K. Henning, N. Netherton, and L. C. Peterson. Austin: University of Texas Press.

_____. 2006. "The Social Ontology of Intentions." *Discourse Studies* 8, no. 1: 31–40.

Eisenstadt, Shmuel N., ed. 2002. *Multiple Modernities*. New Brunswick, NJ: Transaction Publishers.

Engelke, Matthew. 2008. "The Objects of Evidence." Pp. 1–2 in *The Objects of Evidence: Anthropological Approaches to the Production of Knowledge*, ed. Matthew Engelke. London: Royal Anthropological Institute. (Special issue of *Journal of the Royal Anthropological Institute* 14.)

Feld, Steven, and Keith H. Basso, eds. 1996. *Senses of Place*. Santa Fe, NM: School of American Research Press.

Gingrich, Andre. 2004. "Conceptualising Identities: Anthropological Alternatives to Essentialising Difference and Moralizing about Othering." Pp. 3–17 in *Grammars of Identity/Alterity: A Structural Approach*, ed. G. Baumann and A. Gingrich. Oxford: Berghahn Books.

Gingrich, Andre, and Richard G. Fox. 2002. *Anthropology, by Comparison*. London: Routledge.

Gingrich, Andre, Elinor Ochs, and Alan Swedlund. 2002. "Repertoires of Timekeeping in Anthropology." *Current Anthropology* 43: 3–4, 133–135.

Habermas, Jürgen. 1981. *Theorie des kommunikativen Handelns*. Vol. 2. Frankfurt: Suhrkamp.

Hannerz, Ulf. 1996. *Transnational Connections: Culture, People, Places*. London: Routledge.

Harvey, David. 1990. *The Condition of Postmodernity. An Enquiry into the Origins of Cultural Change*. Oxford: Blackwell.

Hastrup, Kirsten. 2004. "Getting It Right: Knowledge and Evidence in Anthropology." *Anthropological Theory* 4, no. 4: 455–472.

_____. 2005. "Social Anthropology: Towards a Pragmatic Enlightenment?" *Social Anthropology* 13, no. 2: 133–149.

Knorr-Cetina, Karin. 1981. *The Manufacture of Knowledge: An Essay on the Constructivist and Contextual Nature of Science*. Oxford: Pergamon Press.

_____. 1995. "Laboratory Studies: The Cultural Approach to the Study of Science." Pp. 140–166 in *Handbook of Science, Technology and Society*, ed. S. Jasanoff, G. E. Markle, J. C. Petersen, and T. J. Pinch. Thousand Oaks, CA: Sage.

Latour, Bruno. 1988. *The Pasteurization of France*. Cambridge, MA: Harvard University Press.

Leach, Edmund R. 1962. *Rethinking Anthropology*. New York: Athlone Press.

Lévi-Strauss, Claude. [1955] 1993. *Tristes tropiques*. Paris: Plon.

Mbembe, Achille. 2001. *On the Postcolony*. Berkeley: University of California Press.

Mol, Annemarie. [2002] 2005. *The Body Multiple: Ontology in Medical Practice*. 2nd printing. Durham, NC: Duke University Press.

Needham, Rodney. 1975. "Polythetic Classification: Convergence and Consequences." *Man* 10: 347–369.

Rabinow, Paul. 1997. *Essays in the Anthropology of Reason*. Princeton, NJ: Princeton University Press.

Thomas, Nicholas, and Carolyn Humphrey, eds. 1994. *Shamanism, History, and the State*. Ann Arbor: University of Michigan Press.

Toren, Christina. 2002. "Anthropology as the Whole Science of What It Is to Be Human." Pp. 105–124 in *Anthropology Beyond Culture*, ed. R. G. Fox and B. J. King. London: Berg.

Waldenfels, Bernhard. [1990] 1998. *Der Stachel des Fremden*. Frankfurt am Main: Suhrkamp.

Young, Michael W. 2004. *Malinowski: Odyssey of an Anthropologist, 1884–1920*. New Haven, CT: Yale University Press.

Chapter 11

STRANGE TALES FROM THE ROAD
A Lesson Learned in an Epistemology for Anthropology

Yoshinobu Ota

Modernity sometimes manifests itself in a rather surprising form in 'faraway' places, for example, in post–Peace Accords Guatemala, where the country's economy has been deeply transformed through the processes of restructuring and neo-liberalism, and its political procedures have been, for the first time in history, opened up to indigenous participation. At the present time, uncertainty looms large in Guatemala. I hope for a direction of reform, while fearing, at the same time, signs of recurrence of repression. I have been hearing stories and reading in newspapers about a series of, to my mind, incredible events. These stories do not fall neatly into my perspective on the political, economic, and social changes that have been taking place in Guatemala, and I am at loss as to how to make sense of them. Following are two such examples.

The first example involves an incident that took place in August 2006. The authority (*juicio Maya*) of Santa Catarina Ixtauacán, a small village in the department of Sololá, arrested several indigenous women and men for the alleged crime of selling their own children, for about $300 each, to adoption agencies operating illegally inside Guatemala.[1] The intended destination of these children was said to be the United States. The parents were summarily punished by the same authority according to the communal law, an application of what is now widely known in Guatemala as 'Mayan justice' (*justicia Maya*). The punishment took an archaic form: the women, with their hair slashed, sat with the men for several hours on crushed stones with extremely sharp edges.[2]

In a Kaqchikel village in the department of Chimaltenango, located in the northwestern highland of Guatemala, where I was staying when the event was reported in the press, I noticed that the people had started commenting on it (although it is possible that they had already known about the practice through rumors). Some compared such a practice with the similar, but more violent, event that had happened several months previously near their own village, and praised the fact that they now controlled their own lives.[3] But more people were taken aback by the news of selling one's own children to adoption agencies. While the villagers practice adoption within the confines of kin networks, they were disturbed by the immoral element in selling one's own children for monetary gain.[4] I often heard the question, "What will become of these children shipped to the United States?"[5] Many had their own answers: "I heard it from a friend that they are used for transplanting organs. Their hearts, livers, and kidneys are used for the sick people in America. The rich use the poor for their organs. Sometimes the bodies are found without organs, thrown by the roadside. I am not sure if it is true, but I heard it as so."[6]

The second example occurred a few years ago. A man who had been working as the driver of a small pick-up truck, transporting things and people from a nearby town on market days, bought a larger truck and also built a two-story house. Some months later, a daughter of the man, a young girl in her teens, got sick and suddenly died. After her death, I started hearing from some villagers that this man had consulted a sorcerer (*ajitz'*) in another village. The sorcerer went to the mountain, where he made an offering to the 'master of the mountain' (*rajawal juyu'*) so that the driver could obtain money. In one version that I heard, this action was described in more detail. The sorcerer put a list of names of the driver's relatives on a piece of paper inside the doll and left it buried for a month. When he returned, he found money in the belly of the doll. He gave the money to the driver, who had paid for the sorcerer's service. The list was said to contain the names of relatives whose lives the driver had offered to the master of the mountain in exchange for money. Who would die next? Even if they were uncertain about what the man was really up to, many were anxious to see what would happen as a result.[7]

These incidents of the 'fantastic'—some in rearticulated forms—embody elements of what the Comaroffs (2000: 297) have called "millennial capitalism" (see also Comaroff and Comaroff 1999). With its casino-like speculative tendency, it not only dominates the international market but also infiltrates deep into the heart of the national economy. As I write this chapter in a small Kaqchikel village in the Western Highlands of Guatemala, I am reminded by the Comaroffs' work that I should be more cautious and careful about how I tell these stories.

I note the following two points. First, the circulation of these seemingly fantastic tales is not necessarily restricted to faraway places, such as, in the Comaroffs' case, post-colonial South Africa and, in my case, post–Peace Accords Guatemala. Rather, these tales are spread globally, producing enigmatic accounts of instant capital gain, sometimes enmeshed in immoral practices (Comaroff and Comaroff 2000: 312).[8] It is wrong to locate these tales in a world disconnected with mine, as if those in that world take the fantastic as reality, while I live in an unenchanted world. Second, the Comaroffs also mention that understanding these tales calls for an examination of the ways in which people "fabricate social reality," their "imaginings," as it were (Comaroff and Comaroff 1999: 295; 2000: 298).[9] But the term 'fabricate' might introduce another level of complication, since it insinuates a fictional quality of the reality thus fabricated. It might therefore contribute more to 'othering' than to understanding. At any rate, the nature of the millennial capitalism that the Comaroffs discuss is not in itself strange and fantastic, but appears to be so only to certain kinds of consciousness or imagining. Consequently, it requires us to approach these tales, although 'fabricated', not apart from the reality in which they circulate. The point here might be summarized succinctly in reference to an important question that Michael Taussig (1993: xvi) has raised: "If life is constructed, how come it appears so immutable? How come culture appears so natural?"

In this chapter, I consider the epistemological implications of the tales mentioned above, attempting to make sense of them as part of my fieldwork experience. Such implications might include classic issues such as, for example, the nature of belief; the role that consciousness plays in the construction of reality and the power of reality thus constructed on the individual consciousness; and fundamental assumptions about the nature of anthropological knowledge.[10] Before considering these implications, I first narrate in the following section an amalgamation of thoughts—a very personal narrative, indeed—from which comes my perspective on these issues, since I regard it important to admit that knowledge is produced within a limited historical circumstance. To my mind, anthropology, however universal it imagines itself to be from its inception, always stops short due to its recognition of the mediated nature of knowledge produced in cultural crossings.[11]

A Perspective on Mediation

The history of anthropology has often been narrated in terms of clashes between contrasting perspectives on the nature of what constitutes ethnographic reality. One of the more notorious is Sahlins's (1976) distinction between 'cultural logic' and 'practical reason'. Sometimes it is understood as a critique of utilitarianism—so-called practical reason—as a cultural logic of the West, as simply a reflection of capitalism. So pervasive is the power of this reasoning that even the 'later' Marx, despite mounting the staunchest critique of capitalism, fell prey to the reason that he had set out to criticize. Sahlins depicts, of course, the ultimate triumph of structuralism as an alternative to Marxism. The distinction that Sahlins makes, however, might be interpreted differently, I think. It could be viewed as the choice that anthropologists have made regarding the nature and degree of 'cultural mediation', although Sahlins (ibid.) seems to stop short when he excludes his own perspective—French structuralism—from such mediation.[12] Sahlins's perspective is important because it redraws the line of contention: what is at stake is not so much truth versus the narrative representation of it, but rather how seriously one takes the nature of cultural mediation. This is the point that I seek to exemplify in the following two cases.

First, to show how deeply inscribed this point of contention is in anthropology, I refer to James Clifford's interpretation of Marcel Griaule's ethnographic approaches.[13] According to Clifford (1988), Griaule's so-called documentary system—using comments from Dogon informants to supplement observable/collectable data—was based on the fact that Griaule feared that his informants always withheld important information from him—in short, that they hid the truth from him. An abundance of "judicial metaphors" reveals the extent to which Griaule sought out truth by orchestrating various forms of "evidence" and "witness" statements (ibid.: 67–68). The truth about the Dogon culture waited to be revealed, as Griaule removed blocks on the road to the core of the culture. Clifford notes the changes in Griaule's method—and its related assumption about the nature of the informants' role—after Griaule encountered Ogotemmêli, a sage well-versed in Dogon cosmology. According to Clifford (ibid.: 65), after meeting with Ogotemmêli, Griaule's ethnographic style evolved from a "documentary system" into a more "dialogic" one of "initiatory complex (where dialogical processes of education and exegesis come to the fore)."

In contrast to this narrative of rupture or radical break offered by Clifford, Hamamoto (2005b) considers that Griaule's basic assumption about what needs to be revealed—the core of the Dogon culture, which is, to Griaule, something essentially African—has not changed much, especially, in view of the fact that Griaule continued to believe that an ethnographic investigation is a matter of access to truth.[14] In his documentary phase, Griaule seeks truth from the outside looking in, as it were. In such situations, access to truth is often blocked when informants withhold information. However, in what Clifford calls his 'dialogic' phase, Griaule situates himself alongside the Dogon sage, from whom truth about the Dogon culture then freely flows. Rather than being dialogic, Griaule creates an image of himself as being inside the culture, as someone who has privileged access to Dogon truth.[15] Dialogue is only a term of disguise; hence, Griaule's basic epistemological stance on the Dogon ethnography has not changed.

What characterizes Griaule's ethnographic approach is a 'realist' epistemology that postulates the existence of reality apart from the consciousness that perceives it. Whatever is perceived is the same for everyone, leaving no room for singularity in the 'native's point of view'. Hence, an ethnographic investigation becomes a matter of access to such reality, a matter of right or wrong. In the case of Griaule, the impediments in his access to Dogon truth are the 'lies' that Dogon informants present to him, not his cultural assumptions that mediate. In other words, he does not acknowledge that the dialectic of mediation makes possible his 'understanding' of the Dogon culture.[16]

Before continuing, I would like to elaborate on the notion of mediation. I do not believe that mediation in anthropology should be looked on as a feature of failure or as "unscientific" residue (Geertz 1983: 16). It derives from the fact that, even in the age of globalization, all human beings are culturally constituted in distinct ways through which cultural differences are re-created and renewed, returning to haunt us like apparitions or ghosts. It motivates us to see the world connected, not through similarity, but in difference, as we strive to foreground our cultural assumptions for the purpose of rescuing the Other from the prison of the already-understood.

The second case that exemplifies my point on the nature of cultural mediation involves a controversy about Samoan adolescence involving Derek Freeman and Margaret Mead. This case is so well known that I hardly need to go into detail, except to note that it also pivots around what counts as truth in anthropological knowledge. In his efforts to refute Mead's claims regarding Samoan society, Freeman (1999) pursued his critique on the conviction that Mead had taken seriously 'jokes' that had been supplied by her Samoan informants—Fa'apu'a Fa'amû, in particular. Freeman found the person who had pulled Mead's leg, as it were, and recorded in testimonial fashion Fa'apu'a Fa'amû's words. By revealing the truth about Mead's source for her understanding about Samoan adolescence, Freeman thought to discredit her. However, I do not think that Freeman had the final word in this case, since there is no guarantee that he himself had not been taken in by jokes as much as Mead had been. It might be an unproductive line of argument to pursue the veracity of the informant's words, as in court testimonies that are typical of unmediated truth utterances.[17]

Anthropologists usually inhabit more opaque and vague social environments in which terms such as 'truth' and 'lie' are less suitable than those more open-ended, such as 'opinion', that need to be tested among the community members (Taussig 1999). Ethnographic accounts might better be regarded as opinions; therefore, they remain "essentially contestable," as Geertz (1973) has pointed out. Some see this as a virtue of ethnography, while others see it as a vice.

In developing my perspective presented here so far, I wish to note my debt to four thinkers, who would be considered an unlikely group to many: Ruth Benedict, a 'ghost' who has haunted me; Michael Taussig and James Clifford, my intellectual guides, so to speak; and Georges Bataille, a 'sign' from the 1980s anthropological discourse in Japan. As a Japanese citizen studying anthropology at a university in the United States, I was haunted by Ruth Benedict's *The Chrysanthemum and the Sword* (1946).[18] This text, already viewed by that time as nothing more than a work of historical interest, has become important to me because of two lessons it has taught me with regard to an ethnographic approach that is reflected in the two tales I introduced at the beginning of this chapter.[19] The first is that Benedict has tried to see Japanese society as mediated by Japanese culture, in juxtaposition with American society as mediated by American culture. Her anthropological approach toward the former is to make explicit the lens through which the latter understands the former (ibid.: 13–14).

Although I recognize, of course, that such a gross characterization of two societies begs so many questions that it might be viewed as nothing but an outdated anthropological pronouncement, I want to rescue from the text Benedict's deep appreciation of cultural mediation, which I think is still worth saving. Her insistence on mediation requires, first, that American readers to bring to the surface of their consciousness what is taken for granted in their daily lives. Geertz (1988: 121) has noted as follows: "Japan comes to look, somehow, less and less erratic and arbitrary while the United States comes to look, somehow, more and more so ... This peculiar passage from perversity to pragmatism on the Asian hand and from level-headedness to provinciality on the American, rigidity and flexibility passing one another somewhere in the mid-Pacific, is the real story *The Chrysanthemum and the Sword* has to tell." These two societies—both the object and the subject of investigation—are always placed in a dialectic tension: the former becomes more understandable as the latter's assumptions about itself become increasingly untenable. Benedict avoids the trap of making the Japanese alien and 'Other' to the American reader, while remaining cautious about not making the Japanese so easily understandable—without unsettling taken-for-granted assumptions in US society—to Americans.

The second lesson I have gained from Benedict's work is about the nature of cultural mediation. Benedict (1946) has constructed her text with an understanding of the difficulty of examining one's own culture.[20] Here, the concept of culture is defined as assumptions that are taken for granted by a group of people, those beliefs that make it possible for them to identify themselves in the world (ibid.: 9). The way in which they imagine the world to be is so natural that they do not talk about it, much less question it, as they go about their daily lives—unless something extraordinary happens. Such extraordinary events might include an occasion when they need to make sense of the people whose lives appear so alien to their eyes. Of course, 'alien' is a term of perspective that immediately brings forth a question: "Alien to whom?" Benedict's anthropological understanding is evidenced in the way that she foregrounds the taken-for-granted assumptions that an ethnographer shares with the reader: such tacit assumptions might penetrate the heart of contemporary social theories. Benedict (1934: 9) thus notes: "[C]ustom did not challenge the attention of social theorists because it was the very staff of their own thinking: it was the lens without which they could not see at all." The discipline thus conceived becomes critical of the society in which it is born: "[Anthropology] challenges customary opinions and causes those who have been bred to them acute discomfort. It rouses pessimism because it throws old formulas into question, not because it contains anything intrinsically difficult" (ibid.: 278).

In a more contemporary vocabulary, exposing taken-for-granted assumptions is similar to what a constructivist does when pointing out the 'constructive' and 'imaginary' quality of various entities—nation, tradition, culture, community, the primitive, the Other, to name only the most obvious—once taken as real. I have learned from Taussig to recast/deepen this (simple) 'unmasking' approach so that it raises a question that Benedict has failed to raise.

Taussig (1987) has stated that every society lives a fiction taken as reality. This could be misleading, if understood as a statement about the fictional, imaginary quality of reality. In his discussion of the 'Putomayo atrocities' that took place in Colombia in the early 1900s, Taussig has examined why this fictional quality of reality that lurks in epistemic murk could produce violence so profound that the British had to send a consular official, Roger Casement, to investigate. The relation between fiction and reality is more complex than that, as Taussig (1993: xvi) seems to hold.[21] I interpret him to be saying that reality emerges through imagining, yet reality thus created somehow restricts the way that we imagine it. How, then, does this 'forced imagination' happen?[22]

Writing in the interwar years, Georges Bataille, among others, developed an approach that continues to undermine the taken-for-granted. In his *The Predicament of Culture*, Clifford (1988: 117) views Bataille's stance as a "modern" one that shows a skeptical attitude toward order. I have come to appreciate more of Bataille's thought through working on the translation of *The Predicament of Culture*. Not properly surrealist as such, Bataille's ideas—his notion of 'heterology', in particular—question the naturalness inherent in one's own thought and lead us to "think outside of our own thought" (Yuasa 1997).[23] The affinity between Bataille's thoughts and those of Taussig seems more substantial since the latter recently expressed his debt in reinterpreting his own analysis of devil worship in Colombia (Taussig 2004, 2006). In addition, Bataille's thoughts echo—through mutual interests in Nietzsche, perhaps—those of Benedict, as I come to understand the latter.[24] I add that skepticism toward order is shared among the three: Benedict has always left a space for the misfit and the abnormal, Bataille has desired to think outside of the common thought, and Taussig sees a 'nervous system' in place of system and order.[25]

Although James Clifford has been understood as someone who has signaled a literary turn in anthropology by "treating ethnography as a literary genre," as Adam Kuper (1999: 214) would have it, his contribution to anthropology needs, by now, to be re-evaluated. Here I mention only Clifford's often overlooked view on ethnography—that writing continues after ethnography is published, for it includes rescuing the text through reading. Ethnographic writing, often thought of as a solitary act, now becomes a "social" process (Clifford 2003: 102).[26] In thinking through epistemological issues in anthropology, writing as a social process is an important realization for me because often we tend to think in terms of the binary—the self and the world, for example—not in terms of the world infused with social relations.

In summary, my perspective that has emerged from theoretical trajectories that have come into focus since I began practicing anthropology in Japan in the early 1990s might be characterized as containing three theoretical elements: (1) mediation; (2) a dialectic of reality and imagining; (3) social process as a frame of thought.

Considerations on Some Epistemological Issues

In introducing two stories from Guatemala, I have referred to economic renew-als that have affected the country. However, such changes do not affect the people in a way that is unmediated by their own imaginings. In other words, I do not think that their actions and imaginations are direct (i.e., unmediated) products of such economic changes. They interpret such changes and act in terms that they understand—through their imagination, so to speak. Yet at the same time, this does not mean that they live in a fantastic world in which a pact with the master of the mountain, for example, guarantees a large sum of money. This is because, as I address later, they are quite uncertain about such a pact, even if they talk about it a lot. Furthermore, it is too easy to say that these tales are simply native/local 'commentaries' on upheavals brought about by economic changes. One such interpretation might point to an immoral aspect of capital gain made possible by illicit means. In this view, the tales have become critiques of such immoral, anti-social acts and, as a consequence, have "maintained egalitarianism" (Montejo 2004: 242).[27] In fact, the crux of the issue resides here: how mediation becomes a part of reality that constrains the imagination of the people.

Before addressing the issue mentioned above, I would first like to expli-cate in more concrete terms my perspective as it might bear on the matter. I hold a position—expressed long ago by Franz Boas's ([1889] 1974) writing on 'alternating sounds', the article that George Stocking (1968) has pointed to as seminal in American anthropology—that perception is an 'apperception'. An implication derived from such an idea is that reality—in the case of ethnog-raphy, reality as it appears to the people under investigation—is constituted through imaginings.[28] Of course, ethnographers are also mediated through their own imaginings: ethnography is thus the result of double mediation. For example, according to Hamamoto (2005a), Charles Darwin was very meticu-lous in his descriptions of fauna found in different locales, and his descriptions of the people of the Tierra del Fuego in his journal are also full of detail. Yet Darwin never makes explicit the horizon of his own perspective: terms such as 'strange'—to whom is the object or activity strange?—are freely employed in descriptions of both fauna and the islanders.[29] Moreover, Darwin's perception of the islanders is structured in terms of the categories already implicit in the discourse on the primitive then current in Europe. Anthropological knowledge emerged, so to speak, when such categories became foregrounded so that a space for the Other was opened up.

Let us now return to the issue at hand. The fact that reality is mediated through imaginings does not mean that it could disappear when imagined oth-erwise or when imagining stops altogether. A characteristic about these tales is that they seem to emerge on the horizon of the possible, a narrow space between what is feasible and infeasible from the vistas of the Mayan people from whom I heard them. As Taussig (1980) states about the devil worship in Colombia, this practice appears in an area recently reorganized by large planta-tions in which work based on wage labor dominates. He notes that the devil worship is always narrated as a second- or even third-hand tale. He has never met anyone who has actually made a pact with the devil, a very important feature of the belief (ibid.: 95).

The tales of the fantastic, in my own investigations, all share this remoteness from direct experience. I have never met anyone who has actually done or witnessed any of the acts referred to in those tales. Are they simply what we refer to as rumors, totally unfounded and nothing more? Yet the people in the village are quite concerned, especially when they see, in the media, news that appears to confirm the tales that they hear.[30] I find it important to understand the tales as beliefs whose veracity is constantly tested and retested, as they circulate in the community.

In connection with an epistemological issue of long-standing concern, I comment briefly on the nature of this sort of belief, drawing on a recent work by Hamamoto (2007a). As a result of his examination of various uses of the word 'belief' in many societies, Needham (1972) came to the conclusion that in many languages there is no referent—a certain state of mind—that corresponds to this English word, and, consequently, its utility in anthropological analysis remains questionable. If belief does not correspond to the state of mind, then, Hamamoto (2007a: 58) suggests, it might be more fruitful to examine what is meant when one says that one believes in something. Hamamoto explicates that when people say that they believe in something, they are not concerned with whether the statement is right or wrong; rather, they are concerned with what others in the community might think of it. In contrast to discussion on belief in epistemology, Hamamoto (ibid.: 66) seems to indicate that an examination of belief should be thrown into a network or community of people, instead of postulating a knowing subject acting solitarily in the world. To know, on the one hand, clearly indicates a degree of certainty within the community, whereas to believe, on the other hand, lacks such a certainty, since it becomes an expression of an attitude, a way of relating oneself to the world.

As much as writing is not a solitary act but a social process, as suggested by Clifford, belief is about a kind of attitude in the world. It might be called, as does Hamamoto (2007a: 67), a "[Jamesian] pragmatic turn" in epistemology.[31] William James ([1907] 1987) redefines a question of epistemology in terms of transitory, indeterminable language, away from the terms of approximation to truth: "We say this theory solves it on the whole more satisfactorily than that theory; but that means more satisfactorily to ourselves, and individuals will emphasize their points of satisfaction differently" (ibid.: 513). Within a community of people, these tales are exchanged, always accompanied with a great deal of uncertainty; in other words, people's opinions are always open to redefinition and reinterpretation.

Here I encounter yet another epistemological issue: the relation between reality and imagining. I have suggested that Taussig's (1993) position is to regard the lives of the people as fiction taken as reality. He has added another twist to this issue—an advance, indeed—by asking why it is so real. His way of approaching a thorny issue in epistemology—realism versus anti-foundationalism—nullifies the line of contention between reality and imagining, since it denies the existence of reality independent of consciousness and, at the same time, affirms the realness of the world created by such imagining.

Uncertainty appears on the horizon of the feasible and the infeasible—what one knows for sure and what one believes. But the horizon itself is constantly changing, as the community becomes less and less self-contained, its moral values being continually contested. In other words, due to infusions of information made available through technology, the community is currently losing the boundaries that used to define a social order. People are in need of aligning themselves with the world that they have imagined, or, as Hamamoto (2007b: 143) has it, of 'tuning in' to it. Their imagining is constrained as they try to adapt to active participation in a world created through imagination. As Taussig's (1992: 3) 'nervous system', the world thus created might be fragile, ready to be unhinged at any moment, since such a system constantly requires a fix, the need for 'tuning in' from those in it (cf. Garfinkel 1967).

Conclusion

When faced with fantastic tales in the field, anthropologists seem to have two alternatives. One is to describe them in terms of the rules internal to a culture—a "Wittgensteinian approach," to borrow a term from Wilson (2004). However, this might run the risk of making it appear that the people who narrate these tales experience the world as totally fantastic. The other is to describe these tales with reference to a reality that exists independent of the consciousness that mediates it, a more 'realist' approach. In this alternative, the tales are reduced to some comments that people make on a reality that anthropologists could also identify as really happening, such as, for instance, global economic changes.[32]

I have proposed yet anther alternative, one that has been produced from an amalgam of theoretical trajectories that do not constitute a clear genealogy, some being personal and some derived from my location in the Japanese anthropological discourse.[33] In any case, none of them is new. I want to give them a second life through interpretation, a goal that Walter Benjamin (1969: 80) has described when referring to translation as a means "to liberate the language imprisoned in a work in [the] re-creation of that work."

The alternative proposed here is to see reality mediated through imagining, through consciousness, which appears so real that it would not be wished away. This is simply a call for an approach rather than an analysis, I must admit. Reality seems to be unsettled, because the line between what the people are certain of and what they are not so sure about is shifting to the extent that what might be feasible is expanding rapidly in their imaginings. The power of neo-liberalism and the global economy stimulates this expansion through redefinition. As a consequence, 'strange tales' circulate in a large number, the kind of tales that thrive between what might be feasible and what might not be—that is, what is not possible for me, but what others might be able to do, or, alternately, what is not possible for them, but what I might be able to do (Hamamoto 2007b). They seem to evade a net of epistemology that presupposes the existence of verifiable truth independent of knowing consciousness. Rather, they create, as Taussig (1987: 121) has concluded, "an uncertain reality out of fiction, giving shape and voice to the formless form of the reality in which an unstable interplay of truth and illusion becomes a phantasmic social force."

My report from post–Peace Accords Guatemala is full of strange tales, which I do not quite know how to interpret yet. I do not think that they are meaningless or any less important than, say, more 'socially relevant'—relevant to whom?—testimonies, for example. On the contrary, I value them, for they suggest a direction in which anthropology might move—or might re-create itself again—by rearticulating old ideas in the present as it struggles with them. Where does 'strangeness' come from? It is certainly not inherent in these tales.

Acknowledgments

I would first like to thank the two organizers of the symposium on epistemology in anthropology, João Pina-Cabral and Christina Toren, for having given me a chance to participate in a series of extremely stimulating discussions. I am also grateful for the institutions that funded the symposium, the Wenner-Gren Foundation for Anthropological Research, the Portuguese Foundation for Science and Technology, and the Institute of Social Sciences (ICS), University of Lisbon. Margarida Bernado at ICS was very helpful in making the conference run smoothly and made me feel welcome in Lisbon. I express my gratitude to all the symposium participants, who made me think again about how diverse anthropology is today—a realization that I find encouraging. Finally, at the last stage of publication I have received valuable editorial assistance from Shawn Kendrick, who has contributed greatly to increasing the readability of this chapter.

Yoshinobu Ota is Professor of Cultural Anthropology at the Graduate School of Social and Cultural Studies, Kyushu University, Fukuoka, Japan. His fieldwork sites include the southern Ryukyu Islands and the Western Highlands of Guatemala. He is the author of several books on anthropological theories. Among them, the most recent is *Bourei toshiteno Rekishi* (Ghost Histories: Anthropology of Traces and Surprises) (2008).

Notes

1. The number of illegally operated adoption agencies has increased to such a degree that the Guatemalan Congress has been debating whether to enact new legislation to make these agencies more difficult to operate. In August 2007, the police searched one such private agency in Antigua and found 48 babies, ready for adoption, some of which might have been robbed from the arms of their parents. In the same year, I heard about a woman whose son was stolen from her at gunpoint just outside of Guatemala City.

2. This cannot be rightly called a form of communal justice, as the mass media tend to describe it, since, among the Mayas, this sort of punishment is alien. It struck some Mayan Kaqchikel people I have spoken with as "extreme" and "hard punishment" (E k'o patijoj poqonal).

3. Several months prior to the event, three thieves were caught and burned to death in small settlements (*ral tinamit*) near the village where I stayed in 2006.

4. With reference to adoption, an expression in Kaqchikel uses a term for 'orphan': "K'o jun ti kimeb'a" (They have an orphan). 'Orphan' could be used as *xajanil*, a secret method of obtaining what one wants. It is believed that by adopting and raising an orphan, a couple will later become capable of having babies of their own. The act of *xajanil* is widespread throughout the daily lives of Mayans.

5. In Kaqchikel, "Achike rub'anikil nk'atzin re akwala' re taq ye'apon kela?"

6. In Kaqchikel, "Ri jun wachib'il xutzijoj chwe, qitz'ij o man qitz'ij ta, man q'aläj ta. Po, tazu', ri *ranima* ri ak'wal nqasäx chire jun chïk ak'wal. Ri winaq rik'in pwaq ri nitikir nilöq ri *organos*, sase', *riñon*, achike na nikatzin ri ch'akul. K'o b'ey re xtorix jun ch'akul richin ma jun *organos* chupän. Re xaxe jun tzijonen chi xinwakaxaj."

7. When one makes this kind of pact (*nk'ayij ri'*, lit., selling oneself), one usually repays oneself when one dies as follows: one is transfigured into a house pole (*xata't*), enduring the burden of the entire roof on one's shoulders, or into a pig (*aq*), getting slaughtered every Saturday. I allude to this local lore not because I regard the telling of the tale as a case of 'tradition' being simply repeated—as a notion of the 'limited goods' might imply—but because I consider it a case of articulation in the emergent condition. But viewing it as articulation does not make me give up asking an epistemological question to be discussed in the third section of this chapter. The question I raise concerns an alternative to a simple reductive explanation, which clarifies it by 'supplying contexts' for the question. See note 32 below.

8. In Japan, the baby-boomer generation, now approaching retirement age, has been the target of alluring but totally unsound investment schemes. Consequently, some baby-boomers, with their eyes toward post-retirement security, become penniless in a matter of months. This happens as they watch news programs in which young executives boast about their overnight success. The fact that these tales of the fantastic are circulating globally indicates that many people now see their relations with the world transformed by millennial capitalism.

9. I have learned this perspective from reading publications by Japanese scholars now working on the issue of sorcery/witchcraft in modern African societies. In particular, see Hamamoto (2007b).

10. Since I am here concerned only with the epistemological aspects of these tales, I will not discuss the merits and demerits of the various explanations offered. However, I want to add, at least, that such epistemological aspects would become illuminated only when they are not subjected to sociological reductionism (as explanation), which gives us a 'false' sense of understanding. See notes 7 and 32.

11. Richard Wilson (2004: 14), writing from post–Peace Accords Guatemala, laments the inability of anthropologists to "evaluate the plausibility of evidence," due to their exclusive concern with the "representational form of the narrative," the condition caused by their acceptance of "a weak, relativist theory of knowledge." His worries come from his experiences of working with truth commissions and international tribunals, for which all but a few anthropologists remain reluctant to "assess ... who did what to whom" (ibid.). The denial of veracity of an anthropological account would result in a political denial. In Latin American anthropological studies, many scholars have adopted an 'activist' stance, which includes conducting research together with the people for whom that knowledge might become 'useful', however the term might be defined (Hale 2006). Writing out of concern for the same political body, yet not completely glossed in the terms that Wilson offers, I am more ambivalent than Wilson about the nature of anthropological knowledge, not because of its overt interest with a representational form of narrative, but due

to its reflexivity to its condition of knowledge production, as I aim to show more fully in the following section.

12. Sahlins has continued to exclude his own perspective from mediation, it seems to me, a point accentuated by Obeyesekere's (1992) critical intervention in his description of the encounters between Captain Cook and the Hawaiians.

13. I am not a historian of French anthropology. The reading I reproduce here is based on my work of translating, along with several other Japanese scholars, James Clifford's *The Predicament of Culture* into Japanese, and of editing, with Mitsuru Hamamoto, a collection of articles, *Meikingu Bunka Jinruigaku* (The Making of Cultural Anthropology). As indicated in the main text, I am indebted to my co-editor's rereading of Clifford's seminal work on Griaule.

14. Although Hamamoto seems to have constructed his own critique of Clifford's interpretation of Griaule's work, Clifford (1988) himself is aware of "important underlying assumptions," one of which is the "existence of secrets." "Cultural truth is structured in both cases [documentary system and initiatory complex] as something to be revealed" (ibid.: 83–84).

15. In *Conversations with Ogotemmêli*, Griaule (1965) belabors at length how he has been selected as someone who is on a par with the sage Ogotemmêli and who has access to extremely esoteric knowledge (Hamamoto 2005b: 106).

16. 'Understanding' is also synonymous with 'misunderstanding' in the dialectic of mediation. One sort of understanding is based on the assumptions that could not be foregrounded, while another might reveal them later. Therefore, from hindsight, the former now might be called 'misunderstanding'.

17. As already observed in the case of Griaule, the judicial language does not seem to fit well when discussing the nature of anthropological knowledge. Unlike Wilson (2004), I do not believe that this uncomfortable fit would result in political denial, since anthropology aims to unsettle precisely the ground of certitude on which truth/false becomes a question to be contested. There is more than one way of being politically engaged and socially relevant, even in a place like Latin America.

18. Faced with this text, I have always felt obliged, strange as it may seem to some, to respond as a Japanese national who can verify or discredit Benedict's interpretations. It has taken a long time for me to free myself from this 'positioning' that the text creates and move toward a reading exemplified here.

19. In the 1960s and 1970s, 'symbolic anthropologists' referred to Benedict's text as an important theoretical source. Beside Clifford Geertz (1988), see also David Schneider (1968).

20. Benedict had already expressed her thoughts clearly on this topic in her previous work, *Patterns of Culture* (1934).

21. During the early 1980s, while attending the University of Michigan, I took at least three of Taussig's seminars and was one of his PhD thesis advisees. To my great shame, I have to admit that during those days I hardly understood his thoughts as expressed in his seminars, when he was working on his magnum opus, *Shamanism, Colonialism, and the Wild Man* (1987). I have revisited Taussig's works many times since my graduation from that institution in 1987; however, only when I began working in Guatemala did I begin to fathom important questions that Taussig raised repeatedly in his seminars and, since then, in a number of his books.

22. In the Japanese anthropological discourse, it was Mitsuru Hamamoto who first suggested this sort of forced imagination involved in so-called occult economies as discussed by the Comaroffs. Hamamoto does not mention his debt to Taussig; however, his rereading of the Comaroffs' articles seems to arrive at the point that I attribute here to Taussig.

23. Many works by Bataille in Japanese translation have been in circulation since the late 1960s. The early 1980s saw several books on 'economic anthropology' that have been heavily influenced by Bataille's notion of *consommation* (consumption).

24. Benedict was an avid reader of Nietzsche during her Vassar days. His influence on her later thought is more profound than her recycling of concepts such as 'Dionysian' and

'Apollonian', taken from Nietzsche's *The Birth of Tragedy*, in her earlier *Patterns of Culture* (Caffrey 1989: 54).

25. Reflecting back on the 1980s, Taussig (2003: 126) states as follows: "[T]his was also a time when instability and contradiction were beginning to be valued—not devalued—by some of us working in the human sciences which, up to that point, had been geared to making sense of the social world as if it were like a machine responding to high pressure and low pressure ... But the version of reality was not the hallucinatory one we were facing."

26. Clifford (1988: 109), in discussing the importance of the idea of rescue in Joseph Conrad's work, *Heart of Darkness*, states that "the act of writing always reaches toward rescue in an imagined act of reading."

27. Hamamoto (2007b: 122–123) states that this interpretation attributes to the actor a motive for which an investigator can hardly supply evidence. The problem, according to him, resides not in the interpretation itself but in the lack of evidence in order to support it. The actor might be quite surprised to hear the investigator's interpretation of a local tale. The investigator might attribute this to the unconscious nature of the meaning of these tales. This line of argument, however, might lead the investigator even deeper into the same problem of supplying evidence, the lack of which simply makes his or her statement an assertion.

28. I might be described as holding an 'anti-realist, anti-foundationalist position'. Yet the question of veracity and evidence is important to me, although not in the same way as some critics of these positions maintain. As I discuss later, such critics often overlook the communities of the people/critics who debate such evidence. When Geertz (1973: 29) describes this interpretation as "essentially contestable," he points to, I think, the existence of these communities.

29. Clifford (2007: 214) states that "the main problem with much descriptive realism is that it projects its vision of what is really there and what is really possible from an unacknowledged vantage point in time and space."

30. At the time of my fieldwork, several sensationalist tabloids were full of shocking photos of people assaulted in the street, houses burned to ashes, and buses overturned. A photo of the illegal adoption agency caught by the police force was in the Guatemalan newspaper *Prensa Libre*.

31. Further, I point out that a similar kind of 'turn' was taken when Marx moved from the stance expressed in his Paris manuscripts of 1844 to that in *The German Ideology*. In the former, the subject of human labor and the world created by it constitute two aspects of a dialectic; however, in the latter, the subject of labor is already thrown into the world, caught in a web of relationships and interconnected through a network of exchanges (Hiromatsu 1974). The latter stance clearly presupposes the sociality of human labor, a step toward Marx's argument in *Capital*. In Japan, Marxist scholar Wataru Hiromatsu has noted the importance of *German Ideology* and has edited a version of the text.

32. In some literature of British social anthropology on Africa that I read in the past, what was 'really happening' was said to be the social structure, the Durkheimian foundation. For example, witchcraft accusations were indexed as contradictions in social structure. This is an approach that supplies contexts—social structure or economic changes—that anthropologists can easily identify for the purpose of explaining the phenomenon. Consequently, a question that addresses the phenomenon itself (rather than its contexts)— that is, why do the people get caught up by this forced imagination?—is never raised.

33. As an invited participant from Japan in an international forum, I am cognizant of a kind of expectation—a 'burden of representation', to use a term borrowed from Stuart Hall—to show references to the local (read Japanese) anthropological discourse. I am more than happy to comply with this sort of tacit request because I have learned from my experience of being situated in the discourse, as this chapter amply demonstrates. It is my belief that heterogeneity still exists in anthropological knowledge, and thus the possibility for surprises remains undiminished, even if some forms of that knowledge are more hegemonic than others.

References

Benedict, Ruth. 1934. *Patterns of Culture*. Boston, MA: Houghton and Mifflin.
_____. 1946. *The Chrysanthemum and the Sword*. New York: Meridian Books.
Benjamin, Walter. 1969. *Illumination*. Trans. Harry Zohn. Boston, MA: Free Press.
Boas, Franz. [1889] 1974. "On Alternating Sound." Pp. 72–77 in *Franz Boas Reader*, ed. George Stocking, Jr. Chicago, IL: University of Chicago Press.
Caffrey, Margaret. 1989. *Ruth Benedict*. Austin: University of Texas Press.
Clifford, James. 1988. *The Predicament of Culture*. Cambridge, MA: Harvard University Press.
_____. 2003. *On the Edges of Anthropology (Interviews)*. Chicago, IL: Prickly Paradigm Press.
_____. 2007. "Varieties of Indigenous Experiences." Pp. 197–223 in *Indigenous Experience Today*, ed. Marisol de la Cadena and Orin Starn. Oxford: Berg.
Comaroff, Jean, and John Comaroff. 1999. "Occult Economies and the Violence of the Abstraction: Notes from the South Africa Postcolony." *American Ethnologist* 26, no. 2: 279–303.
_____. 2000. "Millennial Capitalism: First Thoughts on a Second Coming." *Public Culture* 12, no. 2: 291–343.
Freeman, Derek. 1999. *The Fateful Hoaxing of Margaret Mead*. Boulder, CO: Westview.
Garfinkel, Harold. 1967. *Studies in Ethnomethodology*. Englewood Cliffs, NJ: Prentice-Hall.
Geertz, Clifford. 1973. *The Interpretation of Cultures*. New York: Basic Books.
_____. 1983. *Local Knowledge*. New York: Basic Books.
_____. 1988. *Works and Lives*. Stanford, CA: Stanford University Press.
Griaule, Marcel. 1965. *Conversations with Ogotemmêli*. Trans. Ralph Butler, and Audrey Richards, and Beatrice Hooke. Oxford: Oxford University Press.
Hale, Charles. 2006. "Activist Research v. Cultural Critique." *Cultural Anthropology* 21: 96–120
Hamamoto, Mitsuru. 2005a. "Fâsuto Kontakuto no Saigen" [Restaging of the First Contact]. Pp. 15–38 in Ota and Hamamoto 2005.
_____. 2005b. "Miharashi no Yoibasho" [Place with a View]. Pp. 91–112 in Ota and Hamamoto 2005.
_____. 2007a. "Tasha no Shinnen wo Kijutsusuru" [Describing Other People's Belief]. *Kyushu Daigaku Daigakuin Kyôikugakukenkyû Kiyô* [Research Bulletin, Education, Kyushu University] 9: 53–70.
_____. 2007b. "Yôjutsu to Kindai" [Modernity and Witchcraft]. Pp. 113–150 in *Jujutsukasuru Modanitî* [Modernity Ensorcelled], ed. Toshiharu Abe et al. Tokyo: Fûkyôsha.
Hiromatsu, Wataru. 1974. *Marukusushugi no Riro* [Theoretical Trajectories of Marxism]. Tokyo: Keisôshobô.
James, William. [1907] 1987. "Pragmatism: A New Name for Some Old Ways of Thinking." Pp. 479–624 in *William James: Writings 1902–1910*. Ed. Bruce Kuklick. New York: Library of America.
Kuper, Adam. 1999. *Culture: The Anthropologists' Account*. Cambridge, MA: Harvard University Press.
Montejo, Victor. 2004. "Angering the Ancestors." Pp. 231–255 in *Pluralizing Ethnography*, ed. John Watanabe and Edward Fischer. Santa Fe, NM: School of American Research Press.
Needham, Rodney. 1972. *Belief, Language, and Experience*. Chicago, IL: University of Chicago Press.
Obeyesekere, Gananath. 1992. *The Apotheosis of Captain Cook*. Princeton, NJ: Princeton University Press.
Ota, Yoshinobu, and Mitsuru Hamamoto, eds. 2005. *Meikingu Bunka Jinruigaku* [The Making of Cultural Anthropology]. Kyoto: Sekai Shisôsha.

Sahlins, Marshall. 1976. *Culture and Practical Reason*. Chicago, IL: University of Chicago Press.

Schneider, David. 1968. *American Kinship*. Chicago, IL: University of Chicago Press.

Stocking, George, Jr. 1968. *Language, Culture, and Evolution*. Boston, MA: Free Press.

Taussig, Michael. 1980. *The Devil and Commodity Fetishism in South America*. Chapel Hill: University of North Carolina Press.

_____. 1987. *Shamanism, Colonialism, and the Wild Man*. Chicago, IL: University of Chicago Press.

_____. 1992. *The Nervous System*. London: Routledge.

_____. 1993. *Mimesis and Alterity: A Particular History of the Senses*. London: Routledge.

_____. 1999. *Defacement: Public Secrecy and the Labor of the Negative*. Palo Alto, CA: Stanford University Press.

_____. 2003. *Law in a Lawless Land: Diary of a Limpieza in Colombia*. Chicago, IL: University of Chicago Press.

_____. 2004. *My Cocaine Museum*. Chicago, IL: University of Chicago Press.

_____. 2006. *Walter Benjamin's Grave*. Chicago, IL: University of Chicago Press.

Wilson, Richard. 2004. "The Trouble with Truth." *Anthropology Today* 20, no. 5: 14–17.

Yuasa, Hiroshi. 1997. *Bataille*. Tokyo: Kôdansha.

Chapter 12

EPISTEMOLOGY AND ETHICS
Perspectives from Africa

Henrietta L. Moore

Africa is often portrayed as a place that demonstrates the limits of globalization, a place so excluded from the benefits of markets, information flows, and consumption patterns that the image of it as the continent where most people have "never made a telephone call in their lives" seems perfectly fitting (Ferguson 2002: 143; 2006). Part of the problem here is the way that the Internet and information transfer have become a dominant metaphor shaping our conceptions of globalization (Castells 1996; Cooper 2005: 96). Not only is the information society the engine that is driving change and increasing integration, but it also functions as the conceptual and performative framing for the pretheoretical assumptions that characterize the nature of the global. What happens, then, to those processes, events, aspirations, and experiences that are not captured by this particular model and its derivatives? These include not only

Notes for this chapter are located on page 218.

forms of interconnection, mobility, and flows that have existed historically—long-distance trade routes, empires, migrations, etc.—but also those contemporary life-ways and livelihoods that are so often recorded by ethnographers but cannot be mapped adequately within the existing models of globalization. The history of the African continent has been shaped by long-distance trade, population movements, religious networks, and exchanges across the Indian and Atlantic Oceans, and yet it is still portrayed as the excluded other, the place outside the network(s) (Amselle 2002; Cooper 2005: 92). While recent scholarship has begun to develop a more conceptually nuanced critique of the historical development and contemporary character of globalization, this has not necessarily extended to recognizing Africa as a player in the process of globalization (Bayart 2000: 240).

Jean-François Bayart is one scholar who has taken up this challenge robustly, arguing that Africa is part of whatever we might mean by 'the global' because of its long commitment to different forms of 'extraversion', that is, the mobilization of resources derived from (usually unequal) relationships with external environments for social, political, and economic ends (Bayart 2000). In this model, external environments constitute key resources in processes of political consolidation, economic accumulation, and social and discursive struggles. This would be true, albeit in historically specific ways, of such diverse things as long-distance trade routes and colonial governments, as well as of structural adjustment programs, the HIV pandemic, transitions to democracy, and NGOs (ibid.: 227). Bayart's argument is that the interlocking relationships characteristic of extraversion produce not a structure but rather a dynamic context, "a matrix for action" within which African citizens are agents within their own history (ibid.: 234–235). As Bayart demonstrates, it is important not to conflate two distinct set of facts: the limited degree of the entry of African economics into the capitalist world economy, on the one hand, and the accompanying marginalization or disconnection of Africa in relation to the world economy and the international system, on the other, where strategies of extraversion have actually been the means for Africa's integration into the main currents of world history (ibid.: 241). As Frederick Cooper (2001: 206) argues, the problem with making capitalist integration the standard for globalization and characterizing Africa as a non-globalized continent is that it fails to draw attention to what is actually happening in Africa.

I want to use these few reflections on the global nature of African history and experience to situate a reframed theorization of problems of belief and knowledge in anthropology and their connection to ideas of cultural difference, or to what Webb Keane (2003) has recently termed the epistemologies of 'intimacy and estrangement', that is, the curious way in which we make assumptions about the moral continuities and discontinuities between researchers and researched. It is in this context that I want to explore various concerns with the manner in which we formulate the interconnections between belief, knowledge, and agency. In his 'interested reading' of epistemological frameworks in anthropology, Keane identifies the changing efforts of the discipline to place people's self-interpretations at the center of study, and thus the struggle to privilege intimacy over estrangement as the source of legitimate understanding and ethics in anthropology (ibid.: 224). This is, of course, part of a more general emphasis on agents and the particularity of their social experiences and meanings, as opposed to any effort to adumbrate general laws. At certain moments in the recent past, this has involved anthropologists refusing comparison and generalization as acceptable goals, both scientifically and/or morally (Moore 1999: 1).

A commitment to particularism has been a powerful force in ethnography in the last three decades, but the accompanying allegiance to context carries assumptions about localism or strategies for determining the local ways of knowing when we are in and out of context. This has epistemological consequences, since it most often presupposes cultural difference—that is, the existence of different life-worlds, forms of belief and knowledge, and, ultimately, types of agency. Anthropology has historically resolved some of the challenges inherent in the presumption of incommensurability by resorting to the notion of rationality. Actions, beliefs, and motivations, however strange, are rational in context. This ethical position is underpinned by prior—but often unstated—assumptions about a common and shared humanity.

I want to suggest here that while such an ethical stance is laudable and indeed desirable from many perspectives, it has little theoretical purchase when it comes to studying forms of knowledge and agency in a large number of contemporary contexts. This is primarily because an ethical commitment to rationality-in-difference runs the risk of overattaching us to our differences and our contexts. In the case of Africa, what this achieves is a kind of parochialism, a view of African worlds as not only distinct but disconnected from the worlds outside them, whether this be the world of the global or that of the anthropological researcher. This difficulty cannot, however, be resolved simply by broadening the frame of the context, recognizing the interconnections between Africa and the West, granting people a history (Eric Wolf), situating them within the networks and depredations of capitalism (Sidney Mintz and Michael Taussig), or discussing the movements and hesitations of flows and frictions (Arjun Appadurai and Anna Tsing). This is not just about conceptualizing and analyzing interconnections, interdependencies, articulations, networks, and resistances, that is, the impact of various external factors on Africa. Rather, it is about the epistemological challenges inherent in recognizing that the new forms of agency and subjectification that are arising in Africa will likely have a profound effect in the coming decades on the moral economies, political configurations, and cultural conflicts that will shape the future of the next stage of what we now term globalization and will also change the way that we think about and practice social science. In order to reformulate the ethical and epistemological frameworks of the discipline to meet these challenges, we will need to go a lot further than declaring that we are all rational in context, or that the interactions between researchers and researched can be explained by the incommensurabilities of different forms of rationality and their accompanying knowledge economies.

At the core of the problem is perhaps the kinds of subjects we imagine others to be. There is no single model of the subject or of subjectification to which all anthropologists hold, but several important strands of thought need reflection. The first is the relationship of social construction to cultural relativism, the non-contentious assumption within anthropology that people are in some reasonably direct sense the product of the world they live in, the product of their culture. But as Ernest Gellner ([1959] 1968: 15) pointed out in his acerbic attack on Wittgenstein, the idea that categories and concepts are functional within a "form of life" logically implies that the world is unproblematic as a corollary of the presumption that things are true within their context. It also places a premium on understanding local experiences and local categories as if there were nothing problematic about ordinary language, and as if the interpretation of experiences and categories were self-evident and uncontested. The difficulty with such a model is that it is in danger simultaneously of confining people to their worlds in a way that would ultimately be unreasonable and also of overprivileging the understanding of experiences and categories as obvious, self-contained, and 'natural'. Individuals' self-interpretations are never completely transparent, nor are they completely determined by context, however culturally defined (Moore 2005).

Recent work in anthropology has struggled to link individual agency to culture through a reformulation of theories of the experiencing and acting self. The model of the self that has emerged is one that is self-produced in interaction with others and with cultural categories, but one that cannot be wholly determined by either the relations or the categories and that retains a capacity for creation, refraction, and transformation (Moore 2007). Such a model sets limits—albeit unspecified ones—to cultural determinism through its assumption that culture can never be held simply to determine individual agency, although it does set out the patterns within which that agency becomes intelligible and through which it is open to consideration and self reflection by the acting individual and by others. The notion of a self developed in interaction with others is what provides for the potential for transformation, both historically and through the lifetime of any individual, but it is also closely linked to the capacity for self-objectification and self-description, for reflection on the capacities and qualities of the self and its relation to a world of values, constraints, and aspirations.

There are different kinds of epistemological difficulty to be considered here, and none of them are resolved by a straightforward commitment to particularism with its accompanying epistemology of intimacy (Keane 2003: 236–237). One kind of difficulty relates to the assumption that forms of objectification or meta-languages must necessarily be the converse of experience and agency, and that they are somehow the preserve of the researcher. It is this assumption that accounts for the way that some anthropologists have spoken out against comparison and generalization, insisting that it casts the details of the lives of others into frameworks, narratives, or accounts that are alienating, ultimately making these individuals objects rather than subjects within their own domains. It is curious in the context of the mass of ethnographic work that now exists on scientists, financiers, development consultants, and the like that this view should still have the salience it has in anthropological theorizing, because these are contexts where researchers and researcher frequently share meta-languages.

However, as Webb Keane (2003: 238–239) points out, a commitment to personal experience does not preclude attention to forms of objectification. Languages of self-description are necessarily meta-languages, requiring a certain distance from experience, and are, as Keane suggests, a prerequisite for agency. They are not simply private and conceptual but are addressed to others, and as such they circulate publicly and are subject to contestation, recontextualization, and reinterpretation, providing a link between moral evaluations and actions in the world. Local meta-languages do not in themselves impart an explanation for agency (ibid.: 240), nor are they exhaustive, but we should not accept without question the analytic assumption that such languages are necessarily local in their origins and/or in their pretensions.

One of the many guises in which anthropology has framed its inquiry into meta-languages is through the notion of discourse. A number of ethnographies examine the discourses that arise within social institutions and the impact of those discourses and their associated practices on life-ways and the constitution of particular kinds of subject. Notable examples would be Aihwa Ong's work on Malaysia or the Comaroffs' on South Africa. Mission stations, workplaces, and schools are key sites and social institutions in this regard. Much of this work is implicitly or explicitly informed by a particular reading of Foucault and tends to overemphasize both the effectiveness of these institutions and resistance to them. This is perhaps not surprising, since these contexts are often ones where techniques of domination come into rather brutal contact with techniques of the self.

However, what is less frequently addressed in the literature is the fact that the mechanisms and the means involved in creating specific cultures of the self—and thus in forming ideas about moral subjects—are as relevant to the researchers as they are to the people whom are they are studying, and that everyone is involved in using meta-languages to evaluate the actions and motivations of the 'moral subjects' around them. In certain contexts, such as the one I work in, the meta-languages are substantially shared, but different individuals, including the researcher, have very different positions vis-à-vis them. The result is that differences cannot be simply glossed as cultural, nor can they be explained or addressed simply by stating that my informants are rational in context. The question of belief and its relationship to knowledge and agency takes on a completely different character in consequence. This is aggravated by the apparently still commonly held view in anthropology that local meta-languages are always subject to the threat of encompassment by those of the researcher—rather than the other way round—and by the assumption that the purchase or relevance of local meta-languages must evidently be local (Moore 1996). What is particularly worrying with regard to this is the implicit idea that only certain kinds of subject have access to the forms of self-consciousness and the associated capacities for conceptual framing provided by meta-languages. Put in rather bald terms, this amounts to an unstated claim that nothing could ever come out of Africa that would encompass or reframe the meta-languages of a Western researcher, and thus, by extension, that no framing concepts could arise in that context that could shape the future direction of social science.

I want to use these brief comments on languages of self-description to frame a discussion about the new forms of subjectivity and agency that are arising in some contexts across the African continent. These forms of subjectivity and agency are intimately linked to ideas about knowledge and how knowledge and knowledge transfer are connected to processes of social change and transformation. In such contexts, conflicts over knowledge become a way of assigning value and of reflecting on the moral dispositions of agents. In consequence, problems about knowledge and the various forms it takes become tied to broader questions of ethics. In many parts of the world, including Africa, subjectivities—and particularly gendered subjectivities—are undergoing rapid transformation. Neo-liberalism, state aggression, and globalized consumption patterns are all processes that necessarily both engage with and work through changing theories of the self and of subjectivity.

There is nothing new about the making and remaking of selves. Such processes are an essential part of the making of any history, but they have taken on a particular force in the context of many social movements, experiences, and emerging ways of livelihood and belief that are actively premised on transforming the self. In the context of Africa, radical Christianity is one of the most powerful advocates for and vectors of self-fashioning and social transformation. It is premised on people's desire for a change in the very nature of who they are and of how they represent themselves to themselves. This desire takes on a particular potency and poignancy because it develops all too frequently in conditions of poverty, immiseration, and discrimination, all of which are traumas closely allied in the most ironic fashion to new forms of aspiration. Christianity is not only one of the major forms of social mobilization and transformation in Africa, but as Bayart (2000: 262) points out, it is the leading means by which Sub-Saharan Africa integrates itself into the international system. At the beginning of the twenty-first century, one-third of the world's population is Christian, and tens of millions of the faith's adherents live in Africa. However, it is not just the scale of Christian conversion in the continent that proves difficult for the anthropologist, but the problems it poses in understanding the relations between knowledge and agency, between universal truths and cultural specifics.

New Forms of Knowledge and Agency

My thoughts on these matters have been heavily influenced by my recent fieldwork experiences in Marakwet District in northern Kenya, where the epistemological and ethical difficulties I face have all centered on familiarity rather than difference. Changes in the Kerio Valley over the last 25 years, between 1980 when I first went there and 2005 when I returned, have been dramatic. Most of the significant changes in culture and in ritual practices have taken place over a much shorter period of time, beginning in 1999, and have been the result of intensive activity on the part of churches, local NGOs, and the government. These changes are encapsulated for many by the incomplete, but nonetheless substantial, abandonment of the female circumcision ritual and its replacement by a new ritual, the alternative rite of passage (ARP), designed by NGOs.

One significant factor here is the way that the very notion of Marakwet culture has become reified in the contemporary moment in a way that would have seemed inconceivable in 1980. The speed of this transformation in the nature of 'culture as object' is rather dramatic, having taken place very largely in the last 10 years. The reification of certain cultural practices and their disinterment or distinction from a broader understanding of life-world are intentional on the part of those who see themselves as 'agents of social change' in Marakwet. Indeed, this transformation owes much to the discourse and discipline of anthropology as it is mediated through social consultants employed by NGOs, as well as through local pastors, many of whom have received training in African traditional religions in their theological colleges as part of a broader education about the proper relationship of Christianity to local cultures. Religion and culture have in fact emerged together as discursive constructions and as social facts in the context of a broader set of ideas about the relationship of knowledge to the world and how knowledge underpins agency. Some of these ideas are a direct reflection of assumptions built into the project of development itself, which assumes uncontested links between knowledge, power, and progress. Others, however, are bound up with shifts in the knowledge economies of Marakwet society. The campaign against female circumcision is one such example.

My contention is that the reification of female circumcision as a distinctive aspect of something called culture is a necessary step in any program of eradication. I make this argument because in order for female circumcision to become an object of action, it first has to undergo a transformation that constructs it as a new kind of object of knowledge, one that would then be potentially susceptible to new forms of agency and governance. In the past, circumcision was the fulcrum of a rite of social transformation that prepared girls to be mothers and wives, and intense secrecy surrounded the activities and teachings of *kapkore*, the girls' initiation house.

These forms of knowledge were based on a model of revelation through progress, and initiation for both girls and boys marked the assumption of social adulthood because it began that process of revelation (Moore 2010). I have interviewed men and women extensively as to whether they talk over aspects of this corpus of knowledge when they meet privately among themselves, but all my informants have always been adamant that these matters are never spoken of except when their performance is required. Knowledge and its interpretation constitute a type of practical understanding that is taught primarily by example and is highly sensitive to particular circumstances and sets of social relations. It is not to be imagined as an extant body of knowledge that is stored and transmitted as a corpus, or as a body of knowledge that can be drawn on and elaborated on in the manner that text-based religions can be, for example. These forms of knowledge are bound together, but not by rules or by systematic relations between the system's components. Rather, they cohere through habitus, through situated practice that is often discontinuous in space and time, and yet is always potentially applicable. It makes of adulthood a sort of mastery, but a mastery without explicit and stable content.

Marakwet culture is about living tradition, but the situated and enacted nature of traditional knowledge depended for its success on a lack of explicit reification. Therein lay its power and its purpose. The lived habitus of a world so constructed is both flexible and resistant to change. In order to bring about the upheaval required to displace female circumcision and girls' initiation from their fulcrum position in terms of social and societal continuity and well-being, something had to happen that made these practices cultural objects around which contests of value could legitimately take place. These contests of value were not like the old ones concerned with the appropriateness, or not, of specific situated practices; instead, they were about the nature of knowledge itself and its effectiveness in modern contexts. In this process, the very idea of culture, as opposed to that of a lived world, was created. My point here is that culture in this form proved more amenable to change because it could be objectified and acted on in a new way.

Different categories of actors in Marakwet hold different views about exactly what Marakwet culture is, both in terms of its content and in terms of what kind of object it is. These differing views provide individuals with different capacities or potentialities for action. The notion of Marakwet culture that has recently emerged is a specific kind of object of knowledge, one that, as I have said, is potentially subject to new forms of agency and governance. It is also one that is linked for many individuals to specific forms of self-fashioning, with their accompanying forms of self-objectification. The drivers of change here are Protestant Christianity and education—the history of their development in the valley is in any event intertwined—and together they have produced new sets of ideas about individuals who are specific sorts of moral selves and who also have responsibilities for fashioning themselves and for changing their communities.

Take, for example, one young woman who is now 20 years old. She is one of a group of girls who, with the help of a local NGO, brought court cases against their parents in 2001 to prevent themselves from being circumcised. In talking to this young woman about how she sees her future, she replied by saying. "You have to realize that I am unique, that there is no one else in this world quite like me. God has a special purpose for me, and I will fulfill it." Although the details of this 'special purpose' are a little vague, what is consistent is the strongly held view that remaking the world involves remaking oneself as a moral agent. All the young women involved in the court cases use the terms 'agents of social change' and 'role models for the community' (in English) when referring to themselves and their aspirations. They have a very clear sense of themselves as agents, and they equally believe that the knowledge they have acquired from school and from the church is superior to traditional knowledge. When I ask them about the traditions of their parents and grandparents, an oft repeated response is "What has culture ever done for us?" When asked about the knowledge that girls acquired in the past in *kapkore*, the seclusion house, the most common reply is "It is useless" or "It is rubbish." Doubtless this is because the campaign against female circumcision makes much of the fact that the teachings of *kapkore* are useless, that they have no value in a modern world. What is intriguing is the way that young people now think about culture and about how they can act on it. It is commonplace in the valley now to hear people saying, "Well, we can choose which bits of our culture to keep. We don't have to retain the bad parts like female circumcision, but we can keep the good parts." Choosing the 'good parts' has become emblematic of modern ways of thinking and doing, as people increasingly engage with a process of self-fashioning cast in the idiom of new forms of knowledge. As one girl said: "We are now in dot.com because we have left the old practices behind."

When thinking about new forms of knowledge and their explicit link to enhanced agency, it is important to recall the use by NGOs and the church of such fora as seminars, workshops, training camps, school advocacy clubs, and the like. These occasions take individuals out of their usual sets of social relations and create novel social contexts for them in which they can forge new bonds, identities, and aspirations. In such settings, the use of particular discursive strategies is decisive. One example would be the stitching together of the transformation involved in being 'born again' with notions of enhanced agency in a changed world, as well as ideas about individual rights. This theme not only is central to most training and advocacy sessions related to the anti-FGM (female genital mutilation) campaign, as the campaign against female circumcision is known locally, but also forms the unambiguous subtext for many of the songs and speeches involved in ARP, as in the text of this song:

Decide for yourself
Decide for yourself. Circumcision is not a must
We want girls' development
We want girls' development
You girls, let us not retreat
Let us not retreat, we proceed with Jesus
We've refused to be circumcised
We've refused to be circumcised
I will not go back
I will not go back to circumcision
I will not go back where my mother went
Where my sister went
Grandmother, I will not follow you

In many of the songs and dances at the ARP graduation, the refusal of FGM is linked to enhanced chances for education and for future success, as put in this dance poem:

I visited my neighbor when there was circumcision for girls
I wish I was told
You girls, you study hard in school
I wish I was told

To go to other countries for study
I wish I was told
To bring degree
I wish I was told
N-O
No
F-G-M
FGM

One of the constant refrains concerns the issue of certificates. All girls (and boys) who pass through ARP receive a certificate. The children are explicitly encouraged to see this document as being linked to other kinds of certificates signaling educational attainment. Stories are often told in the ARP speeches about how girls seeking college places were preferentially treated because they were able to produce their ARP certificate. *Kapkore*, it is said, has no certificate. Its knowledge is therefore useless.

In 2007, Raila Odinga, then a presidential hopeful in Kenya's election (and subsequently prime minister), addressed a pre-election meeting in Marakwet District that was designed to canvas the Kalenjin vote. He was heard to declare that what is important is to be "circumcised upstairs." He asked the people present, "Which is more important—to be circumcised in the mind or in the flesh?" This distinction was readily taken up by young people in the valley and others, who could be heard saying, "I want to vote for Raila. He's circumcised upstairs"—meaning that he is educated, knowledgeable about the modern world, and clever (Moore 2010).

Conclusion

New informational economies arise when people have to manage new forms of knowledge in the context of changed social interactions, and these are accompanied by new meta-languages of self-description that provide very particular linkages between moral evaluations and actions in the world (Keane 2003: 232–234). There is now a good deal of ethnography from Africa on how Christianity and development have impacted on traditional societies and local contexts, but much of this work focuses at the level of discourse and is Foucauldian in inspiration, examining the effectiveness of these institutions and/or resistance to them. What is beginning to emerge—as a consequence of the prolonged contact of anthropological researchers in Africa and elsewhere with radical Protestantism—is a quite different approach to subjectification and agency. This is being forced by the hyper-agency of radical Christian belief and by the way individuals and their ideas about knowledge and action have become part of international Christian networks. The radical equality of human beings before God has immense transformative power in the African context, where many believers see themselves as part of a global moral community. Their moral responsibility for the well-being of that community is encapsulated, among other things, in formidable critiques of globalization, social inequality, and moral relativism. Particular Christian churches and movements have differing frameworks for understanding the character of this global community and the nature of the moral challenges it presupposes. Debate within the Anglican communion over sexuality and the rights of homosexuals to participate in the ministry and the life of the church have been bitterly divisive at the Lambeth conferences of 1998 and 2008, because the African Anglican Church will not accept what its members see as an attack on the moral authority of the scriptures and the church stemming from 'Western values'. While they are joined in opposition by other Anglican communities and individuals, this debate has brought cultural differences to the fore, as well as opening public discussion on the nature and character of modern morality, specifically, the centrality of marriage.[1]

The Anglican Church has always claimed universality, and sexual politics (at earlier moments, divorce, polygyny, and contraception) has always threatened its claims to moral coherence (Hoad 2004: 55–58). The human rights discourse, which sees homosexuality as a sexual orientation that is part of the definition of humanity, has its universalist assumptions challenged by the competing universal claims of a global faith whose morality is sustained by the Scriptures. The debate that rages on such matters in African churches of many denominations is sustained by the claims of the faith's adherents to speak with moral authority concerning and on behalf of our common humanity. The debates in Africa will have a profound impact on moral discourses and global political alignments over the coming years, and the allocation of many important resources—such as bilateral and multilateral aid money for work on sexual health, development, children's rights, etc.—will be determined by their outcome.

What seems likely is that the future of Christianity, the character and content of its belief, and its relationship to political, social, and economic transformation will be substantially determined outside the West. This produces particular epistemological and ethical problems for anthropological researchers regarding the relationship between Christian beliefs, knowledge, and agency that are explicitly not local in scope, even if they are located within a defined context. We can no longer base our own disciplinary ethics on an uninterrogated commitment to particularism, to acknowledging cultural difference, where our informants are simply figured as rational in context, as exemplars of their locality. We have to recognize instead that incommensurability is not the major epistemological challenge in certain contexts; that we are dealing with moral worldviews and claims, forms of self-description and self-objectification, which actively endeavor to guide moral action and make universalist claims; and that such evaluations may well seek to encompass our own meta-languages and find them wanting. This situation sets out the terms for a very different form of social science, one that will need to be based on a thoroughgoing revision of its epistemological claims and ethical practices.

Henrietta L. Moore is the William Wyse Professor of Social Anthropology at the University of Cambridge and Director of the Culture and Globalisation Programme at the Centre for Global Governance, London School of Economics. She has a long-standing research interest in Africa. Her most recent monograph is *The Subject of Anthropology: Gender, Symbolism and Psychoanalysis* (2006). She co-edited with Todd Sanders *Magical Interpretations, Material Realities* (2001) and *Anthropology in Theory: Issues in Epistemology* (2005).

Notes

1. See http://www.anglicancommunion.org/listening/.

References

Amselle, Jean-Loup. 2002. "Globalization and the Future of Anthropology." *African Affairs* 101: 213–229.

Bayart, Jean-François. 2000. "Africa in the World: A History of Extraversion." *African Affairs* 99: 217–267.

Castells, Manuel. 1996. *The Rise of the Network Society*. Oxford: Blackwell.

Cooper, Frederick. 2001. "What Is the Concept of Globalization Good For? An African Historian's Perspective." *African Affairs* 100: 189–213.

_____. 2005. *Colonialism in Question: Theory, Knowledge, History*. Berkeley: University of California Press.

Ferguson, James. 2002. "Global Disconnect: Abjection and the Aftermath of Modernism." Pp. 136–153 in *The Anthropology of Globalization: A Reader*, Jonathan X. Inda and Renato Rosaldo. Oxford: Blackwell.

_____. 2006. *Global Shadows: Africa in the Neoliberal World Order*. Durham, NC: Duke University Press.

Gellner, Ernest. [1959] 1968. *Words and Things: A Critical Account of Linguistic Philosophy and a Study in Ideology*. Boston, MA: Beacon Press.

Hoad, Neville. 2004. "Homosexuality, Africa, Neoliberalism and the Anglican Church: The Lambeth Conference of Anglican Bishops, 1998." Pp. 54–79 in *Producing African Futures: Ritual and Reproduction in a Neoliberal Age*, ed. Brad Weiss. Leiden: Brill.

Keane, Webb. 2003. "Self-Interpretation, Agency, and the Objects of Anthropology: Reflections on a Genealogy." *Comparative Studies in Society and History* 45: 222–248.

Moore, Henrietta L. 1996. "The Changing Nature of Anthropological Knowledge: An Introduction." Pp. 1–15 in *The Future of Anthropological Knowledge*, ed. Henrietta L. Moore. London: Routledge.

_____. 1999. "Anthropological Theory at the Turn of the Century." Pp. 1–23 in *Anthropological Theory Today*, ed. Henrietta L. Moore. Cambridge: Polity Press.

_____. 2005. "The Truths of Anthropology." *Cambridge Anthropology* 25, no. 1: 52–59.

_____. 2007. *The Subject of Anthropology: Gender, Symbolism and Psychoanalysis*. Cambridge: Polity Press.

_____. 2010. "Forms of Knowing and Un-knowing: Secrets about Society, Sexuality and God in Northern Kenya." Pp. 30–41 in *Secrecy and Silence in the Research Process: Feminist Reflections*, ed. Róisín Ryan-Flood and Rosalind Gill. London: Routledge.

Index

academic disciplines, 24, 60, 61, 70–75
Africa, 15, 37, 193–4, 202n32, 207–216
Afro-Brazilian religions, 108, 110–112, 117, 126n6
agency, 15, 50, 56n16, 109, 116, 119, 120, 126n10, 126n17, 127n19, 142n6, 150, 186, 201n1, 208, 209–118
all-or-nothing syndrome, 11, 163–174
alterity, 8, 13–14, 80–92
Amazonia, 20–21, 37, 38, 158–160
analytical categories, 9, 16, 135, 140
anti-foundationalism, 67, 199
autopoiesis, 12, 14, 139–140, 142n7

Barth, Fredrik, 9, 94–100, 105–106, 182, 189
Bataille, Georges, 195, 197, 202n23, 206
becoming, 10, 117, 118, 121–123, 127n21, 136, 140, 149, 173
belief, 15, 28, 29–30, 64, 73, 84, 87, 104, 106, 112, 142n4, 150, 165–169, 175n3, 193, 196, 199, 208–212, 216
belonging, feelings of, 146–149, 154
Benedict, Ruth, 195–197, 203n20, 203n24, 205
Bloch, Maurice, 18, 20, 37, 38, 80, 91, 92
Bolivip, 9, 100–104
Bourdieu, Pierre, 173, 180, 18

candomblé (Afro-Brazilian religion), 9–10, 112–125, 126n13
Castoriadis, Cornelius, 7, 43, 49, 51, 55n4, 56n11, 57
Christianity, 56n15, 212–217
Clifford, James, 56n15, 57, 95, 107, 182, 189, 194–197, 203n13, 203n14, 203n19, 204n26, 205

cognition, 17, 51, 139, 142n6
comparison, 17, 68, 80, 99, 115, 152–154, 157–159, 159n5, 179, 187, 209–210
consciousness, 4, 14–15, 41, 45–46, 50, 53, 142–143n8, 193, 194, 196, 200–201
contextualization, 3, 153, 158–159, 211
creation, 15, 25, 45, 53–54, 87, 110, 120–123, 127n19, 188, 200, 210
self-creation, 134–136
Cuba, 4, 6, 8, 81–92, 126n8

Davidson, Donald, 5, 13, 18, 164–174, 176
Deleuze, Gilles, 87, 92, 120, 123, 124, 126n12, 126n16, 127n22, 127, 175n1
Devereux, George, 43–44, 53–54, 56
dialogical pluralism, 8, 61–62, 69–74

ethnographic encounter, 2, 45, 47, 166, 172
ethnographic reality, 198
ethnographic writing, 197
ethnography
    and epistemology, 6, 8–9, 15–16, 20, 106, 139, 141, 168, 171–174, 178
    and generalization, 148–149, 151
    power of, 12
    as self-reflective exercise, 45–46, 53–54
    and theory building, 2–3, 172–174
    and truth, 82, 90, 195
evidence, 14, 17n7, 18, 35, 55n4, 67, 93, 99, 135, 144n13, 160, 161, 172, 175n2, 177–188, 194, 196, 202n11, 204n27, 204n28

female circumcision, 213–215
fetishism, 8, 64, 79, 108–115, 120–122,
    127n20, 128, 206
four stages of society (Adam Smith), 33

Gell, Alfred, 56n16, 57, 109, 116, 120,
    125n1, 126n10, 126n17, 128
generalizations, 11, 79, 147–159
genetic epistemology, 138–140, 141,
    143n15
Griaule, Marcel, 194–195, 203n14,
    203n15, 203n17, 205
Guatemala, 14–15, 190–197, 200, 200n1,
    202n11, 203n21, 204n30

Habermas, Jurgen, 64, 64–70, 77, 186,
    190
Highland Clearances, 6, 28
history, 5, 16, 19, 35, 38, 38n2, 39, 58,
    65, 72, 76, 78, 93
    and anthropology, 6–7, 153
    and explanation, 61, 140–141
    and fetish, 109, 122–123, 125n3
    of ideas, 8, 12, 67, 70, 165
    and intersubjectivity, 136, 140–142,
        144n3
    and mind, 145, 164
    and Scottish Enlightenment, 25
    and Tupi, 10–11, 158–159, 160
Honneth, Axel, 8, 61, 69–70, 77, 78
human condition, 2–4, 12, 13, 135,
    140–141, 163, 168–70, 174–5, 176,
    179, 183
human sciences, 5, 12, 16, 62, 67, 142n7,
    151, 204n25
Husserl, Edmund, 44, 55n9, 57, 142n4,
    142n7, 144n14, 145, 185, 186, 188
Hutton, James, 6, 23–27, 31–35, 39

Ifá divination, 8, 82, 85, 89
imaginings, 14, 193, 198, 200
indeterminacy, 14, 165–167, 171–174
intersubjectivity, 5–6, 10, 44, 53, 130–141,
    143n9, 143n10, 144n13, 159,
    186–188

Kapferer, Bruce, 17n2, 17n6, 18, 81, 93,
    144n16, 145
Kenya, 6, 212, 216
knowledge-making, 96–99, 105

Latour, Bruno, 82, 87–89, 93, 109, 111–
    113, 116, 121–124, 128, 180, 190
Lévi-Strauss, Claude, 20, 23, 34, 35, 39,
    42, 45, 55n3, 56n19, 57, 58, 113,
    116, 117, 125, 126n9, 128, 186, 190
life-world, 5, 7, 40–53
lived experience, 11, 143, 157–158

Malinowski, Bronislaw, 20, 29, 37, 42–44,
    55n5, 58, 135, 142n4, 145, 147,
    167, 172, 176, 190
Mannheim, Karl, 65
Mayan justice, 192
mediation, 14, 51, 162, 193–198
Min, 9, 96–100, 105
modernity, 7–8, 13, 16, 17n8, 60–76, 112,
    182–183, 187–188, 191
    second modernity, 178, 183, 186, 188
    multiple modernities, 62, 68, 75–75

nation-state, 60–61, 72, 75–76
Needham, Rodney, 173, 175n3, 176, 184,
    190, 199, 205
negation, 83–85, 173
New Guinea, 6–7, 40, 47–48, 55n8, 96–97
new realism, 14–15, 181–186

objectivism, 180–183, 186
objectivity, 51, 63, 95, 148
    relative, 95, 105
ontogeny, 2, 6, 10, 19, 135–141, 142n7
ontology, 2, 3, 8, 9–11, 13–14, 48, 56n16,
    108, 112, 114, 116, 123, 163, 169,
    185
oracles, 8, 84–90, 92n2

particularism, 3, 80–81, 178–180, 185,
    209–210, 217
performance, 47, 61, 75–76, 82, 97–98,
    117, 181, 213
phenomenology, 15, 43–46, 141, 142n5,
    142n7, 185–188
psychoanalysis, 15, 40–57

rajawal juyu' (master of the mountain),
    192
reality, 5, 7, 14–15, 34, 41, 45, 47–53,
    56n11, 62, 65, 73–75, 98, 108, 110,
    112, 117, 180, 193–200
reasoning, 13, 25, 135, 164, 185, 193

redefinition, 11, 62, 75, 82, 199–200
ritual, 15, 16, 97, 99–100, 110, 114, 116–
119, 123, 127n20

scientific observation, 6, 22–28, 30, 34
Scottish Enlightenment, 6, 24–26, 31–34
secrecy, 9, 97–100, 105, 213
self-reflection, 3, 45–48, 210
self-similarity, 95–96, 105–106
skepticism, 165, 180, 184–185, 197
social process, 16, 143, 197, 199
social relations, 10, 15, 30, 96, 98, 110,
111, 126n17, 135, 137, 144n13,
144n14, 197, 213–214
Stafford, Charles, 17n7, 18, 151, 153, 161
Strathern, Marilyn, 17n5, 18, 51, 56n16,
58, 87, 93, 96, 107, 113, 116, 124,
128, 152, 153, 158, 159, 161, 164,
166, 175n4, 176
subjectivism, 152, 180–183, 187
symmetrical anthropology, 112–113

Tarde, Gabriel, 127n17, 129
Taussig, Michael, 14, 81, 93, 193, 195–
200, 203n25, 205, 209

truth, 8, 11, 13–15, 35, 41, 45–49, 54, 63,
80–92, 92n1, 97–98, 110–113, 164–
167, 185, 194–195, 201, 202n11,
203n14, 212
Tupinamba, 2, 10–11, 148–149, 154–158

underdetermination, 171–173

Viveiros de Castro, Eduardo, 17n5, 18,
82, 87, 93, 124, 125n1, 129, 152,
153, 158, 159, 160, 162, 164, 169,
172, 176

Wagner, Roy, 9, 55n8, 87, 93, 94, 95–96,
105–106, 107
Wilson, Richard, 17n4, 18, 148, 162,
175n2, 176, 200, 202n11, 203n17,
206
Wittgenstein, Ludwig, 8, 52, 62–64, 76,
79, 165, 176, 184–186, 189, 200,
210

Yagwoia, 7, 39, 41, 47–51, 54, 55n8, 58